Hidden Lives

Stories from Child Survivors of the Holocaust

Edited by Rachelle L. Goldstein
and the Hidden Child Foundation/ADL

Library and Archives Canada Cataloguing in Publication

Title: Hidden lives : stories from child survivors of the Holocaust / edited by Rachelle L. Goldstein and the Hidden Child Foundation/ADL.
Other titles: Hidden lives (2025)
Names: Goldstein, Rachelle L., editor. | Hidden Child Foundation/ADL, editor.
Identifiers: Canadiana (print) 20250173476 | Canadiana (ebook) 20250173506 | ISBN 9781772604429 (hardcover) | ISBN 9781772604436 (EPUB)
Subjects: LCSH: Hidden children (Holocaust)—Biography. | LCSH: Holocaust, Jewish (1939-1945)—Personal narratives. | LCSH: Holocaust survivors—Biography. | LCGFT: Personal narratives.
Classification: LCC D804.48 .H53 2025 | DDC 940.53/1809253—dc23

Cover design and layout by Laura Atherton

Printed in China

All efforts have been made to obtain permissions to reproduce all the photos in this book from their copyright holders, as listed on page 329.

Special thanks to ADL and Jonathan Greenblatt, CEO and National Director, for their contributions and unwavering support of the Hidden Children, which made this book possible.

Second Story Press gratefully acknowledges the support of the Ontario Arts Council and the Canada Council for the Arts for our publishing program. We acknowledge the financial support of the Government of Canada through the Canada Book Fund.

Canada Council for the Arts

Funded by the Government of Canada
Financé par le gouvernement du Canada | Canada

Published by
Second Story Press
120 Carlton Street, Suite 412
Toronto, ON M5A 4K2
www.secondstorypress.ca

We dedicate this book to our rescuers. Throughout Nazi-occupied Europe, they risked it all—from imprisonment to immediate death—to protect us.

May their courage be a shining example for generations to come.

Each extra day that we lived was because of luck and not because we were smart, or brave, or cunning.

—**Susan Thumin Silk**,
a hidden child of the Holocaust

...only my mother and I survived in the ghetto in Budapest, Hungary, in 1944. Only gradually and slowly and in silence did I learn my mother's story, yet from that silence, my sensitivity and compassion were born. To keep that story alive, I became vocal in educating about the Holocaust and spoke in schools, synagogues, and senior centers. The retelling of my story keeps my past alive, a past that gives me strength and resilience. A past that generates compassion for people, animals, and the earth. A past that lets me listen and hear the children and the earth crying for justice. There is no "off" button here; I am living my history.

—**Susan Kalev**,
an infant survivor of the Holocaust

Table of Contents

Historical Note vii
Preface by Rachelle L. Goldstein ix
Foreword: What I Learned from My Father
by Abraham Foxman xvii

Introduction: Silent No More by Robert Krell, MD 1

PART I: SEPARATION & DISPLACEMENT
Introduction: The Consequences of the Separation of the Family by Dr. Bloeme Evers-Emden, PhD 4
Alone in a World Full of Others by Chava Kolar 7
Severed, like a Tree from Its Roots
by Lillian Boraks-Nemetz 10
Beyond Secret Tears by Lili Silberman 14
Memories and Reality: A Dilemma by Moshe Bar-Semech ... 18
Miracles and Mysteries by Jack Goldstein 20
From Bohemia to the Netherlands by Cordula Hahn 29
My Return to Judaism by Yetty Derschowitz 34

PART II: BETWEEN TWO RELIGIONS
Introduction: Conflicts of Identity
by Nechama Tec, PhD 38
Born in Austria, Saved in Belgium
by Ruth Wallach Bachner 40

Growing up in Occupied France: A Dual Experience by Renée Roth-Hano 46
Am I Still a Little Catholic Inside? by William H. Donat 50
Converting to Catholicism Saved Me and Changed My Life by Zula Hass 54

PART III: THE YOUNGEST SURVIVORS
Introduction: The Targeting of Babies and Toddlers by Elisheva van der Hal, PhD, and Danny Brom, PhD 62
The Mystery and Dignity of a Very Young Survivor by Robert Krell 64
Legacies of a Very Young Survivor by Maya Freed Brown 67
I Was an Infant Survivor in Greece by Esther Franco 70
Still Searching for the Hidden Child by Andrew Griffel 75

PART IV: THE TEENAGERS
"I Would Rather Have the Pain of Memory than to Forget" by Dasha Werdygier Rittenberg 84
My First Kaddish by Alexander Kimel 94
Clara Haras Strahl Tells Her Story to Her Grandchildren by Joanne Ashe and Pepi Strahl 99
Hidden in Berlin by Manfred Segal 111
The Magic School by Salomea Kape-Jay, MD 117

PART V: SURVIVAL
Notes from the Holocaust by Susan Thumin Silk 126
Memoirs of a Girl in Hiding by Erna Stopper Bindelglas..... 132
One of the Last to Tell About the Holocaust by Leo Vogel.. 144
A Survivor's Affirmation of Life by Eva Paula Nathanson..... 148

The Irony and Mystery of Survival
by Henry R. Huttenbach, PhD 155
The Rescue of a Jewish Family in Greece
by Yolanda Avram Willis 163

PART VI: THE LIBERATION
Waiting for Liberation in Poland by Alexander Kimel 168
Yom Kippur: After the Liberation by Leon Wells................. 171
The Liberation in Belgium by Rudy Rosenberg 173

PART VII: THE POSTWAR ORPHANS
Remembrances of 1945 in Poland by Jakub Gutenbaum..... 178
To Palestine: August 8, 1947 by Ruth Lavie-Jourgrau.......... 181
Letting Go of Hate by Pinchas Zajonc................................ 185
Bits and Pieces of Our Lives by Mechel Jamenfeld............... 188
Uncovering My Past by Richard Ned Lebow........................ 196

PART VIII: THE RESCUERS: **Individuals & Organizations**
The Righteous Among the Nations: The Courage to Care
by Mordecai Paldiel, PhD.. 206
My Hidden Childhood in Vert Galant by René Lichtman ... 210
A Beacon of Light by Eva Kuper.. 213
One Family's Wartime Chronicle by Jacques Silberman....... 225
A Childhood on the Run by Albert Hepner 233
A Public Thank-you to Chavagnes-en-Paillers
by Odette Meyers.. 241
Rabbi Zalman Schneerson Saved the Teitelbaum Sisters
by Bertha Teitelbaum Schwarz.. 245
Jews Rescuing Jews by Mordecai Paldiel, PhD 252

PART IX: REFUGEES ON THE RUN

Editor's Note: The World's Response to the Crisis of War in Europe by Rachelle L. Goldstein 262
I Remember by Johanna Franklin Saper 266
An Ill-fated Voyage and Return to Danger by Judith Koeppel Steel 271
Survival in Shanghai, China, During World War II by Evelyn Pike Rubin 278
The Saga of the Tehran Children by Dorit B. Whiteman, PhD 285
Escape to Russia and Beyond by Ruth L. Weiss Hohberg 290

PART X: THE AFTERMATH

Yaakov's Story: A Jewish Child in Christian Disguise by Jack Kuper 298
Reuniting with Family by Dr. Rose Kfar Rose, PhD 303
Brussels, 1945–1947 by Albert Hepner 309
The Postwar Years, 1945–1953 by Joseph Gosler 312
An American Summer Camp by William Donat 318
Return to My Mother, Yiddish Culture, and Jewish Identity by René Lichtman 325

Photo Credits 329

About the Contributors 330

Historical Note

Before Hitler and the Nazis came into power in Germany, in January 1933, there were many vibrant Jewish communities throughout Europe. By 1945, two out of every three European Jews had been killed, and their communities had vanished. Two-thirds, or six million, of Europe's Jews were murdered by Nazi Germany and its collaborators. Of the six million who were murdered, about 75 percent, or 4.5 million, had lived in Poland, the Soviet Union, and other eastern European lands.

In 1942, Nazi Germany dominated most of Europe. Greater Germany had been enlarged at the expense of its neighbors. Austria and Luxembourg were completely incorporated. Territories from Czechoslovakia, Poland, France, Belgium, and the Baltic states were seized by Greater Germany. Nazi military forces occupied Norway, Denmark, Belgium, northern France, Serbia, parts of northern Greece, and vast tracts of territory in eastern Europe. Italy, Hungary, Romania, Bulgaria, Slovakia, Finland, Croatia, and Vichy France were all either allied to Nazi Germany or subject to heavy Nazi influence. Between 1942 and 1944, Nazi military forces extended the area under their occupation to southern France, central and northern Italy, Slovakia, and Hungary.

Text and photo courtesy of the United States Holocaust Memorial Museum.

Preface

By Rachelle L. Goldstein

To bring about the complete eradication of the Jewish population in occupied Europe, Nazi strategy demanded that not only adults but children be targeted for destruction as well. Thus, one and a half million children—from infants to teens—were murdered during World War II (WWII). Nine out of ten Jewish children were killed simply because they were Jewish. Such deliberate and systematic killing of children was unprecedented in human history.

Very few Jewish children escaped the Nazi plan of annihilation. Most under the age of fourteen or fifteen were put to death immediately upon arriving at extermination camps. Not only in camps, but in the ghettos and in hiding, Jewish children in Nazi-occupied Europe were often the first to die. Only 6 to 11 percent of Jewish children survived, versus 33 percent of the adults. (The statistics for surviving children vary because many were never recovered and remained with their rescuers.)

Those who eluded the Nazis survived primarily because they were hidden from their persecutors, living out of their captors' sight, in convents, orphanages, haylofts, woods, basements, or sewers. Some lived openly under concealed names, pretending to be Christian.

Desperation compelled parents to make the agonizing decision to leave their children with strangers or to let them fend on their own, wandering through forests and villages in search of food and shelter. But such separations often saved children from the fate of their parents: by the end of the war, 80 percent of the surviving hidden children were orphaned.

Although we—the hidden children—were once thought to have been "too young" to be affected by our experiences, today, we know better. Yes, with time, most of us overcame our burdens, buried our memories, and grew up to become valued members of society. Now, we are the last witnesses to this period of terror, and it is with this realization that we—the last survivors of the Holocaust—bring these stories to you and to future generations.

Until 1991, I rarely spoke about my background—not with friends, not even with family. When asked "Where are you from?" I would generally answer "the Bronx." I wasn't alone in attempting to forget about WWII and the Nazis' attempt to eradicate every Jew from the face of the earth. Ever since 1945, I've been surrounded by a universal amnesia of the Holocaust. This lack of memory seems intentional among people of all backgrounds—old and young, savvy and less-so. This isn't surprising. Who wishes to revisit the apex of man's cruelty toward his fellow human beings? No one. Survivors, least of all.

We, who witnessed these horrors as children, also buried our memories and went on with our lives. By the end of the war, my immediate family was one of the few to remain intact. I was born in Brussels, Belgium, in 1939, and was forced into hiding when I was nearly three years old. After a separation of two and a half years, I was reunited with my parents in the fall of 1944. I had been hidden in two places, first with my brother and cousins in a Protestant orphanage in Uccle for about ten months, and then for about eighteen months on my own at the *crèche* (nursery) of the Convent of the Franciscan Sisters in Bruges. All along, I knew neither why I had been removed from my family, nor why people, called *les Allemands* (the Germans), wanted to kill me.

My Jewish origins were kept secret from me because, at that age, I could not be trusted with such dangerous knowledge. This wasn't a problem in the orphanage, but among the ardent nuns, I was reminded each day that my soul would not enter heaven if I died. The vision of my burning in hell forever was as frightening and mystifying to me as the wartime bombings. So too were the times I spent with two other children in the coal cellar when the Nazis visited the convent to capture Jewish children. The three of us were ushered down a coal chute with the dire warning that we would be killed if the Nazis heard us. I understood the threat and trembled in silence. I still recall fearing the sound of my own breathing.

I was promised the war would be over some day, but this hope was tinged with apprehension. I could no longer recall my parents' faces, so how would I know them? And since they had not brought me to the convent, how would they find me? My distress was only relieved by a sensory retention of them. The memory of my mother's embrace is what comforted me through the bombings, the coal cellar, the harshness of my caretakers, and most of all, the separation from my family.

In Europe in 1945, everyone—Jew or Gentile, adult or child—had a war story to tell. It took me a while to realize the difference: while the Nazis wanted to dominate all people in the conquered countries, they were more fixated on exterminating the Jews, including my family and me.

In the immediate aftermath of WWII, everyone simply wanted to resume a peaceful life. My parents returned to their work (manufacturing hats from our home), my brother went back to school, and I began kindergarten. My most vivid memories of 1945 are of going nearly each day with my mother to various agencies to scrutinize their lists of survivors, and of listening to the few survivors who visited us. These were days of great anxiety and dashed hopes. My uncle Maurice was the only of my mother's three siblings to survive the camps. Discovering this news, my mother was the most joyful I had ever seen.

Life went on with little discussion of the war. There were no allowances made for missing school or work, and no mention of mental health problems resulting from the war. Adult or child, one just picked oneself up and went on.

By the time my family and I arrived in the US in September of 1950, the world's attention had shifted to the Korean War, the threats of the Atom Bomb, the Russians, and the communists.

No teacher or student in the US ever asked me about my experiences during the war years, and in truth, that was just fine with me. I wanted so much to be "normal" like everyone else. I envied my classmates who reveled in silliness. I still remember my sixth-grade teacher, Mrs. Berger, miming and writing my first English word, "SMILE," on the blackboard.

In the postwar years, neither I nor my parents thought of ourselves as "Holocaust survivors." Simply "hiding" did not compare with experiencing the camps. Yet, the fear of capture remained with my parents throughout their lives. I remember being awakened by my mother's frequent screams in the middle of the night.

The evildoers of our nightmares were always the Germans. We never called them "Nazis." So, how did so many people come to embrace Nazism? I have seen the films and photos of what happened in the camps and ghettos and wondered how an ordinary man who loves his family, his community, his church, his pets, can become so detached from his morality—and others' humanity—as to kill, face-to-face, a man, a woman, a child? These films and images were taken by regular foot soldiers as souvenirs or trophies. They took pride in their brutality.

Throughout history, children of combatants were generally ancillary victims of the ravages of war. But, when the Nazis devised the "Final Solution," every Jew (as defined by Nazi ideology) in occupied Europe, became a target. From the start, the Nazis concealed their intent with euphemistic language to make the transports or "relocations" appear benign. When people were taken away and never heard from again, everyone understood the rumors that had begun to circulate from the east.

Deception is the hallmark of tyrants. Lies were (and still are) effective in gaining and maintaining public support and deceiving the opposition. During WWII, ruses were also used within the conquered populations. In Belgium and elsewhere, the Nazis used the hoax of maintaining children's homes to display their "concern" for Jewish orphans. In these places, such as in Wezembeek-Oppem, young children were tolerated but shipped to the death camps as soon as they turned sixteen. The Nazis' hatred of Jewish children trumped any vestige of mercy or rationality.

Adolf Hitler did not ascend to power alone. He was duly appointed as Chancellor of Germany by President Paul von Hindenburg in January 1933, after the Nazis garnered a majority in the elections of 1932. So, how did nearly an entire country become besotted with such evil? Where and how did it breed? Was it ignorance? Lack of education? Or just plain naïveté within an overwhelming majority of the population?

Now that misinformation is sent instantaneously to millions around the world, we can no longer afford blameless passivity. The deniers—who have sown doubts and untruths since 1945—are multiplying their lies exponentially with each passing hour. Even in democracies such as the United States there are intensifying parallels to the autocratic Nazi era, and we are seeing the highest levels of antisemitism since the war. With such disregard for memory and history, how do we guard against the lies and prevent any genocide, or another Holocaust?

I fear greatly for the future. Our organization, the Hidden Child Foundation, regularly gets a spate of hate mail filled with vile and wild accusations. There are plenty of good history books to turn to if one wants to have an accurate picture of what happened during WWII, but who is learning from them? A 2020 Claims Conference state-by-state analysis points to disturbing statistics in the US: In New York, for instance, nearly 20 percent of Millennials and Gen Z feel the Jews caused the Holocaust. Nationally, 63 percent did not know that six million Jews were murdered, and 36 percent thought that "two million or fewer Jews" were killed during the Holocaust. Also, out of more than forty thousand camps and ghettos in Europe during the Holocaust, 48 percent could not name one. (See the 2020 Claims Conference article "First-ever 50-State Survey on Holocaust Knowledge of American Millennials and Gen Z Reveals Shocking Results".)

On January 23, 2025, the Claims Conference released the first ever eight-country (US, UK, France, Austria, Germany, Poland, Hungary, and Romania) Holocaust Knowledge and Awareness Index, which shows a growing gap in knowledge about the Holocaust, especially in young adults. Yet, in almost every country surveyed, a majority feels another Holocaust can happen again. This later survey only reinforces that in the US and elsewhere, we must do better about educating young people about the dangers of looming antisemitism.

Hence, the necessity for these warning tales from the last remaining survivors of the Holocaust. Our numbers are dwindling with each passing day, and we care too much about our world to see our history repeat itself. We tell our stories in the hope that these narratives will live on longer than history "lessons" in the memories of the young (and the older).

If there is a single bright light in the accounts of the Child Survivors, it is that of the rescuers. Most of us who survived in hiding made it through those horrible years with the help of some humane and righteous people.

Who will be the righteous of today? Who will rescue today's democracies that are teetering on the brink of autocracy? If we do not understand the Nazification of an enlightened country, are we doomed to repeat it? Here? Now?

Eventually, the answers will lie in the hands and hearts of our readers. We hope they will learn from us that all humans have the same desires for themselves and their families, that democracies are fragile, and that our leaders must be rational and truthful people who will always preserve what we proudly proclaim in our Pledge of Allegiance, "liberty and justice *for all*."

Before we tell our stories, let's begin with a bit of history. When Nazi Germany surrendered to the Allies in May 1945, we were Jewish children just coming out of hiding. It took another forty-six years—until May 1991, in New York, at our First International Gathering of Children Hidden During WWII—before we would call ourselves "Holocaust survivors." For decades, our plight had been minimized by comments such as, "They're so young, they'll get over it!"

When more than 1,600 people from twenty-eight countries packed into a Manhattan hotel in 1991, it was the first time that our history was acknowledged, and that we were finally recognized as bona fide "survivors" of the Holocaust.

What had brought Hidden Children together after so many years? A film. The documentary, *As If It Were Yesterday*, written and directed by Myriam Abramowitz and Esther Hoffenberg, told the story of the Jewish Belgian Resistance Network, a group that saved more than 4,000 children during the war. Nicole David, a Hidden Child, saw the film and was so moved that she contacted Myriam Abramowicz. During their conversation, Myriam mentioned that every time the film was shown, people who, as children, were hidden during the Holocaust came to her with the same remark: they felt they had lost their childhood and grown up too soon.

Myriam suggested that a get-together be arranged. Shortly thereafter, Nicole and three others who had been similarly hidden met with Dr. Judith Kestenberg, project director of Child Development Research, an organization that studied childhood trauma. Out of that initial meeting came the resolve to find more Hidden Children and the decision to hold an international reunion.

Where do the stories in this book come from? Since its inception in May 1991, the Hidden Child Foundation has been committed to adding the accounts of Child Survivors to the annals of Holocaust history. We've spoken at many schools and to various groups; and we've published an annual bulletin, *The Hidden Child*, from 1991 to 2020. We send out articles, titled *My Story*, via email. After decades of silence, we are committed to remembrance and commemoration.

Rachelle L. Goldstein, *Co-Director of the Hidden Child Foundation*

Hidden Child Foundation Founders, May 1991, left to right: Miriam Rakowski, Nicole David, Renee Roth-Hano, Ava Schonberg, Naomi Waldman, Ann Shore, Shoshana Ron, Cecile Low, Carla Lessing, Lore Baer, and Lusia Ashenberg.

Foreword

By Abraham Foxman

What I Learned from My Father

(Excerpted from the Foreword of the book, In the Shadow of Death, *by Joseph Foxman, Yad Vashem, and the Holocaust Survivors' Memoirs Project, New York • Jerusalem, 2011.)*

Of the many fateful decisions my parents made as they tried to keep one step ahead of the Nazis, none was more fraught with anxiety and fear than their decision to give away their one-year-old son.

It was perhaps the most unnatural decision a parent could make. They entrusted my life to my Polish Catholic nursemaid, a woman they had known for only a short time. They did so on a leap of faith, a belief that I would have a better chance of surviving outside of the burgeoning Jewish ghetto of Vilna under the protection and care of the devout Catholic woman who loved me as her own.

It was an incredible risk, and a dangerous calculation. Yet it worked. I was reunited with both my parents after the war. Unlike the fate of so many families and parents of so many other children, my family unit—because we were separated—survived and was reunited intact.

My father, Joseph, and my mother, Helen, protected me in my youth from hearing about the tough decisions and hard sacrifices they had made during the war years. And after we had left Europe for good and settled into our new life in the United

States, they spoke a great deal of their experiences, but not to me.

Abraham Foxman with his nanny, Bronisława Kurpi.

I did not know that my father, a historian by avocation, had written down, in exacting Yiddish, recollections of his experiences in Lithuania and elsewhere in Eastern Europe. His memoirs describe in careful detail how he repeatedly cheated death in the work camps, in the factories, in the ghetto. Imagine my surprise when, years later, I came across these papers as I was going through his personal effects. I'd had no idea that these memoirs existed. My mother and father had never spoken of them. As I grew older, I began to try to understand why it was that I had survived, why I had been spared the fate of 1.5 million other Jewish children who perished in the Nazi inferno. During the war, I had been kept safe, protected, fed, clothed, and happy by my nanny. She had me baptized and took pains to love and care for me. She took me to church every Sunday and kept my Jewish identity hidden.

I had many questions for my father. And there were many answers, both spoken and unspoken. The realization, for example, of how alone we were when I celebrated my Bar Mitzvah. My friends and classmates were surrounded by many dozens, if not hundreds, of family members—the aunts, uncles, cousins, grandparents, and siblings who crowded the *shuls* of Brooklyn to celebrate the most important rite of passage into Jewish adulthood. For my bar mitzvah, we could barely fill the living room of our one-and-a-half-bedroom apartment—and the guests were friends, not family.

My parents answered some of my questions about Europe and the war with simple *yes*es and *no*s. But they were never able to explain what I saw as the biggest question of my life: How could they have given me away? I asked this sometimes in disbelief and sometimes in anger. My parents were never able to explain this most unnatural decision, which not only saved my life, but theirs as well.

Another question that I struggled with while growing up—and that I ultimately was mature enough to ask my father—was the question of his unflagging and seemingly unquestioning faith in God. How, after everything that had happened to him in Europe, after the killings and the scenes of death he had witnessed, after the near total annihilation of his family and of European Jewry, how could my father believe in and revere God? And how could he make the decision so easily to bring me back to my Jewish roots, my *Yiddishkeit*, after I had been returned to my parents for good?

I was born in 1940, in Baranowicz, Poland. Under the protection of my nanny, I had been baptized in Lithuania as a Catholic boy named Henryk Stanislaw Kurpi, the names of my nanny and my patron saint. I had gone to church every Sunday, and, when passing through the city of Vilna, I would cross myself when I passed a church. When I met a priest, I kissed his hand; when we saw a Jew, I had been taught to spit at him.

After the war, my father slowly reintroduced me to my Jewish roots without apparent compunction, remorse, or anger at God. His decision was a great mystery to me until, years later, I asked him about his faith. The answer surprised me. He told me that the evil that had created the Shoah was not God's—it was man's. Essentially, it was man's inhumanity toward man. This idea is reflected in his memoirs, in which he recounts the moments in his survival odyssey when he truly believes that God intervened to spare his life and the lives of his wife and child. My father saw faith in those interventions, and he was unafraid to express his sincere belief in miracles.

The first time my father took me to shul was in Vilnius on Simchat Torah. I guess it was because he figured I'd like it, since it is a joyous festival full of singing and dancing. A Soviet officer in uniform, who was Jewish, came up to my father and asked if he could include me in the dancing. He put me on his shoulders and began to dance, saying, "This is the Jewish flag." The Jewish children picked me up and danced with me, and I came home and told my mother, "Hey, I like the Jewish church!" It was the beginning of my return to Judaism.

Incidentally, sixty-five years later, I would meet this officer again. Unbeknownst to my family and me, the soldier had moved to the United States, where he became an Orthodox rabbi and an educator. We were reunited in his home in Detroit, Michigan, in April 2010. His name is Rabbi Leo Goldman, and he was ninety-one at the time of our meeting.

Something else I didn't understand for a long time was my parents' insistence that I retain my fond memories and love for Bronisława Kurpi, my nanny, the woman who saved my life. This was even after everything that had transpired to taint the relationship, and though we were unable to stay in touch with her after the war. Why, I wondered, would they permit me to keep her memory alive, and even to hold on to photos of the woman who once claimed me as her son, and who, after the war, had done everything to keep me from being rightfully returned to my parents? She had had me kidnapped twice, and had told terrible lies to the Soviet authorities about my father in an effort to have him imprisoned.

There had been a painful custody battle, of which to this day I have no memory, so searing, so emotionally traumatic was this ordeal on the psyche of a five-year-old boy. We had left Eastern Europe to get away from all of this and more, yet my parents obstinately insisted on keeping her memory alive.

When I finally gathered up the courage to ask my father about my nanny, the answer again surprised me, and served as a powerful and early life lesson. "Son," he told me in Yiddish, "everything in excess is no good—too smart, too stupid, too nice, too poor...."

Here was a good woman who had suffered from too much love. And too much love sometimes transforms itself into hate. Yet my parents wanted me to remember for the rest of my life the woman who had risked her life so that I could live.

Another question I had occasion to ask my father: Why did people in the ghettos go to such lengths to keep diaries of what was happening to them? I didn't understand how people bartered bread for paper, when a piece of bread meant the difference between life and death; how people could barter soup, when soup was the only meal they had that day.

My father's answer was that they feared that no one would know that they had lived. He explained that, in the Jewish tradition, we had an obligation of *Zahor* and *Yizkor*, to remember and to eulogize and preserve the memory of the dead.

This is the most important message and lesson of the Holocaust and, for me, explains everything about why my father felt it necessary to put pen to paper and to write about his experiences. There are many universal questions that arise out of the evil of the Holocaust; there are no easy answers and, perhaps, there will never be. But our children and our children's children need to understand how it happened, why it happened, so that they can carry on the imperative of *Never Again*.

Abraham Foxman *is world-renowned as a leader in the fight against antisemitism, bigotry, and discrimination and regularly speaks out on issues of global antisemitism, the war on terrorism, church/state issues, and issues relating to the Holocaust, which he survived as a hidden child. He is a passionate supporter of the State of Israel and a voice for peace in the Middle East.*

Mr. Foxman is National Director Emeritus of the Anti-Defamation League (ADL), from which he retired in 2015 after fifty years with the organization, including serving as National Director from 1987 through 2015. Upon retirement, he served as Vice Chairman of the Museum of Jewish Heritage in New York City. He is the author of several books, and co-authored Viral Hate: Containing Its Spread on the Internet.

A Holocaust survivor, Mr. Foxman has been a member of the President's United States Holocaust Memorial Council, appointed by presidents Reagan, George H. W. Bush, Clinton, and Biden.

Introduction: Silent No More

By Robert Krell, MD

(Excerpted from The Hidden Child, *Volume V, Number 1, spring 1994.)*

Silence served us well while hiding in Christian homes, in convents, in caves, in partisan groups, even in concentration camps. Survival so often depended on not being noticed, being inconspicuous; on the ability to suppress tears, ignore pain. Grief was borne in silence; so was rage.

Silence is the language of the child survivor. We might have talked after the war...but adults persuaded us to get on with life, forget the past. Adults, who themselves had survived and suffered so much, inadvertently diminished the experiences of the children. Silence enveloped our existence.

My awareness of being a child survivor crystallized at Jerusalem's 1981 World Gathering of Holocaust Survivors, when Rabbi Israel Meier Lau (then Chief Rabbi of Nethanya) introduced himself as the youngest child liberated from Buchenwald at age eight. Not long after reading Sarah Moskovitz's book, *Love Despite Hate: Child Survivors of the Holocaust and Their Adult Lives*, I was the guest speaker at an early meeting of the fledgling Los Angeles Child Survivor Group. I told them how, between 1981 and 1983, I noticed what should have been obvious—we did not exist. There were Holocaust survivor organizations primarily for older survivors, those who had been young adults at liberation. There were organizations for children of survivors. Even the 1978 book, *Children of the Holocaust*, by Helen Epstein, was about the second generation.

But we were the *real* children of the Holocaust, those who survived the war hidden, without our parents, never knowing whether we would see them again. Our lives unfolded differently. Those sixteen and under at the end of the war were more likely to join adoptive families, resume schooling, and live away from other survivors. And even where child survivors stayed in touch with one another, few identified themselves as such.

With an already shaky identity, and a self-comforting practiced silence, it is no surprise we did not draw attention to ourselves. Older survivors knew something of their Jewishness and had a prewar experience of traditions and learning. They had memories. Often passing for Christians while in hiding, younger child survivors emerged from the war with confused identities and, sometimes, with precious few positive Jewish memories. While adult survivors had a stronger prewar Jewish education, child survivors had a stronger but secular postwar education. No wonder so many child survivors became professionals, lost their accents, and disappeared into the landscape of "ordinary" life.

Would it have been possible to live our entire lives behind the facade of normalcy and ordinariness? I don't think so. We faced a formidable adversary—aging. The inevitable assault of nostalgia was bound to trigger memory. Our experience of the world simply does not fit with that of our non-European contemporaries, whether Jew or non-Jew.

Prior to the 1991 First International Gathering of Children Hidden During WWII, Abe Foxman (then-national director of the Anti-Defamation League) and I sat and talked for three hours about the similarities in our experiences of hiding, the adjustment to the fortunate return of parents, a subsequent struggle with Christian versus Jewish identity, and so much more. One fact was obvious: A floodgate of memory needed to be released or it would devour us. Our discussion committed us to the proposed 1991 meeting for we knew that facing memory required for us to be together.

Robert Krell, *CM, MD, FRCP(C), DFAPA, is professor emeritus, Department of Psychiatry, University of British Columbia, and a noted author of several groundbreaking books, including his memoir* Sounds From Silence: Reflections of a Child Holocaust Survivor, Psychiatrist and Teacher.

PART I

Separation & Displacement

Introduction: The Consequences of the Separation of the Family

By Dr. Bloeme Evers-Emden, PhD

(Excerpted from The Hidden Child, *Volume IX, Number 1, spring 2000.)*

One of the worst consequences of the Holocaust was the disintegration of the family, especially the separation of children from their parents. When the deportations of the Dutch Jews began in July 1942, many people went, trusting they could survive. But when the Nazis' methods became increasingly brutal, it was understood that something terrible was going on.

Starting in the autumn of 1942, more Jews sought to hide. Because an entire family could seldom find a hiding place, parents were confronted with the horrible necessity of "giving away" their children to complete strangers as they faced a dismal and uncertain future.

One parent still trembled at the memory: "You have an appointment with a stranger on the corner of a certain street. She takes your child and disappears with her on the bus. That's how I gave her away...how I survived this, I don't know." Another said, "I still see very clearly how he walked out of our sight at the hand of the 'aunt'...our feelings were of ultimate powerlessness...." No one has written about the pain of it, a pain that never leaves. And nobody imagined the difficulties that arose when you were "lucky enough to survive and get your children back."

Only a small percentage of parents were reunited with their children after 1945 (80 percent of hidden children were orphaned by the end of the war). Most children had no family, and the teenagers among them often had no place to go. Many asked themselves why they had survived. The few surviving parents went in search of their children. On average, children had four to five wartime addresses. And to keep everyone safe, most foster parents did not know the birth name of the child nor the former address. Nevertheless, despite the many obstacles—their traumas, their lack of funds, housing, and transportation—most parents were in desperate pursuit of their children within weeks of liberation.

Often, young children did not know that their foster parents were not their biological parents. They were not interested in strangers who told them that they were their "real" mothers and fathers. They fiercely resisted the separation from their "parents." When taken to their parental home, they would yearn for their foster parents.

The estrangement took a heavy toll. Parents were disappointed that the child they had idealized during the war years did not want them. Although some older children adapted to the new circumstances, many did not. Some ran away to their foster parents, some misbehaved, others wanted nothing—no school, no kisses—but to return to their foster homes.

Researchers have found that a separation of a few years without contact brings about an irreversible estrangement in all children. In the case of hidden children, there is an additional factor. Even very young children seemed to sense that their lives were at stake when they went into hiding. They adapted very quickly to the new surroundings, hardly crying for their parents—an important survival tactic. The reasoning seemed to be, "I must surely have been a bad child that my parents gave me away; I must be a very good child now lest these people give me away." Their grief over losing their parents and their anger about being "given away" stayed mostly hidden. But after the war—past the danger—their fury emerged, and often it was aimed at their parents. For many, the happy life at the end of the nightmare did not come to pass.

Bloeme Evers-Emden *(July 26, 1926–July 18, 2016) was a Dutch Jewish lecturer and child psychologist who researched the topic of "hidden children" and wrote four books on the subject in the 1990s. During WWII, she was forced to go into hiding from the Nazis and was subsequently arrested and deported to Auschwitz on the last transport leaving the Westerbork transit camp on 3 September 1944. With her on the train were Anne Frank and her family, whom she had known in Amsterdam. She was liberated on May 8, 1945.*

Alone in a World Full of Others

By Chava Kolar

(Excerpted from The Hidden Child, *Volume IX, Number 1, spring 2000.)*

It happened so gradually that I did not notice it at the beginning. My twin sister and I were just six and had entered a Jewish school when a pro-fascist regime took over the Slovak part of Czechoslovakia. We had a spacious apartment on the fifth floor of a building on one of Bratislava's main streets, and we watched President Tiso's processions from our balcony.

The adults started talking in whispers around us. Some children mysteriously stopped attending classes, and by mid-semester, the school was shut down altogether. A few of us whose parents either had special permits or had converted to Christianity transferred to state schools, but most children seemed to disappear into oblivion. I never saw any of them again.

Until the uprising in Banska Bystrica in 1944, my own life was harder but it remained bearable. Nobody explained what was happening as we moved from one flat to another, each one smaller and farther away from the city center. Fewer friends visited and for no apparent reason, relatives "went away" or "traveled." I didn't understand why they did not even come to say goodbye. Why they never wrote. My aunts and uncles, my only cousin, my grandparents who loved me so tenderly, all evaporated silently.

The separation from my loved ones became confusing and ominous, even more so because I was discouraged from asking why. One day, my father was taken to a labor camp in Sered. My sister and I stopped attending classes and, with our mother, were crowded into a freezing room. My mother wept silently at night. I clung to her desperately. She was my only link with the world that had abandoned me.

When Father came back—one of the very few prisoners to return—beaten but whole, I felt lucky, and I was sure that things were taking a turn for the better. But after a short while, my sister and I were told that, if we were to survive, we had to leave our parents. They placed us in an evangelical pastorate orphanage in Modra, and they too, went into hiding. I was desperate with grief. I tried, unsuccessfully, to persuade myself that being left in this horrible institution was necessary, a place where the nuns beat children for any tiny offense, and where I had to pretend to be someone else. How could my dear parents have done such a thing to us?

I developed a fear of people and tried to avoid contact with them. I was confused, angry, and infinitely sad. Not quite comprehending the cause of my circumstances, I became distrustful of the whole world and of every person in it. Since then, I have never succeeded in really belonging, in feeling completely at ease with people, even with friends, or in forming one single lasting bond. I have become an outsider in a world full of "others."

Chava Kolar (under the X) and her sister (in plaid dress to the right) in the Modra orphanage.

The separation from most of my beloved, indeed of the world as I knew it, was permanent. They never returned. They have no graves, and their spirits still hound me, as if they have not found their peace. Or is it perhaps I who did not? Yet, I was lucky. A family in Vrbovce kept my parents safe in a hole in their barn, and, despite mortal danger to himself and to his family, the pastor in Modra did not disclose the hiding place to the authorities. After the war, our little family of four reunited, later made *Aliyah*, and started a new life. We were alive, but none of us were ever quite the same.

Chava Kolar, *born Gertruda (Gerda) Kaufmannova, immigrated to Israel in 1949 with Youth Aliyah. She retired from the Weizmann Institute of Science.*

Severed, like a Tree from Its Roots

By Lillian Boraks-Nemetz

(Excerpted from The Hidden Child, *Volume IX, Number 1, spring 2000.)*

When I was given away, I felt severed from my family like a tree from its roots. As a child of nine, I did not understand it was a matter of life and death. I felt abandoned.

The memory of my prewar life was one of bounty, safety, and happiness. A circle of loving family members enfolded me, giving me a secure sense of belonging. My parents, grandparents, uncles, aunts, and cousins met together often, and it was always fun and play. All too soon, the war hit our lives and removed the ground from under our feet.

Even in the Warsaw ghetto, before deportations began, our family gatherings continued. On those occasions, I still felt relatively happy. Despite the fear and deprivation of ghetto life, being with family allowed me to have some sense of continuity. Suddenly, the gatherings ceased. All my aunts, uncles, and cousins disappeared. Later, we learned they had been deported to Treblinka.

Things got worse. Our ghetto became an antechamber to the death camps. Huge transports of men, women, and children left daily for the so-called resettlements in the East. I was separated from my parents in 1942 when I escaped the Warsaw ghetto with a false set of documents in my pocket. I had to go out alone, my father said, holding my hand tightly. I thought that both he and my mother were coming with me, but soon I realized that they would stay behind. I was to let go of my father's hand and walk away without looking back. I wanted so much to turn around to catch that last glimpse of my beloved father's face. But I did as I was told. Jagna Boraks—my real name—left to become Irena Kominska, a Catholic child of imaginary parents.

Lillian Boraks-Nemetz in the summer of 1939, just before the war broke out.

On the other side of the ghetto wall, a strange woman took me to a Polish village where my paternal grandmother lived with a Catholic man. The village people were told I was a child of a friend who was wounded during the *blitzkrieg*. Baba also had false papers, so I was not allowed to call her Baba. As a result, I was afraid to call my grandma anything. Suddenly, in my mind, Baba became nameless and depersonalized, and I began to feel awkward around her. A pretense, a form of coolness, set in between us lest the village folk guess the truth about our real relationship. Even inside the house we remained distant from one another because the windows across the street had spying eyes behind the white lace curtains.

I felt isolated from the world and everyone I loved. My parents and my little sister had vanished from my life. An awful pain gnawed at my stomach as I worried about my parents' safety. I had nightmares about being left in a field all alone, looking for my mother, crying out "Mama, Mama"—in a voice that did not want to come out but felt like a scream. All my days in the country were spent alone as Grandma busied herself with chores.

I accepted my aloneness with great responsibility and carried out the requirements for that condition diligently. I was not allowed to go to school, to have friends, or to wander away from the house. I was given daily chores of weeding the garden, digging for and peeling potatoes. In winter, in addition to my regular chores, I had to trudge off, knee-deep in snow, to a neighbor for milk. My feet without boots, my hands without gloves, I found these chores tedious and painful. I had no one to talk to and no one talked to me. I had no choice. I did as Grandma and the man told me. I lived in silence.

When my parents returned many months later, they told us that my sister, in a neighboring village, had been informed on and taken away by the Gestapo. We never saw her again, and I never said goodbye. I felt guilty that I had survived. I began to feel undeserving of life. I felt deserted by God since he did not hear my pleas to save my little sister.

When I finally went to live with my parents toward the end of the war, I was to call them "Uncle" and "Aunt" because my false document contained a name different from theirs. Conditioned not to feel out loud, lest I cry or laugh and give away our secret, I became numb. I felt separated and confused. In my mind, they were not my parents but someone else's. My father had taught me the virtues of honesty and truth, but here, life took on a form of deception and unreality. It seemed that we were hiding our identities not only from the enemy but also from ourselves.

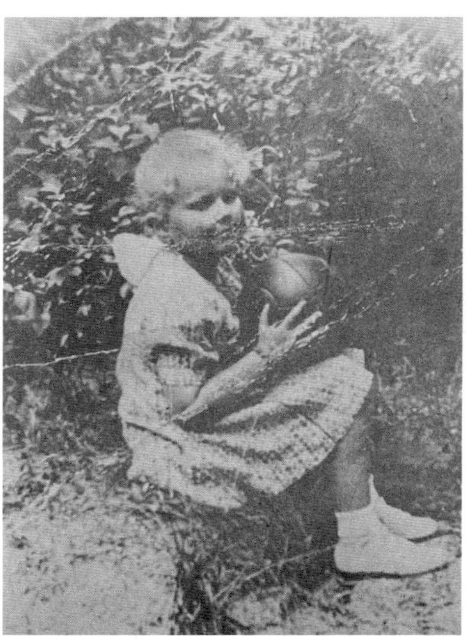

Lillian (pre-hiding period).

A systematic disintegration of principles I had been taught was taking place. Now illusion, not reality, of who I was and who I was not distorted my family values. This condition perpetuated itself into my teenage and adult life, most of which seemed unreal. Later, I viewed my own children with love but through an estranged lens, as if these children did not quite belong to me but more to my husband—as if I did not deserve to have them as my own. I began to question my own identity, as a mother, a wife, a daughter, and a Jew.

In the '60s, I called it existentialism. I simply lived from day to day and thought little about my feelings and attitudes. At the same time, I was strongly urged to forget all about my past. So, inside me there lived another self, very well hidden from the world. I recall feeling that there were two of me—my adult self and my child self that had never integrated. It was as if the child that ceased to exist during the war was struggling to fulfill itself inside a grown woman's mind and body. The whole saga of teenage experience was also missing from my life since, during the war, I had entered adulthood far too early. I became increasingly aware that while my life progressed in a seemingly normal manner, chaos loomed in my soul. I had not really survived the emotional and physical implications of war, of hiding, and mostly, of the separation from my family.

Lillian Boraks-Nemetz *is the author of a trilogy for young readers (*The Old Brown Suitcase, The Sunflower Diary, *and* The Lenski File*) and two volumes of poetry. She has translated and co-translated into English two poetry collections written by Polish émigré poets. She taught creative writing in the Department of Continuing Studies at the University of British Columbia.*

Beyond Secret Tears

By Lili Silberman

(Excerpted from The Hidden Child, *Volume V, Number 2, fall/ winter 1995.)*

I was four years old, and my brother was five and a half when we were first separated from our parents and placed in a Protestant orphanage in Belgium. I was a depressed and confused child, but with the passing of time, I began to believe that all children lived away from their parents. After several months, the director of the orphanage had reason to suspect that the Nazis might discover the few Jewish children hidden there, and my brother and I were suddenly returned to our parents.

They were not expecting us when our escort knocked on their door. My parents were certain the Nazis had come for them. The terror on my mother's face as she opened the door devastated me. I had expected her to be happy at my homecoming; instead, gloom and despair permeated our home.

Shortly thereafter, a strange man came to the house, removed my brother and me, and accompanied us by train to a convent in Bruges. I was sure I had done something terrible. The convent had two separate facilities, one for boys and one for girls. I was immediately separated from my brother. My fifth birthday had just passed, and I was now alone in a strange place.

The nuns were strict disciplinarians. But as terrified as I was of the nuns, I was equally afraid of the older children. When unsupervised, some of them would abuse the younger ones. As one of the youngest and smallest, I lived in constant terror. There was no place to hide, and I did whatever I could not to bring attention to myself.

What little food we had often had worms, and the bread was always rancid and moldy. We lacked clothing, heat, and medical attention. I don't remember ever bathing. I never saw a toothbrush, a handkerchief, or toilet paper. When I did not see newspaper scraps, I used my clothing. I was awakened at night by lice crawling inside my ear and I had a chronic bloody infection on my scalp. Even in the freezing winter, we were sent outside. I was swollen and numb from the cold, and my hands, blistered from frostbite, were scarred for years. I knew that I was diseased from filth and neglect, but I thought this existence was normal.

Lili and her brother, Charles, c. late 1938/early 1939.

I hungered to be with my mother and father. I clung to their memory. I desperately yearned for my mother's gentleness. I longed to be noticed, to be touched and caressed. I craved so intensely, I remember my body always aching. Yet I seemed unable to cry and I dared not make noise. I thought that if I were good, the nuns would tell my parents and they would come for me. I would play by myself, always pretending that I was talking with my mother, always pleading with her to come for me.

I longed to see my brother, believing that he could protect me. He was then six and a half years old. Hoping I might see him, I routinely looked through a keyhole when no one was looking. When Mother Superior occasionally appeared, I would plead with my eyes for her to notice me, to see my loneliness, my despair. I was a beggar for a look, a touch. From the age of four, I never saw the world outside, never knew that children lived together with their parents, never knew that they played in the park while their mothers watched over them. Everything had been taken from me. I was to remain only with a distant memory of my parents' faces. I came to feel that I was nothing in this world, and, at the age of five, I felt old and worn out.

It would be four years before we were reunited with our parents. Their own ordeal and terror, their grief at the loss of so many cherished family members, their long and mournful separation from us, all had emotionally weakened them. As I became aware of how broken these two gentle people were, I began to grieve for them. I became overly cautious of my behavior and my main concern was to not cause them any distress.

Ours was a home where memories were not welcome, a home with no past. I was encouraged to believe that I was too young to understand, and that the only thing that mattered was that we were all very lucky to be alive and together again. While I grew up waiting for my parents to ask about that once-orphaned child, I was to remain secretly tormented by my painful memories.

My brother tried to dissociate himself from his past and in so doing, he distanced himself from me. Our common history was never discussed. We were to become a family of strangers. After having once begged for a touch, I was to spend years hungering for an ear. When I tried to break the silence, I was always quickly reminded how lucky I was, far luckier than most. When I began to realize that my parents had no awareness of

Charles and Lili when they first arrived at the convent in Bruges in 1943.

the sorrow I carried, and no desire to know of my hidden past, I came to believe that my feelings had never been important to anyone.

When, through the years, I encountered unexpected kindnesses from strangers, the tears began to flow, and I welcomed them. And, today, I can finally say I have found my peace.

Lili Silberman, *now deceased, worked in New York as a paralegal. The man who brought Lili and her brother to the convent was Father Bruno Reynders, the Benedictine priest, who hid close to four hundred Jewish children in Christian homes and institutions and was recognized by Yad Vashem as a "Righteous Among the Nations."*

Memories and Reality: A Dilemma

By Moshe Bar-Semech

(From The Hidden Child, *Volume VIII, Number 1, winter 1998/1999.)*

I was born in the little town of Giraltovce in East Slovakia on June 29, 1942, a few weeks before the Jews of that area were taken to the local prison for deportation to Auschwitz. A few hours before we were to be transported, the local sheriff, a friend of the family, rescued my parents and me.

My father joined the Partisans in the forest of the Tatra Mountains, and my mother managed to go to Budapest, Hungary, where she could hide. But after several months, she ran out of money, and, too scared and hungry to take care of a baby, she handed me over to a relative who was married to a Hungarian woman, who sent me to her sister in the village of Nagyrede. I ended up with her daughter, who became my mother for almost two and a half years.

It wasn't until three months after the end of the war that my father and his comrades found out they were free. He set upon finding his family. After finding my mother, he found me—a thin, starved little boy, ill with tuberculosis, refusing to leave his "family" to go with the strange man. After several days, my father took me away by force. It took me many years to accept my parents as my parents. Only when I had children of my own did it occur to me that, had I been in their place at that time, I might have done the same.

Ten years ago, I presented a workshop at a family therapy conference in Budapest. I had a free day before returning to Israel, and I found myself in a taxi, determined to locate the woman who had raised me for two and a half critical years. I had no name, only that of the village. My parents said they forgot her name, and "in any case, you don't owe her anything. Your father gave her all the money he could."

Mrs. Czörgo Miklósne in 1947.

After a lot of detective work, I found her—Mrs. Czörgo Miklósne. For me, this was a most important achievement for two reasons. First, I finally rejected my parents' demand to forget her and to accept them as my only parents. I have proven that one does not have to choose one over the other. I can have them both: my parents as my "biological parents" and parents after the Holocaust, and Mrs. Czörgo Miklósne as my Holocaust-mother. Secondly, visiting that Hungarian village brought me great relief. I found out that all those foggy, frightening memories were real remnants of real places, people, and occurrences. What I vaguely felt and remembered was a reality! These two internal understandings changed my life more than any therapy could. A great deal of my tension and depression simply disappeared.

Why am I compelled to write this now? For two reasons: Now, I seek forgiveness from my parents for being angry with them for many years. I felt that they did something terrible in leaving me and in letting me lose my innocent childhood. Now I know they are not to blame. The Nazis are the villains. Additionally, I want to thank this wonderful and courageous Hungarian woman, Mrs. Czörgo Miklósne from Nagyrede, who at only age twenty, was a real mother to me.

Moshe Bar Semech, *married with four children, was a clinical psychologist and a couples and family therapist.*

Miracles and Mysteries

By Jack Goldstein

(From My Story, *Volume XXXI, April 2023; as told to his granddaughter for a school project.)*

My earliest, most vivid memory is of Sunday, March 13, 1938, one of the fateful days that marked the beginning of the end to our family's way of life and everything we held dear. It was my and my twin brother Bruno's third birthday, and our family had gathered at our grandparents' apartment to celebrate. From the balcony, the adults watched with alarm the cheering crowds in the street as the Nazi army paraded into Vienna to thunderous shouts of "*Heil* Hitler!" Bruno and I stood there, not quite understanding what to make of this ominous scene.

With Austria's annexation into Nazi Germany, life became immediately difficult for Austrian Jews. Those who had the prospect

Mother, Regina Goldstein, née Sussman, with (left) Jack, and (right) Bruno. Vienna, c. 1937.

Mother, Regina Goldstein, and twins, in Brussels, c. December 1939.

and means to leave, did so—including many members of my family. On my mother's side, they went to Palestine, France, and Switzerland. On my father's side, only one uncle was able to find safety for himself and his family in the US in 1938. One uncle made it as far as Italy; another and his wife were able to get to London by obtaining jobs as butler and maid for a wealthy household. Quite a disillusionment for young people who spent summers at the beaches and winters on the ski slopes!

By early November 1938, our extended family in Austria was down to my two sets of grandparents, my mother's sister, brother, and his family. My mother was very attached to her parents, and fearing for their welfare, she refused to leave.

Then came *Kristallnacht*! A man from the SS came to our apartment and ordered my father to come with him. My father asked, "Can I first say goodbye to my children?" My father entered our bedroom, and as the soldier looked on, he kissed us both as we slept in our beds.

What happened next will always remain a mystery and a miracle to me. The soldier walked my father down the stairs, then along the street, but when they reached the corner, he was told to vanish!

After this close call, there was no longer any wavering or uncertainty. My father had hoped his brother in the US would be able to obtain visas for us, but this did not materialize. With conditions becoming more dangerous with each day, we flew from Vienna to Frankfurt, and from there to Belgium—the one country that allowed us to pass through, because we had preliminary applications that would eventually secure visas to the US.

Once in Belgium, we got by. The Nazis had confiscated most of our assets and we had fled with whatever fit in a few suitcases. My father sold accessories for clothing, and my mother used her sewing skills to produce women's undergarments. In May 1940, just before the Nazi invasion, my father was arrested by the Belgian police, along with thousands of other men now considered "enemy aliens," most of whom were Jews from Germany and its newly conquered territories. (My father wound up in a series of French internment camps—Saint-Cyprien, from May 1940 to October 1940; Gurs, from October 1940 to May 1941; and Camp des Milles, from May 1941 to August 1941.)

With two five-year-old boys, my mother thought it best to join the thousands of refugees on the roads trying to escape the continent. My Aunt Fanny, who had entered Belgium illegally, joined us. One truck driver agreed to give us a lift to Dunkirk for a fee, but when he discovered that my aunt had no identification "papers," he said she had to get off.

So, we started walking. It was very hot and the road was strewn with dead soldiers and horses. At night, we slept in shelters. I have no memory of what we ate or how my mother paid for it. But somehow, we kept going—walking during the days and trying to sleep under the din of bombardments at night. As we approached Dunkirk, we learned that only British and French soldiers were being evacuated. We were forced to re-

Father, Heinrich, with twins, in 1944, just before Liberation. Father is hiding his yellow star with a briefcase.

turn to Brussels, which was now under Nazi military administration.

It wasn't easy for my mother to fend for us alone, but she managed somehow. Though we missed our father terribly, we carried on, trying to maintain some sense of routine by attending our local public school.

Then, another miracle! In August of 1941, my father escaped from the Camp des Milles, in France, and eventually made his way to Brussels. When Bruno and I first saw him, we didn't recognize him. He had a beard, wore a beret, and he'd lost a lot of weight. My father spoke about the harshness of the camps, the death rate, and how lucky he was to have endured. One of his uncles, who had been with him, had not survived the malnutrition, the lack of medical care, and the cold.

In 1942, with the implementation of the Final Solution, the Gestapo took over the reins of government, and the Nazis became more determined than ever to capture every Jew. Bruno and I, by then age seven, were ousted from our school; we were no longer safe outside, and wearing the yellow star became mandatory.

Even being in our apartment became dangerous. With the *rafles* (raids) increasing in frequency, no Jewish home was safe. My parents risked going outside to barter for food. While they were out, I worried. They could be arrested at any time, and I began to live in fear.

Being stuck indoors for such a long time was also boring. I taught myself to read German, and one day I saw a notice in my father's German newspaper about deer hunting that listed all the restrictions—the seasons, the days, even the hours. When my father came home, I said, "Dad, the deer have it better than we do. They're protected by the police. We're worse off than the deer." Then I asked, "Why? What have we done?" My father just looked at me and shook his head.

My mother was always fretting about her parents, her brother Moritz, his wife Stefi, and their two boys, Jackie and Kurt. Moritz had sacrificed himself and his family by remaining in Vienna to care for his aging parents. All were transported from Vienna to the ghetto of Debica in Poland. My mother corresponded with them and sent packages until early 1943, when they were rounded up

Left to right: Aunt Stefi, Grandmother Cilli, Grandfather Josef, and Uncle Moritz in the ghetto of Dębica, Poland.

and later murdered by the Nazis. (The letters are available at the United States Holocaust Memorial Museum as "Goldstein family letters".)

I was a very religious kid, especially during the war. I believed in God and in angels, and that I would be protected as long as I believed in Him. My father set an example by putting on his *tefillin* and *tallit* every morning. I admired both my parents—my father for his devotion to our faith, and my mother for keeping kosher even in the darkest times. Each Friday night, my mother set the table with a white tablecloth and, though there was very little food to place on the table, she lit the Shabbos candles. During these trying times, it was very important to my parents to maintain our rituals.

We survived in this way until early 1944. One day, as my parents were out, probably to find some food, the Nazis blocked off both ends of our street with their trucks. There was no way to hide or to escape this *rafle*. They banged on our door with the butt of their rifles. I was slow to answer because I was in the middle of a prayer. When I finally opened the door, they shouted at me, "Why didn't you answer the door?" I told them I was praying.

Two tall, uniformed, and helmeted soldiers, along with the infamous Jewish traitor known as "*Gros Jacques*," loomed over

Bruno and me, asking where our parents were and when they would be back. We answered that we didn't know. Then they said, "Get ready, you're coming with us. Pack some clothes, some water and food, we'll be back for you in fifteen minutes."

As the soldier spoke, I remembered my father had previously worked in a factory that produced fur hats and gloves for the Germans fighting on the Russian Front. I knew he had a document that had once exempted him from arrest. Though no longer valid, it was stored by my parents in a side compartment of our stove, which, with no coal to heat our home, was rendered useless.

"I want to show you something," I said, retrieving the document from the stove and showing it to the soldier. He read it, passed it to the other soldier, who read it, folded it, and returned it to me. They walked out.

Once they were out, I said to Bruno, "We're not going to do anything, they're not going to take us, God is going to take care of us." From the hallways and stairs, we heard the screams as people and suitcases were shoved down the stairs. Those sounds will remain with me forever.

When they returned to our apartment, one soldier asked the other in German, "What shall we do with the boys?" After a few moments, the other soldier said, "*Lass sie*" (leave them). And they walked out. Another miracle!

We were the only people remaining in the building. The concierge came to our apartment and said, "You boys better leave because the Nazis will come back." We didn't know what to do. There were curfews at night, so we waited, sitting on the floor, hoping for our parents' return.

Wedding photo of Sophie and Israel Goldstein.

Sophie and Israel in Opole, shortly before they were murdered.

Before our parents reached our building, a gentile neighbor ran up to them. "Don't go to your apartment, the Nazis have taken everybody, and they usually come back at night."

"But my children are there," my mother said.

The neighbor repeated, "They took every Jew from the building and from the entire street. Your children aren't there."

My mother fainted in the street. After my father revived her, she told him, "My boys are there, I know it." They went back and found us! Hugging and kissing us, they knew we couldn't stay.

We found a discarded baby carriage, put whatever we could into it, and walked to stay with our aunt in a different part of Brussels. A neighbor said to my mother, "You know you're putting your children in jeopardy. There's a priest, Father Bruno, who hides Jewish children. You should contact him, and he'll hide your children."

She contacted him, and he selected a railroad station and time to meet. "I'll have a flower in my lapel and when you see me, let the boys walk over to me. Don't cry. When you see them with me, walk away." We followed the instructions, but I remember looking at my mother, thinking this may well be the last time I will ever see her. I will always remember the love I saw in her eyes before we parted.

Though we were separating, it felt good to be outside and on a train. After being cooped up in our apartment for such a long time, there was some relief in that. Bruno became playful and was climbing onto luggage racks, going from one to the other. Always the careful one, I said to Bruno, "Stop! You're bringing attention to us." Father Bruno wasn't at all bothered by my brother's high spirits. I remember thinking, "That priest is such a nice man, a good man."

Kolonie Saint Jan Berchmans, Maaseik, June 28, 1944. Bruno is the second boy from the right in the second row; Jack is behind him.

We arrived at a station where a doctor was waiting for us. He took us to his house with a circular driveway and encouraged us to ride his children's bicycles. Since we were learning on a gravel surface, we weren't too successful. Still, that day, free from fear, remains etched in my mind.

The next day, we were taken by car to a convent, the Kolonie St. Jan Berchmans, in Maaseik. The doctor drove, with Father Bruno at his side, and with us in the back, under a blanket. We were told there would be lots of checkpoints with Nazi soldiers, and that we had to pretend to be his very sick patients, so sick that he was transporting us to a hospital. The ruse worked.

The convent was a very different experience. There was very little to eat, save for a watery oatmeal three times a day. I was very homesick, particularly on Sundays, when some of the children had visitors. Nobody came to see us, and I wept for my parents. The only treat we all had on Sundays was sardines. I remember enjoying dipping some bread into oil.

As the liberation neared, I became very ill, and was placed in isolation in the attic, even as bombs fell and everyone else ran to the shelter. I was feverish, feeling rather sorry for myself, when suddenly my mother appeared! It had been very dangerous for her to come, but she said she had to take a chance because she'd had a "premonition." Seeing our poor condition, she took us home, where two or three weeks later, Brussels was liberated.

My immediate postwar years were also difficult. My father insisted I be placed in the third grade French section, although I spoke none. Previously, I had attended the Flemish section, and I hadn't gone to school for nearly three years. My first year in the French section was probably the hardest I'd ever worked. The next year I did very well—I was third in my class. The year after, I was number one, and I remained number one for the rest of my schooling in Belgium. If there's one thing that the war years did for me, it is that my setbacks made me very ambitious. At an early age, I said to myself, "Hitler didn't win this!"

Jack Goldstein, *a retired civil engineer, worked on international projects for decades after his graduation from CCNY in 1957. Bruno Goldstein also graduated from CCNY in 1957, and until his retirement, he worked as a civil engineer for US governmental agencies.*

From Bohemia to the Netherlands

By Cordula Hahn

(From My Story, *Volume XXI, June 2022.)*

My parents, Renate and Karl, grew up on different sides of the tracks in Karlsbad, Bohemia—my mother, the rich Jewish girl and only daughter of a successful lawyer, and my father, the son of a successful house painter, who grew up with four siblings in a noisy Christian household. They had the same last name, Hahn, a quite common—Jewish and non-Jewish—name in that area. They met when my father was hired as a math tutor for my mother. They fell in love and while still in high school, they decided they would get married after finishing their degrees at the university of Prague, where they eventually earned their PhDs.

Despite the prevalent economic depression at the time, a magical period awaited them upon their return to Karlsbad. My father taught my mother biking, skiing, hiking—all that she had not been allowed to do by her overprotective mother. They went camping in the Bohemian countryside; they hiked with a friend to Luxembourg. In Karlsbad, they went to tea dances in the luxurious hotels of the famous spa resort. They took long walks in the Karlsbad woods with my grandfather Oscar, my mother's melancholic, severely asthmatic father, taking their adored little dog, Schorschl, with them. For now, life was still good and comfortable: summers were for summer sports, winters for winter sports, evenings for music and literature.

For quite some time, my mother's relatives and many others were already involved in political organizations or planning to

Renate and Karl during their magical prewar period in Karlsbad.

fight from abroad. But my mother and father considered moving to Palestine, as some of their friends did, a foolish undertaking.

When my mother's parents divorced, my grandmother moved to Prague. She always had been a difficult woman; it felt like a relief to everybody that she had moved away with her lover.

Many knew the day would arrive when tea dances would be replaced by death marches. It certainly happened in Karlsbad, where during *Kristallnacht*, the Jews were marched to prison. At that horrific time, my mother was pregnant with my brother; my father was the only non-Jew in the miserable group.

Having a common last name was no longer humorous. Several Dr. Hahns were physically abused while imprisoned, including my father, the Aryan Hahn. After a couple of days, the group was released and given five days to pack and leave the annexed Sudetenland. My parents and my increasingly despondent grandfather were able to reach Prague and move in with my difficult grandmother. "When Hitler comes, I die," my grandfather had declared for a long time. And the ever-so-correct, reliable, melancholic, mustached, elegant lawyer did just that when countries appeared uninterested in hosting an asthmatic, old Jewish man.

With each day, the atmosphere in Prague became more threatening. Czech Jews and refugees from Nazi Germany knocked on the doors of consulates, begging for visas. My grandmother managed to snag one to England. My parents were not so lucky. The British were not sympathetic to pregnant women unable to be put to work immediately. My parents' close, wealthy, Swiss friend, Dr. Max Wehrli, guaranteed for them a considerable sum of Swiss francs, which, with the help of a Dutch MP, allowed them into the Netherlands on a transit visa. The plan was to travel on to the US, where very rich relatives, well integrated into New York society, were expected to show empathy toward their family.

Little did my parents know that their relatives, eager to dive into Anglo-American culture, dreaded the arrival of their refugee relatives and the affidavits never arrived.

Nazi Germany invaded the Netherlands in May of 1940, before my brother's first birthday. The first two years were almost tolerable. My parents and brother lived in the blue-collar neighborhood of an affluent area. Their neighbors were not unkind, just surprised about their foreignness. The grocer and his wife from around the corner were a source of support whenever they could be. I was born in June 1942 in a Catholic Hospital in Utrecht, where my mother stayed for nine days so that at least for this period she would be out of danger.

By the summer of 1942, my parents and all others targeted by the Nazis realized they were in a desperate situation. My mother wore the yellow star. No more biking, no more swimming. The pool was affordable and was the center of neighborhood life from May to the end of August. It was just a minute's walk from the house, where one could hear the children screeching with delight in the water. My mother, alone at home, singled out my brother's and my screams among those of the other children as she read or paced nervously from one room to the other until we came home.

Fortunately, Dutch friends, university students active in the Resistance, and the local mayor surrounded my family with their protection. The time came to build a hiding place in the cellar of our house. They placed a forbidden radio there and listened to the BBC and Radio Oranje, the station of the Dutch Government in exile in London. My mother had false papers, also provided

Cordula and brother Christoph in 1944.

by the Resistance. Our very helpful grocer and his wife, a childless couple, wanted to take in my brother and me, but this plan never had to be executed.

If needed, the scheme was to be as follows: my very blond mother with a German name was to pretend to be a German domestic and to feign being mentally disturbed by just roaming around.

Still, danger could not be avoided. My mother was called to the police headquarters, where sterilization was proposed as her only way out. Dutch police banged several times on our doors, causing my brother lifelong trauma. The threat of the summons came closer and closer. Each time my father's protector was there to jump in and save my mother. My father too was not completely out of danger. Since Nazi Germany's annexation of Bohemia, we were automatically considered German citizens and my father was called in for duty to serve at the Eastern Front. Through careful study of German law, he found a way to avoid serving because of his star-wearing Jewish wife. After the war, they said they saved each other, and they had!

My parents' wartime difficulties became part of our family lore. I grew up with that word "affidavit." As a small child, I knew it had something to do with Jews and I imagined it was King David who decided who could enter America! But at the time, my questions to my mother were mostly those of a very young child, and more pressing.... Why hadn't she taken her dolls when she fled her country? Or the silk dresses she had once owned?

Later, I wondered if my family was punished for being secular and detached from their Jewishness—for trying to belong, and for relying on their service to their country. For many years, I wished they had dreamed less during their tea dances, wasted less time hiking and skiing, listening to classical music, and discussing their literary heroes. They could have spared themselves so much fear and danger—if only they would have been more aware of what was happening around them.

After a long career at the Dutch Consulate in New York City, **Cordula Hahn** *is now a volunteer at the Hidden Child Foundation.*

My Return to Judaism

By Yetty Derschowitz

(From The Hidden Child, *Volume XX, 2012.)*

After the *Anschluss* (annexation) and the distress endured by Jewish families in Vienna, a few Jewish girls and I were allowed to enter Belgium on June 24, 1939. A convoy of boys, including my brother Erich, arrived later, on July 20. Our parents had made the heart-wrenching decision to be separated from their children to prevent us from falling into the hands of the Nazis. I was five and a half years old, the second youngest in the group. I remember being taught rudimentary French words by the older girls on the train: "*S'il vous plaît, merci, bonjour Monsieur, Madame.*" We were greeted at the station by Belgian volunteers, led by Mme de Munter-Latinis, then president of the Association of Women Lawyers, who organized the transfer.

During the entire war, I was cared for by a French-speaking Belgian couple, Irma and Arthur Scauflaire-Lemaire, whom I called "Papa" and "Maman." My foster parents were shopkeepers who, prior to the war, had managed to put away some savings. But once the war began, their small nest egg melted away with the increased cost of food and the medical expenses incurred after Papa became ill in 1941. He died in 1948.

At war's end, no one came to claim me. So, I stayed with Maman, who by this time had very little left. We led an extremely modest existence; I would say on the threshold of real poverty. Maman and I remained together until I married in 1954.

My personal experience of the war was on the whole rather positive. I had been protected by the entire village, all of whom,

Jewish girls' convoy from Vienna, arriving in Brussels on June 24, 1939. Yetty is the little girl in front, on the far left. A copy of this photo was sent to Yetty by Mr. de Munter, the son of Mrs. de Munter-Latinis, the attorney who organized the transfer. Mr. de Munter found this photo among his mother's effects.

even the mayor, knew I was Jewish. At the end of the war, when I tried to see where my name had been entered in the "register of foreigners," I discovered that the page in question had been torn out. Thanks to that, the Gestapo never found me. On the other hand, to the enormous relief of my foster parents, each year the mayor signed an extension to my residency permit.

However, Maman later told me that a German officer once entered the shop and said to her, "Madam, I know you have a little girl living with you who is not your daughter." Maman was too shocked to reply. He said that the mother of one of the girls in my class had informed on me. The woman, his former mistress, had perhaps hoped to ingratiate herself with him. He continued, "I am a German officer but not a Nazi and I shall not be returning to that woman." He assured Maman that our secret was safe with him, but repeated that we should be very careful. My classmate and I were both just eight years old.

I had been baptized into the Catholic faith back in Austria, this being a condition for my leaving the country and entering Belgium. But upon my arrival, the village priest was not convinced that my baptism had been done correctly, so he made me go through the ceremony a second time. I cannot blame the priest for feeling that he was simply doing his duty. Moreover, how many people can boast of being baptized twice? Nevertheless, after having been brought up as a Christian, it was only much later, and after much reflection, that I joined the Jewish community.

Almost immediately after the war ended, I started to write my real name in my exercise books. Maman, who had wanted to adopt me officially, gave up the idea, reasoning that if she were to adopt me, I would only make her life a misery. Thus, I kept my real name but, at the same time, maintained all my affection for this woman to whom I owed my life, my good health, and my education.

In 2002, at a ceremony at the Israeli Embassy in Brussels, my foster parents, Irma and Arthur Scauflaire-Lemaire, were posthumously awarded the title of "Righteous Among the Nations." It is an honor they richly deserve.

Yetty Derschowitz *resides in Belgium.*

PART II

Between Two Religions

Introduction: Conflicts of Identity

By Nechama Tec, PhD

(Excerpted From The Hidden Child*, Volume VII, Number 1, fall/winter 1997.)*

As hidden children, our lives were dominated by two basic demands: giving up our Jewish identity and silence. Complying to both, even temporarily, implied a rejection of our families. In part, it was also a denial of our religion. Most of us came from secular homes—Jewish Orthodox children hardly ever made it to the Christian world. And yet, religion assumed an important place in our lives. We knew that being Jewish had deprived us of our right to live. Being Jewish meant something bad, something for which we could be killed. Being Christian meant being protected.

Of the different Christian religions, Catholicism was particularly influential in the lives of the hidden children. Many who were old enough to realize what was happening welcomed Catholicism. Those who were very young embraced it blindly. From the perspective of the Jewish child, baptism and Catholicism were positive forces. Each shielded him from danger. Each offered a feeling of security and comfort.

Inevitably, the influence of religion spilled over into the postwar lives of the hidden children. For the children, their very survival was proof that they had adjusted well to their roles as Christians. But at the end of the war, they were asked to switch again. For many of us, the return to Jewish identity was a drawn-out process. Some never returned. Acceptance, hostility, ambivalence, resentment, shame, and regret were only some of the emotions we hidden children had. Some of us may still continue to have such feelings about our Jewishness, about our religion. At times mixed together, appearing and disappearing, these emotions are not surprising.

We could not easily give up that which had helped us to survive. If being Jewish meant danger, disapproval, something one could be killed for, why would a child want to take it back? Most of us were conflicted about these issues. For a while, we were suspended in two worlds: the Christian and the Jewish. Some of us could not reconcile the two. Still others have taken a definite step toward Christianity or Judaism.

Has becoming a part of two different worlds given us a broader, less prejudiced perspective on life, on people? Perhaps.

Nechama Tec *(née Bawnik) (1931–2023) was a Professor Emerita of Sociology at the University of Connecticut. She received her PhD in sociology at Columbia University and was a Holocaust scholar. Her book* When Light Pierced the Darkness *(1986) and her memoir* Dry Tears: The Story of a Lost Childhood *(1984) both received the Merit of Distinction Award from the Anti-Defamation League of B'nai B'rith. She also wrote* Defiance: The Bielski Partisans *on which the film* Defiance *(2008) is based, and for which she won the 1994 International Anne Frank Special Recognition prize.*

Born in Austria, Saved in Belgium

By Ruth Wallach Bachner

(Excerpted from My Story, *December 2022, Volume XXVII.)*

In 1988, I returned to Vienna to see the building where I had lived. I was startled when I saw the name *WIMMER* on the door of my family's apartment, and I sobbed uncontrollably. A man in his 70s opened the door. When I told him my name, he looked as if he'd seen someone who'd come back from the dead. The last time he had seen me, I was the one inside the apartment and he was ordering my family to leave. Now he was denying it. "You made a mistake—you lived next door. I have nothing to do with this. I was on the Russian front." He refused to let me in. I thought of all that my family endured while he spent the last fifty years in the comfort of our home—with our possessions.

Postwar photo of Ruth Wallach Bachner.

I was born in Vienna in 1930 and lived with my parents and younger brother in the twentieth district, a neighborhood with a large Jewish presence. My parents, who fled Poland when they were teenagers, enjoyed being away from the chronic antisemitism and pogroms that had plagued their childhoods. I grew up surrounded with love, family, friends, and Judaism.

My carefree childhood ended in March of 1938—the day I stood among the thousands of Austrians who swarmed the streets of Vienna to celebrate the *Anschluss*—the unification of Germany and Austria. What I witnessed that day still haunts me. The crowd was frenetic, waving Nazi flags, saluting, and screaming, "*Sieg Heil! Heil Hitler!*" The man standing next to me reprimanded me for not saluting Hitler. I was petrified and felt threatened.

Public displays of antisemitism were now an acceptable part of everyday life. My classmates kicked me, pulled my hair, and spit at me in front of the teachers who did nothing to stop it. Things escalated quickly. Jewish people were dragged out of their stores and were beaten while crowds stood and watched.

On November 9 and 10, 1938, *Kristallnacht*, the night of broken glass, synagogues and Jewish stores throughout Austria and Germany were destroyed, including my father's haberdashery. A few days later, the building's superintendent, a young man wearing a Nazi SS uniform, knocked on our door. He yelled, "I am taking your apartment. If you don't leave by tomorrow, I will report you to the Gestapo."

We left our belongings and ran. Using forged passports, we took a train to Aachen, Germany, and were smuggled across the border into Belgium. In Belgium, we lived in Marneffe, in government housing set up for refugees. I went to school and made friends. We enjoyed a temporary sense of normalcy but continued trying to get visas to leave Europe.

On May 10, 1940, when Nazi Germany invaded Belgium, our lives again changed dramatically. Soon Jewish people were required to register with the police, and by the spring of 1942, they had to wear yellow stars. Once again, as in Austria, we were overcome with a sense of doom. We saw Nazis hunting Jews, grabbing them from the streets and out of buildings. None were ever heard from again. We had several close calls, returning to our building minutes after a raid. My cousin Betty, her two-year-old son, and her husband weren't as lucky. They were sent to the gas chambers of Auschwitz.

Sensing we needed help, a neighbor in our building introduced us to Father Bruno Reynders, a Benedictine priest who would later be recognized by Yad Vashem as a Righteous Among the Nations for saving almost four hundred Jewish people—mostly children. Through his large network of clergy, family, and friends, *Père* Bruno found places for my family to hide. I was twelve years old; my brother was eight, and we needed to be separated from our parents and from each other. My brother was placed in an orphanage and my parents were hidden as domestics at the Prion family's *château* in Liège.

I was hidden in a convent, Our Lady of Seven Sorrows in Ruiselede. Only the Mother Superior knew I was Jewish. My name and identity were changed; I became "Marie Renée LeRoi," the only Jewish girl living among girls from wealthy farmer families.

I said goodbye to my parents and brother. I hugged them tightly and hoped they didn't see me cry. For four long years we had been living with turmoil and uncertainty. With little food, no belongings, and no place to call home, the only solace I had was the comfort and security of being with my parents. Now that too was being taken away from me.

Although I was treated well at the convent, I lived in constant fear someone would find out I was Jewish. I tried to look and act

Ruth is on the right side of the aisle, fifth row, second girl from the aisle.

like the other girls. I wore the same uniform, said the same Latin prayers, and lived in the same room. I went to mass, crossed myself, and went to confession. Inside, I was always on guard, expecting the Nazis to barge in at any minute and take me away.

I missed my family. My stomach was in knots. I worried about where they were—or if they were alive. The three American $100 bills and the piece of paper with my uncle's address in New York my mother had stitched into the hem of my coat were constant reminders I would probably never see them again. I wanted to believe my family and I would not be murdered. I started to embrace Christianity and found comfort in praying.

It was expected that all girls at the school would be baptized. I felt terrible pressure from the nuns who repeatedly told me if I wasn't baptized, I would have a blemish on my soul and die in hell. In a way, I was brainwashed. I had promised my father I would always be Jewish, and I didn't know what to do. I wondered if being baptized would make me safe from the Nazis. I went to the Mother Superior for guidance. On one of his visits to the convent, Père Bruno was given a letter to take to my father, asking his permission for me to be baptized. My father replied, "If it will save her life, she has my blessing."

So, I was baptized. The Mother Superior found godparents for me, kind people with whom I stayed during school breaks. The convent became my cocoon. I felt somewhat insulated from the outside world.

The war in Belgium ended when I was fourteen. I was grateful my parents and brother had survived but also had mixed feelings about leaving the convent. I wanted to become a nun, but the nuns explained that I was too young. I left the convent with my bible, a statue of the Virgin Mary, and with plans to continue studying and to return in a few years.

Living with my family in Brussels, I continued to practice my adopted religion in secret. I read the Bible under the covers and snuck out of the house Sunday mornings to go to Mass. My parents found out and insisted I stop. Christianity had been a huge part of my life and I felt lost without it. My parents understood it had been important for me when I was in the convent, but now that the Holocaust was over, they expected me to return

Ruth with her parents and brother in 1947, when they went to say goodbye to the Prion family before their departure for the US.

to Judaism. Within a few months, I gave up Christianity and started going to synagogue regularly with my parents.

We left Belgium in 1947 and settled in New York where my parents' siblings and my cousins lived. Adjusting to a new country was difficult. I was a teenager who spoke with an accent, didn't have friends, and struggled to fit in. I pleaded with the Belgian consulate to send me back to Belgium, but they couldn't.

In time, I adjusted as best I could. I finished high school, joined Jewish organizations, made friends, and attended Hunter College at night. I got married in 1951 to Fred Bachner, a Holocaust survivor. Holocaust education and remembrance was important to us. We gave testimonials and spoke to students for decades.

In 1988, upon my return to Belgium, I stood at the entrance to the convent and was overcome with the fears and uncertainties I had felt when I was twelve. When I saw Sister Marie-Therese, one of the nuns I had been close to, memories of the warmth and caring I had been given came flooding back.

I went to the château in Liège where my parents were hidden. Up until the Prions' death a few years earlier, my parents and the Prions wrote letters to one another. In the 1960s, my parents visited them in Liège. Now I was there to thank them in person. I will forever be grateful to the wonderful people who risked their lives to save me and my family.

des AFFAIRES ÉTRANGÈRES et du COMMERCE EXTÉRIEUR

Direction générale de la Chancellerie et du Contentieux

MINISTERIE van BUITENLANDSCHE ZAKEN en BUITENLANDSCHEN HANDEL

Algemeene Directie der Kanselarij en der Geschillen

MINISTÈRE des AFFAIRES ÉTRANGÈRES et du COMMERCE EXTÉRIEUR
BUREAU SPÉCIAL
PASSEPORTS

LAISSEZ-PASSER
tenant lieu de passeport

DOORGANGSBEWIJS
ter vervanging van een reispas

F 7492

Le présent laissez-passer est délivré à Mademoiselle
Dit doorgangsbewijs wordt afgeleverd aan
WALACH Ruth

de nationalité allemande ... à Vienne
van nationaliteit, geboren te
le 6 août 1930
op (1)

résidant à Saint Josse ten Noode, 26, rue Botanique
verblijvende te

titulaire de la carte d'identité N° 5220
houder van de eenzelvigheidskaart Nr

délivrée à Saint Josse ten Noode, le 31 août 1945
afgeleverd te op

A section of Ruth's Laissez-Passer, dated March 23, 1946.

Ruth Wallach *immigrated to the United States in 1947 and married Fred Bachner, also a survivor. She and her family lived in Westchester until her passing in 2020 from COVID-19.*

Growing up in Occupied France: A Dual Experience

By Renée Roth-Hano

(Excerpted from The Hidden Child, *Volume VII, Number 1, 1997.)*

The very first time I experienced faith—a connection with a world beyond my daily one—was in a Catholic convent in Normandy on a mild, early spring day in 1943. I was eleven. Paris had been bombed and I hadn't heard from my parents, who were hiding there. There was no doubt in my mind: my mother and father were dead, if not from the bombs, then because they had been caught.

I was sitting in the garden, determined to keep my sad thoughts from my two younger sisters. I had settled at the foot of the statue of the Virgin Mary. I thought, she is a mother, isn't she? She, of all people, would know how it feels to be afraid, to feel lonely. And for a moment, it seemed as if she were stretching her arms out for me—a Jewish girl.

After the stormy times we had experienced, it was easy enough to bask in the warm and welcoming atmosphere provided by the nuns. Eagerly, I set out to put into practice what my sisters and I were being taught in the Catholic school we attended: performing my daily good deed, saying grace before meals, and participating in prayers and songs in a church that embraced us totally.

How I admired the nuns' selflessness and brave spirit—their risking their lives by taking us in. They were always respectful of our differences, ushering us into church through the side door so we wouldn't have to genuflect in front of the altar. Yet they were mindful that we blended in. Only when the Nazis invaded our

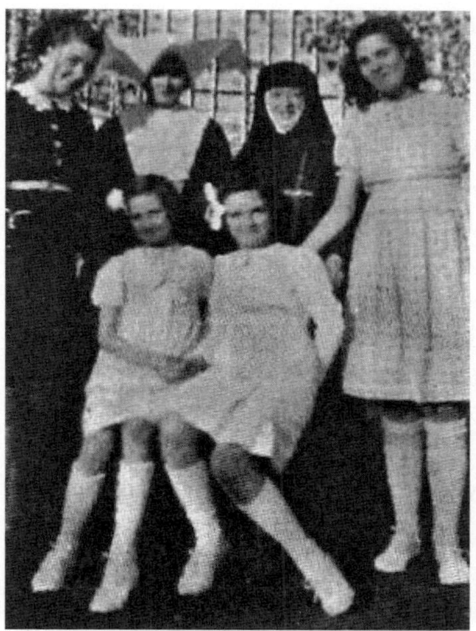

Standing, left to right: classmate, Mother Superior, Sister Charles of the Little Sisters of the Poor, and Renée. Sitting: sisters Lily and Denise, spring 1944.

town were we secretly baptized to complete our disguise.

Baptism had not been easy. As the oldest, I felt responsible for my sisters, then ages nine and eight. I felt that it was a betrayal of sorts and that things would never be the same again. But I could not stop it. I began to sleepwalk and to suffer from attacks of breathlessness so severe that I feared I would die. And I had nightmares that we would go to Heaven without our parents.

So, when a few months later, our nunnery and town were bombed on that fateful D-Day, it felt right for me to vow, if God let us live, to become a nun. It was the least I could do, and the most. The truth is I had been terribly hurt and scarred as a Jew. I had gone to bed one evening an ordinary, innocent eight-year-old, barely knowledgeable about her Jewish faith, and I woke up the next day, forced to flee my home. I had been startled by the open displays of hatred around me in Paris. I was branded as a Jew: compelled to wear the Star of David, banned from movies, cafés, and parks, denied a radio, and subjected to curfews.

But the real hurt had started long before the war when I learned that Jews preferred boys. When I was born, my father gave me a boy's name. He did the same for my middle sister. And when my youngest sister was born, he told everyone she was a boy.

My mother's messages were hardly more positive. Women don't count at all in a "minyan," she reminded me. They are not allowed to touch the Torah or pronounce the name of God. Being a *balabusta* was my only chance in the world. I was in no hurry to grow up.

In the Catholic religion, at least, God is kinder to women, I thought. He made Mary the mother of Jesus, and little Thérèse of Lisieux a saint! The nuns were not afraid of Him—they were married to Him. Still, I couldn't trust Him. What if He were the same God Jews prayed to and feared, He who couldn't care less about the plight of the Jews—even little children. So, I turned to the saints invoked daily at the convent: St. Anthony, who would unfailingly turn up a lost key, a stray sock, and Sainte Thérèse, who was from a neighboring town. I didn't really believe in them, but that's all I had. I knew very little about Jewish history and, feeling abandoned by my parents, the saints kept me company and soothed my pain.

The isolation—the alienation, really—continued in postwar France. For a long time, I couldn't look into people's eyes lest they'd find out I was Jewish. Even when I felt safe enough to bring up my Jewish background, I would clam up, my throat choking out the words. I had never told anyone about my vow, but it was on my mind. Partly out of rebellion because I could not forget the war years, as my parents wished, I would sneak out to church for Sunday Mass, until the day my father found out and raged, "You are not going to church! You are a Jew, for God's sake!"

He died three days later. I have not attended Mass since—nor have I wanted to. It was only during a trip to New York that the knot became undone. My very first culture shock occurred when I heard people openly discussing the Seder in a department store. My most liberating experience—my very first hearty laughter—occurred as I was watching TV comedian Sid Caesar peppering his notorious German gibberish with Yiddish words. Only when I began to breathe freely and to keep my head high could I begin to discover and appreciate my Jewish heritage. I decided to make New York my home and, in order to revisit the past, I began to write. In fact, English, I realized later, had become the language of reconciliation for me. It allowed me some distance before setting down my thoughts in French.

But it was the International Gathering of the Hidden Child in May, 1991—and those that followed—which provided me with the most valuable experience of all: a community of peers, an extended family where I—*enfin!*—could feel unconditionally accepted. What am I today? Of course, I am a Jew—though not a conventional Jew. Being able to say, finally, "I am Jewish" without choking or blushing is a wonderful feeling.

Renée Roth-Hano *is the author of* Touch Wood: A Girlhood in Occupied France *and its sequel,* Safe Harbors.

Am I Still a Little Catholic Inside?

By William H. Donat

(Excerpted from The Hidden Child, *Volume VII, Number 1, 1997.)*

In 1943, when I was barely five years old, I was smuggled out of the Warsaw ghetto. I had already survived many hours in the bunker my parents and their neighbors had fashioned, and I had just been rescued from *Umschlagplatz*, the infamous railhead the Nazis had set up to transport Warsaw's Jews to Maidanek and Treblinka. My father had managed to persuade a ghetto policeman to snatch me out.

The close call had been so chilling my parents began a massive effort to place me on the Aryan side. It was difficult enough to place a girl, but to find someone willing to take a boy was unheard of. I had blond hair and blue eyes, and we spoke only Polish at home, but still, I was a Jewish boy bearing the sign of the covenant. After an exhaustive search, they found an older couple, active in the underground, who might be willing to take me. Before the war, the man had worked for my father's newspaper as an editor. His wife, who was to become my "Auntie Maria," came to see me at the printing shop, SS Druckerai, where my father worked. She felt that I could "pass," and arrangements were quickly made: my mother taught me the "Hail Mary" and "Our Father" prayers; I learned my new last name and got my first haircut; I was to forget the ghetto and to remember that my mother was in the country and my father in the army.

I lived with Auntie Maria and Uncle Stefan for about a month when one of the neighbors betrayed me to the local Polish police.

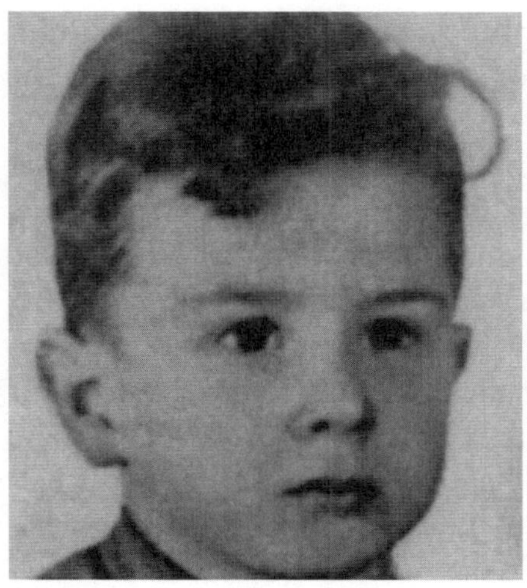
William H. Donat, age seven.

Auntie Maria stood up to the pistol-waving policemen, deftly bargaining for my life with the American $20 gold pieces my father had given her, while reminding them that one day the war would end. A deal was struck—they would not take me to the Gestapo, but she could no longer keep me with her.

I was sent to an orphanage in Otwock, which was run by nuns. Shortly after my arrival in this strange and inhospitable place, I was approached by a young nun. "Admit you're a Jew and I'll help you." I persisted in denying what must have been obvious to all the nuns, until one day, feeling particularly lonely and melancholy—I even remember thinking that it must be my birthday—I confessed my terrible secret, but only after the nun promised to keep the confidence. She told me not to worry, she could fix everything.

She arranged to have me baptized and I threw myself into daily prayers, going to Mass, asking God for more food. This went on for two years: prayer, hunger, learning to read and write, and despite our common unhappy lot, I was hazed by the other boys for being a "*Yidle*." In sharing every aspect of my life, my secret had become obvious to them. But my prayers to Jesus and Mary continued, always fervent and honest.

One day, Russian soldiers arrived, telling us the war had ended. Then Auntie Maria came with a woman I vaguely recognized. I had not seen my auntie for two years, but I knew who she was. As for the other woman, when asked if I knew her, I divined, "You must be my mother."

"Yes," she answered, "would you like to come with me? I promise you will never be hungry again." This was a huge undertaking for someone who had just survived two years in Majdanek, Auschwitz, and Ravensbruck, who had walked back from Germany to Warsaw in ski boots, and who didn't know where she would spend that night.

The plan my young nun and I had devised was already falling apart: if ever the Jewess—my mother—were to come for me, I would run into the woods and not go with her because she wouldn't let me pray to Jesus. Whether it was curiosity, or my need to confront this woman who had abandoned me, or a genuine recognition and recall of the love I had received before our separation, I do not know—after all, she had promised to come back for me after the war, and here she was! And here I was, challenging her: "Can I still pray to Jesus?" I asked. Perceiving what was at play, my mother assured me that I could pray to anyone I wished, she was just happy to see me. And with the pledge that I would never be hungry again, I saw no more obstacles to my going with her.

Miraculously, my father had also survived the two years of horror in the camps; in fact, after the war, people in Warsaw would point us out as an unusual sight, a Jewish family where all the members survived. My fervor for prayer slowly receded, as did the antisemitic comments I often spewed. My parents, although willing for the time being to put up with my Catholicism, would not accept my disparaging remarks. One day, my mother told me that they don't make fun of my religion, therefore I was not to continue such insults, even though I was just repeating what I had heard from other boys in the orphanage, and what seemed to me to be a natural part of the coarse Polish language. Besides, I was told, we were going to America where I would learn a new language. Still, for a long time, I would tell my left hand from my right by secretly making a truncated gesture, imperceptible to others, to check which hand I would have used to cross myself.

I grew up in New York City, where I lived in a predominantly Jewish neighborhood, attended schools with large Jewish populations, and had mostly Jewish friends. By the time I went to college, there was no question of my Jewishness. What impact, then, did my experience with Catholicism have on me as I became an adult? I found myself developing the same outlook toward religion, all religions, that my parents held. I consider myself a Jew. I married a Jewish girl. We raised our three children to be Jewish. My granddaughter is continuing the tradition. But I cannot accept a deity that is defined as "one who acts in human history" yet permitted the horrors I have read about, heard of, and lived through.

Perhaps my exposure to Catholicism made me aware of the relativity of all faiths, each dealing in their own ways with the eternal questions of man. They all help us cope with metaphysical problems we cannot understand. But after the Holocaust, it's difficult for me to accept that one and a half million Jewish children did not survive. It would be the height of egotism for me to thank a God who saved me but walked away from six million Jewish victims. And what about the additional five million non-Jewish victims of the German Reich?

So, who am I and how do I identify myself? I think of myself as ethnically Jewish. My dog tags in the army certainly said "Jewish." I relate to my people, to their joys, to their history, and to their tragedies. I am torn whenever there's a brutal act against my people, or for that matter, whenever a group of my people is irrationally stubborn. Is this my good American liberal arts education, or the emotional harkening to a religion that was, for a short time, mine? Could I still be a little Catholic deep inside? If religion is defined as the fashion in which one prays, or the tenets one accepts, then surely, I am not. I have too long been exposed to another mode of celebrating the yearly cycle of days that are special to my people—those people who would no longer be here if the Nazis had prevailed. What I will not do is to give the Hitlerite a final victory by forsaking my Jewish identity. Too many died because they were Jews for me to abandon them.

William H. Donat, *now deceased, was president of a printing company in New York City.*

Converting to Catholicism Saved Me and Changed My Life

By Zula Hass

(Excerpted from The Hidden Child, *Volume X, Number 1, 2001.)*

Before 1939, before the Soviet occupation of our part of Poland, my elementary school had been part of the Druskin's Gimnazjum in the city of Bialystok. Since 1938 when we moved to Bialystok, my father taught music at our school and my sister Rena attended its junior and senior high schools. I had been ailing with bronchitis during the spring and just as soon as school was over my parents sent me to the Eastern Carpathian Mountains on vacation. I was to stay there, in the small oil town of Boryslaw, with my aunt Rachela who practiced dentistry. Her sister, Aunt Giza, lived with her.

I stood at the Bialystok train station, teary eyed, with a little valise in hand, being reassured by my father that both he and my mother would soon follow and that we would all have a fine summer in a mountain resort. My escort, Mrs. H., was a friend of the family who was traveling to the nearby town of Drohobycz where the crude oil pumped in Boryslaw was refined.

I looked at my father's face and I knew…I just knew that I would never see him again. When I arrived in Boryslaw, my aunts Rachela and Giza greeted me with, "Why did they send you here? Don't they know that war is about to break out?" And indeed, two weeks later, on June 21, I awoke to the blast of guns. Outside, I saw people, mostly Jews with bundles on their backs, marching eastward, following the retreating Soviet army. The shelling of the town continued for three days. When the electricity was cut off, we huddled together in the dark, pondering what to do.

Then the Nazis came. They gathered the Jews in the town square and sent them to the prison to carry out and wash the thousands of bodies of political prisoners supposedly murdered by the Soviet secret police. Ukrainian peasants followed, loudly agreeing with the Nazis that these political prisoners were mostly Ukrainians and that their murderers were Jewish Communists.

Left: Ernestina (Rena) Schepper-Hass. Right: Izabela (Zula) Hass, with parents, c. 1935.

Armed with pitchforks, knives, and axes, the Ukrainians dragged Jews out of their homes, and a vicious pogrom erupted right in front of my eyes! Terror-stricken, I stood behind the curtains of our second-floor windows and watched. A drunken peasant pulled down Stalin's statue from its pedestal, then dragging a Jewish toddler, he smashed his little head against the statue. Other Ukrainians brutally hacked to death the howling mother and father who were hugging the body of their child.

The carnage went on into the night with the Ukrainians brutally butchering all the Jews that they tore out of their homes. Luckily, my aunts had installed heavy iron bars on the front and back doors of our house. But I did not believe that I would be spared, the longest day of my twelve years of life.

The next day, my aunt's dental technician, Eidikus, and I were forced to crawl into a flimsy hideout above our outhouse. We stayed there in silence for the next two days and nights. It was only on the third day that the Jews began to scramble out of their hideouts to mourn and bury their dead. I had suddenly become a grownup, an old person. Dr. Peekarska, my aunt's colleague and protégée, came to us with a basket of food. She had not forgotten the many favors my aunt had done for her at the clinic. In fact, throughout the Nazi occupation, this righteous Polish lady stood ready to help us whenever and however she could.

My older cousin, Wolfus, came to us soon after the start of the Nazi occupation. Wolfus was a freshman at the Lvov School of Engineering. But my aunts sent him back to his parents. A Polish guide was hired to take Wolfus to the ghetto of Bialystok where his parents, along with my parents and Rena, had been interned. This was the first time I was able to send news to my family. After that, I would write to my piano teacher, Mrs. Szatagina, a Russian native, who would smuggle our letters back and forth. Boryslaw's enclaves of Jews who managed to escape death were soon besieged by a terrible hunger. Day after day, I could see emaciated Jews walking the streets, begging for help. But the Ukrainian police killed these poor wretches. We weren't doing too well ourselves. Although Aunt Rachela had substantial savings, she had to use these judiciously. In time, Aunt Rachela was permitted to establish a limited dental practice for her non-Jewish patients, and she was paid in food items.

In December 1941, news came that Nazi killer units, the *Einsatzgruppen*, were on the outskirts of town. Within a day or two, the Nazis and their Ukrainian helpers were dragging Jews out of their homes, transporting them to the woods. Each time, empty trucks would return to carry off more Jews. It took no time to learn that all these Jews were executed and buried in the forest in gigantic mass graves.

The iron bars on our doors had kept us alive, but these could not be relied on again and again. When our Polish friends brought us the news in the spring of 1942 that the Einsatzgruppen were again in our environs, we realized that we had to seek a safer way to hide. Aunt Rachela scanned the list of patients in search of those who would be most likely to hide us in their homes. She had ruled out Mr. Lemecki who had been overheard saying that the Poles ought to thank Hitler for getting rid of the Jews. But it was the same Mr. Lemecki who volunteered to hide all of us in trunks kept in his cellar!

This time, the Jews had anticipated the *Aktion* and many had hidden. The Nazis then resorted to a trick: they discontinued the roundup for twenty-four hours, thereby luring the fugitives, including us, into a trap. My aunts, Eidikus, and I immediately returned to the Lemecki residence. But when we knocked on the door, we overheard Lemecki's antisemitic mother say, "Hide these dirty Yids again? Never!" Yet Lemecki saved our lives once more.

When we returned to Boryslaw after two days in Lemecki's cellar, many of our friends were missing. All of them had been sent to the extermination camp of Belzec. My hopes for survival were gone and I wondered if my parents would ever see me again. In the summer of 1942, there was another Aktion. Once again, a Polish family came to our aid, allowing us to hide in their empty country home. The Aktion was interrupted for twenty-four hours. This time, we were tricked and returned home. During this day of "truce," my aunt had spotted a Ukrainian policeman, Hrycek, who had been her patient. He hinted that he'd be "Coming in soon." But it was now too late to leave the house. This time, all four of us squeezed into the crawl space above the outhouse. We could hardly breathe as we listened to the Ukrainian policemen search every nook and cranny of the apartment. It was lucky that my aunts had not hidden under the beds this time.

We were petrified when the Ukrainians entered the outhouse wondering aloud if there was a space behind the loose boards of the ceiling. I listened to the pounding of my heart and counted the last seconds of my life. But Hrycek urged his pals not to waste time looking in unlikely spaces, and we were spared.

By the fall of 1942, very few Jews were left in Boryslaw. A tiny ghetto was formed, and my aunts, Eidikus, and I were forced to move in with the family of my friend Rena Stiffel. Aunt Rachela opened a tiny dental office and even some Germans came to see her. Those Jews who had proper work certificates would temporarily escape the transport to Belzec, but that of course excluded the children.

Because of this, a hideout was constructed in the cellar for Rena, her unemployed mother, and me. It could be entered through the back of a closet. Three times a day they fed us and removed the bucket serving as our WC. We could light candles but only occasionally. Rena's mother, a cultured woman, fascinated us with talks of the theater, the opera, and her travels. The talks kept my mind off the dangers, but I would daydream about being free again, about walking the streets of Bialystok, about my parents.

Sometime in February 1943, Mrs. Kowicki walked into Aunt Rachela's office. She was clad in black and she told my aunt about the tragic death of her fifteen-year-old daughter. My aunt then asked Mrs. Kowicki if she would be willing to save the life of a Jewish mother's daughter in memory of her own daughter. When the bereaved mother said yes, I became the Kowickis' "niece," and they took me into their home.

To legitimize the enterprise, all kinds of original and forged Aryan documents were purchased for me. These documents included the birth certificate of a dead Polish girl and I became Irena Borek. I loved my "Uncle Emil" and my "Aunt Sophie," but my stay there became precarious. Uncle Emil built a hideout for me over the veranda whose boards would be moved in the evening so that I could come in for the night. But one day, neighbors inquired if it was true that the Kowickis were hiding a Jew in their house.

In view of this new danger, they decided I would live with Uncle Emil's relatives in the town of Sanok. On June 3, 1943, I was secretly baptized, given the rosary beads and prayer book of Janka, the Kowickis' daughter, and taught the essentials of catechism. I was told that St. Mary would now save me. At the age of fourteen, I had to pretend so many things. Would I be able to do it?

I was now the daughter of Wladyslaw and Olga Borek, née Partyka, Polish patriots whom the Soviets had exiled to Siberia. Uncle Emil kept reassuring me that I would be safe. There were trees and flowers around the house, and within this serenity, I began to believe that maybe I would survive. The following Sunday I went to church with my new family. I was a careful observer, mimicking the melodious prayers and the cadence of standing and kneeling. That afternoon, I returned to the empty church and, standing in front of the statue of St. Mary, I pleaded with her for my life, making vows of gratitude: "Save me…please save me…. If you do, I will believe in you until the day I die." Gradually, my fears disappeared. People treated me with kindness but, of course, they weren't aware of my true identity.

In the summer of 1944, the Soviet army fought the Nazis in and around Sanok, and one side or the other alternately occupied the town. We had to stay in the cellar during the final eight weeks of fighting until the Russians liberated us. We resumed a fairly normal life, and I continued my education. A few months later, I heard that Aunt Giza, Aunt Rachela, and her dental technician Eidikus had survived the war and had settled in Walbrzych, the former German-Silesian town (Waldenburg).

In October 1945, I received the news that my sister Rena had survived the concentration camps in Nazi Germany. She had returned to Poland and was staying with our aunts in Walbrzych. How was I, an ardent Catholic, going to live within a family of Jews? Since my parents and the rest of my Jewish family had all been killed, I decided to remain a Polish Catholic for the rest of my life. I went to Walbrzych and told my sister that I would not go with her to Germany and wherever else she would go from there. Rena and I parted ways forever.

Zula Hass *was married to a former minister of public works and member of the Polish Cabinet. They lived in Wroclaw. (Rena Hass became a biology teacher and dean at the Bronx High School of Science in New York.)*

PART III

The Youngest Survivors

Introduction: The Targeting of Babies and Toddlers

By Elisheva van der Hal, PhD, and Danny Brom, PhD

(Excerpted from The Hidden Child, *Volume XXIV, 2016.)*

During the Holocaust, babies were born in open fields and forests, prison cells, labor and concentration camps, in cattle cars, and—if their mothers had forged identity papers—in hospitals. They were born underground, in holes where their mothers hid, and behind the barbed wires of crowded ghettos to parents hidden by non-Jews. When caught by their persecutors, most of these babies were murdered, often sadistically. Some were killed by despairing parents, particularly when it was feared that their crying would endanger the lives of adults.

In concentration camps such as Bergen-Belsen and Theresienstadt, where the inmates succumbed to malnutrition and fatal illness, a very small percentage of babies survived with their families (Garwood, 1999) or without them (Meijer, 2001). But with those exceptions, the few infants who survived did so largely because their parents had connections with non-Jewish caregivers. Though they might not have known what fate awaited them, these parents understood that the "relocations" were dangerous. Some parents entrusted their babies to non-Jewish friends; others had to rely on resistance organizations to find a safe home. Newborn babies were smuggled out of hospitals in laundry baskets and garbage bins or taken from mothers awaiting deportation in transit areas. Desperate parents who did not have connections with non-Jews left them on the doorsteps of houses, churches, convents, and monasteries. Young children were hurled out of deportation trains or over ghetto walls in the hope that a compassionate and courageous soul would save them. The motives of the rescuers ranged from religious or political beliefs, to financial gain, sheer compassion, or even the opportunity to obtain a baby for themselves; whatever their impetus, all of them risked their lives in caring for a Jewish child.

After the Liberation, new problems awaited. If the parents did not survive or did not manage to find their child, some foster parents kept the child that had come their way. But the majority of the infant survivors suffered at least one separation—often several consecutive ones, if they had been moved from one hiding place to another. They were claimed by parents they had never known, by relatives of their murdered parents, or by representatives of the Jewish community. Many were placed in orphanages because parents or other kin were too weak or too ill to care for them. Much more so than older children, such infant survivors were not acknowledged as having experienced wartime traumas or aftereffects. Often, they were considered to have been too young to remember and thus "too young to have suffered."

Dr. **Elisheva van der Hal** *and Dr.* **Danny Brom** *live in Israel. Both were born in the Netherlands.*

The Mystery and Dignity of a Very Young Survivor

By Robert Krell

(Excerpted from The Hidden Child, *Volume VIII, Number 1, winter 1998/99.)*

It is an enduring mystery to child survivors that we still suffer from memories traceable to infancy and early childhood. "How is it possible," we ask, "that after a lifetime of raising families, achieving professional or business successes, contributing to the welfare of our communities, we suffer now from what happened then? We were so little, and it was so long ago."

There are children who went through the war without prewar memories, schooling, or recollection of family to sustain them. For those born during the war or at its beginning, the oldest were no older than five or six in 1945. These children have only fragments of memory, of fear and loss, and perhaps of only a fleeting trace of a consciously remembered parent or parental gesture. But even these pieces of memory are important for they generate traumatic as well as healing recollections. It is a memory not to be denied.

Adults assumed young children had no memories at all, and, therefore, were free from problems. Adult survivors, who remember family life and endured concentration camps and unspeakable atrocities, considered the children to have been "lucky not to know what happened." They were wrong.

As a psychiatrist, I know that much psychological evidence points entirely to the contrary. Since a child's foundation for adulthood is predicated on developing feelings of security and

Robert Krell during his hiding period, c. 1943.

trust—based on parental love, nurturing, shelter, nourishment, and a predictable life—in the first few years, a dramatic disruption is devastating and long-lasting. If the trauma lasts for several years, as it did for so many during the war, and does not abate because of new traumas endured in the postwar years, the structures required for an integrated, mature personality are shaken to the core. Even the pre-verbal memories of a vulnerable existence are engraved along with those recollections that reappear readily. They require only a sound, a smell, a touch.

So, how did we make it? Were the fragments of memory sufficient? Did we dare imagine an ordinary beginning? Did we deceive ourselves by joining the chorus of those who said, "You were too young to remember," implying thereby that "You did not suffer like us"? From where did we draw strength? Perhaps we simply bypassed our traumatic beginnings for these many years with immersion in work, intense commitments to family and friends, busying ourselves with travels and adventures in order to contain the secret, mysterious core of shame and rage. Why shame? In response to a child's feeling that something is wrong with them to be treated so badly. Why rage? In response to the unfathomable experience of persecution so intense that there is no other response but to be enraged.

I function well. I have a successful career, a loving family, dear friends, and a fulfilling life. With all that, when I was fifty-six, I visited an early childhood trauma expert and therapist to secure a letter of support for a victim's claim to be submitted to WUV in Holland (the Dutch Restitution Organization). It was a small quest for justice I had never considered before. Prepared to tell my story of hiding in a rational, sequential manner, I managed only to weep for two hours straight.

Considering the fragile underpinning of our existence, what a miracle to have come this far. The usual prognosis for children entirely deprived of childhood is not promising. We have defied even the conventions of modern developmental psychology. We are living contradictions. We gather our fragments, build on them, reconstruct our foundations, write our stories, read the stories of others, add to our knowledge and self-understanding, derive strength from it all, and struggle to confront our despair.

And mostly, we win. For our despair comes from real origins, not imaginary ones. The struggle is intense but meaningful, the achievements truly astounding.

Robert Krell, *CM, MD, FRCP(C), DFAPA, is professor emeritus, Department of Psychiatry, University of British Columbia, and a noted author of several groundbreaking books, including his memoir* Sounds From Silence: Reflections of a Child Holocaust Survivor, Psychiatrist and Teacher.

Legacies of a Very Young Survivor

By Maya Freed Brown

(Excerpted from The Hidden Child, *Volume VIII, Number 1, winter 1998/99.)*

A childhood is a terrible thing to lose. I was born in transit, somewhere between Poland and Byelorussia, sometime between 1940 and 1942, after my parents escaped from the Warsaw ghetto. The journey ultimately ended in Uzbekistan. Sometimes, I was with my parents; other times, I was left in orphanages or with strangers willing to hide an infant. Months would go by before a parent would retrieve me. I would cry when they left and cry when they returned. Feeling rejected when I did not want to go back with them, my parents would be disappointed and angry. This pattern became set and only worsened as time went on and places changed. My memories are few. But the emotional ramifications of frequent abandonment have marked me for life. Not being able to attach feelings to experiences; being misunderstood only intensifies the pain. Nightmares of lonely train whistles, claustrophobic rooms, loud noises, and hunger dominate my nights.

Maya at eight months in Vitebsk.

Each morning begins with a sinking feeling of imminent danger. Even as an adult, my relationship with my parents was full of anger, bitterness, and misapprehension.

During most of my childhood, I was convinced I had made up my disturbing dreams. With no one to share my confusion, I felt so lonely. I never thought of telling my parents about my nightmares. My problems were either dismissed or interpreted as criticisms. I would be accused of being ungrateful for all they had done for me during the Holocaust.

Although they considered me a "difficult child," I was depicted as happy and carefree. My father would say, "Maya has perceptions, but I know the truth." With no memory of the events, how could I fight that? Their need to view the world through rose-colored glasses was an attempt to deny their own Holocaust experiences. And thus, they believed they were protecting me. But for me, the loneliness was exacerbated, and the self-blame intensified. As time went on, any chance for bonding was lost in a maze of conflict, recrimination, and bitterness.

Maya in Uzbekistan.

With no common understanding, mutual alienation became permanent. When I had my own children, I did not know how to care for them. I was shocked to find myself unable to respond to a crying baby. If the infant had just been fed and changed, why was she still crying? I cared deeply about these two little girls, but I could not attend to their emotional needs. I was unable to comprehend the significance of love, attachment, bonding, and protection. I did not know then that to be a nurturing parent, one needs to have been nurtured as a child.

As an adult, I would ask my mother what I had experienced

as a child during the Holocaust. Her response was that I was "a cute, happy child" whom everyone admired. My emotional memories, however, indicate otherwise. Such a contrast in perception reinforced my own conviction that I had made up my own childhood. Most people say I'm "lucky" because I cannot remember being two, three, and four years old. At some point, I even tried to convince myself that my childhood began at the age of eight in Toronto, Canada. This need to deny my past was an attempt to be like everyone else, to fit in, to be normal. Nobody wanted to hear what I had to say, anyway. I was told to "forget about it." I was "too young to have suffered." Even older Hidden Children assumed that I was more fortunate because I did not remember very much. The opposite is true, of course. Psychologists now know that, in experiencing trauma, the younger the child, the more damaging are the subsequent pains and scarring. The younger the child, the less able she is to tolerate incomprehensible experiences. She cannot process the information and is left with massive, frightening, non-verbal distress.

What most people do not even notice in their daily routines can precipitate hours of anguish for me: sirens, crying babies, stray animals, even leaving the house to go to work. Every separation causes anxiety. Traveling is never enjoyable. So much for a traumatic childhood and its many ramifications.

Maya Freed Brown *is a psychotherapist specializing in individual and family therapy; she married and raised two daughters, who grew up to be professionals and happily married.*

I Was an Infant Survivor in Greece

By Esther Franco

(Excerpted from The Hidden Child, *Volume XXV, 2017.)*

I was born in a hospital on April 1, 1944, in Thessaloniki Greece. My mother, Rebecca Pissirilo-Franco, was twenty-one years old, and my father, Leon Franco, was twenty-four. Both came from educated and prosperous Sephardic Jewish families who were in the textile business. They spoke many languages—Spanish, Ladino, Greek, Yugoslavian, and some French. They met in my mother's hometown of Kastoria, which was still free of Nazis in 1942, when my father and his brother arrived, having fled occupied Bitola. Had they stayed in Bitola, they might have perished with the rest of their family, including their parents and many aunts, uncles, and cousins.

In Kastoria, life was still normal and peaceful under the Italians, young people still gathered for afternoon dances known as *après-midis*. It was there that they met and fell in love, eventually marrying in 1943. My parents were young, good-looking, charming, and I'm told, very much in love. I pieced together their story in the 1960s and 1970s, when I met with relatives in the US, Israel, Yugoslavia, and Greece, and with their former friends and classmates.

Soon after they married, my mother was pregnant with me. But by the beginning of 1944, the Nazis had come to Kastoria, bringing with them their atrocities and violence. They began gathering the Jews, stealing their valuables, and recruiting willing Greeks to cooperate with them. Suddenly, everything changed.

Left: Esther's mother, Rebecca Pissirilo-Franco, as a high school student in Kastoria, c. 1938. Right: Esther's father, Leon Franco, in 1943–44, age twenty-three–twenty-four, in Kastoria, Greece.

On March 25, 1944, all Jews from the northern part of the country were transferred to Thessaloniki, about 125 miles from Kastoria. Here, they were gathered into a transit site, close to the railway station, from which trains, fully packed with our people, were sent to the death camps.

My mother was in the last days of her pregnancy, in the throes of humiliation, hunger, cold, witnessing atrocities, violence, and killings at the hands of the Nazis. Little more than a child herself, she undoubtedly felt fear, agony, anxiety, and depression, and surely, she transmitted all this to me.

When my parents arrived in Thessaloniki, the Red Cross asked the Nazis to let my mother go to a hospital, because she was about to give birth to me. At the last minute before going into the trains, "we" were pulled out of the line. My father and my mother's mother tried to go with my mother, but both were dragged back violently. My mother gave birth to me all alone in an unfamiliar town with strange people. Now we were two; and we only had each other. When my mother understood the impending danger, she begged a nurse to save me. The nurse kept her promise and brought me to her family.

My mother was hiding under a false Greek name trying to avoid arrest, but some said she was betrayed by a Greek woman, a collaborator. Others thought it was the director of the hospital who gave her away.

I was only three months old when my mother was arrested and taken to prison. On the 8th of September 1944, my mother was executed by Greek collaborators, along with seven other Jews. It was the last execution. What irony…my father and his brother, my grandparents, and my mother's younger sister, only sixteen years old, were all executed in Auschwitz. As survivor and writer Victor Frankl said, the best of us perished, and I believe it.

I grew up as Aliki Papadopoulos in a poor, Greek Christian home. My foster parents and their three children were kind and compassionate. They loved me, and I loved them—yet, from early childhood, I was an unhappy, depressed child. I had numerous, difficult issues that are hard to describe. On my first day of high school, at the age of twelve, I was told my real name and about my real parents. They could not have picked a worse moment to tell me the truth!

Twelve is a difficult age, even under the best of circumstances. For me, it was hell. It required too much growth and maturity for one day: first day of high school; first day with my real but new name; first day with my new-real parents and their new names—names I couldn't even pronounce.

I went through all this without any kind of psychological help. Depression was inevitable. Although I experienced great difficulties, I felt somewhat relieved to finally learn "the truth." In a way, I had been expecting such a day. Children sense what's amiss. All through the years, I knew that something was wrong with our family. We were so different in every way, outside and inside. Silence and lies had not helped me. I had always felt tormented. Since then, the word "truth" has become a preoccupation in my life.

From that time on, I began a new journey: a search for my identity. I needed to know about my family, and most of all, about my parents. My foster family became distant and unwilling to help. In fact, they seemed annoyed, even hostile, when I expressed a wish to establish relations with my family and with Jewish people. They hid as much as possible—my family photos, names of relatives, objects that had belonged to my parents. Some were sold, others destroyed. They were sensitive people… why such cruelty, I wondered?

Were they afraid? Afraid that I would stop loving them, or care for them? Were they feeling inadequate, not up to the task of raising a Jewish child? Surely, many complicated and difficult emotions were involved, and I can understand their fears. Still, I could not grasp how loving my real family would make me stop loving them.

On the contrary, I felt obliged and emotionally moved by their kindness. Yet I can't excuse their behavior toward my family and my people. When I was between the ages of three and six, they refused to let me go to my blood relatives, family members living in New York who wanted me. They even hired a lawyer, and with the protection of the Greek court, they kept me away from my relatives.

Why? Was it out of love, or something else? Was it for some financial support they were expecting to receive? The Joint and the Jewish community of my hometown all tried to take me away from my foster family. They wanted me to grow up as a Jew, living under better conditions, with my own people—to live the "truth" of my identity, name, and ethnicity.

But my foster family refused to give me up. I remember very well the chasing and hiding I had to go through during this time. I was afraid of the "bad people" who were coming to take me away from my "mother and family." The "bad people" were the Jews, and the "good" were the Christians. What an irony for a victim of the Holocaust, a small child, to have to go through such lunacy.

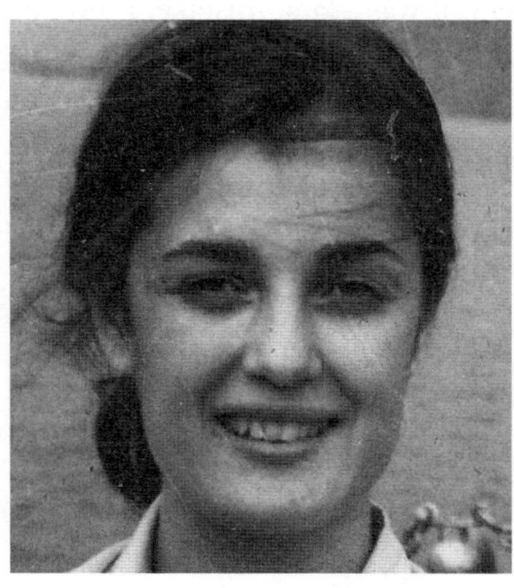

Esther, c. 1963–64.

It would have been much easier for me, and I would have been a happier adult, had I grown up with my own people. Unfortunately, my foster family did not understand the wounds they were adding to my soul, or the problems they laid upon my shoulders. Was it ignorance? Psychologically, my journey was a difficult one. It wasn't until I was twenty-five years old that, for the first time, I had the help of psychotherapy.

I finished high school in 1962 and went to the Aristotle University of Thessaloniki, where I studied literature and received my bachelor's degree. A year later, I earned a full scholarship to study drama, and I obtained my master's degree. I worked as a theater actress for a few years.

In 1977, I decided to go to Israel and learn Hebrew while working on a kibbutz. I stayed ten months. I love Israel. It is the only country that feels like home to me. It brings tears to my eyes for many reasons. I never felt that I belonged in Greece. It is a country where 95 percent of the Jewish population was killed in the Holocaust.

Since childhood, I had wished to make the US my home. In the early 1980s, I hoped to make my life's dream come true. I applied for an audition at the drama department of UCLA because of its excellence in theater studies. I wanted to continue my studies and get a master's degree to be able to teach drama in the US. I was accepted as a student after auditioning in Greek drama and Shakespeare, but the committee was not willing to give me the scholarship I had applied for.

I am afraid it was naïve of me to confess to them how much I wanted to immigrate to the US. It was a fatal mistake. I did not have the money to pay for tuition, board, and expenses. So, with a lot of bitterness, I gave up my dream.

Through the years, I was married and divorced twice. I did not want to have children. I was not qualified for motherhood. Today, I live alone. I have no relatives. I've had a difficult life because of the Holocaust.

Still Searching for the Hidden Child

By Andrew Griffel

(Excerpted from The Hidden Child, *Volume XXV, 2017.)*

I was born in Radom, Poland, in October 1942. My conception coincided with the Wannsee Conference, where the Nazi high leadership signed off on the Final Solution. I came into a world primed for my destruction. When my father died twenty-six years later, shortly after I first moved to Israel in 1968, I found a small slip of paper among his possessions. It bore a single line of Yiddish, in the hand of the Belzer Rebbe, a man my father revered for his wisdom: "Wait until the salvation—*geulah*—to circumcise him." He had kept this note in his wallet for over a quarter century.

My father had regarded the words of the Belzer Rebbe, smuggled to him in 1942 from Krakow, as prophecy, *nevuah*. He had wanted to know, if my mother should give birth to a son, whether he needed to observe Jewish law and have him circumcised

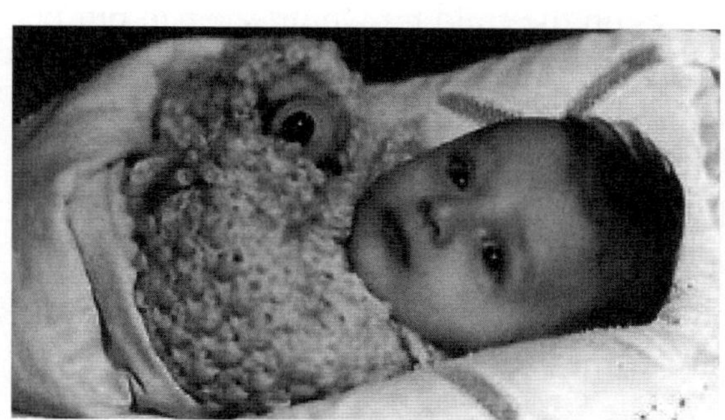

Andrew at three months old.

eight days after entering a world turned upside down. What he had seen in the Rebbe's response was the absence of qualifying words: he would have a son, and the salvation would come to him, my mother, and me.

I have wondered all my life why Henryk and Sura Perl Werchaizer Griffel persisted in having a child amid the Holocaust. Nazi soldiers targeted pregnant Jewish women. They stripped them bare and thrust bayonets into their wombs. There are stories of the Nazis hurling Jewish infants into the air and shooting them for target practice.

In an unimaginably dangerous time, pregnancy put my parents' lives at even greater risk. For three years, they had been imprisoned in the Radom ghetto, which the Nazis had begun to liquidate, sending its denizens to concentration camps. Shortly before I was born, my mother saw the Gestapo drag her brothers and her father into the courtyard of the leather factory he owned and shoot each of them in the head. The Nazis took over the factory, directing its output to the boots that were trampling Europe underfoot.

Just before her due date, my mother was approached on the street by two of her father's employees. They told her to follow. Together, they walked the two miles from the ghetto to the factory, taking care not to be seen. Once there, they climbed a back staircase. In the building's attic, my mother found a midwife waiting. The midwife induced labor while my mother bit down on a piece of wood against the pain. Below and terrifyingly near, Gestapo guards watched over the factory's workers; for my mother to cry out would have cost everyone in the room their lives. When I emerged, my first cries were also stifled with a cloth to my mouth. And then, knowing this was the only way to save me, knowing she might never again lay eyes on the child for whom she had put her own life in jeopardy, she handed me, by previous arrangement, to Jan Szczepanski, a chemical engineer at the factory.

Sometimes the "hidden" part of "Hidden Children" was literal—the child was kept out of sight. In my case, it was my identity. I was given a birth certificate with a new last name and taken in by a Polish Catholic family. For me, though, there has always been another dimension—the experience itself is hidden, beyond the reach of my memory. Whatever it feels like to be a Holocaust survivor, I'm not sure I've ever really felt it. What I did feel, as I grew up with my parents in the United States, was the pervasive sense that I should consider myself a victim.

My parents instilled this in me directly and indirectly. What they had endured during the war had left them broken, and I was stranded on an uneasy bridge between two shores of Holocaust experiences, a first- and second-generation survivor alike. Their unspoken message was that I must in some way be broken too—that I was fragile and should be treated accordingly. I rebelled against this sense of self, much as I wrestled with the feeling that I did not fully belong in my own family. After my birth, my parents spent the remainder of the war hidden by another Polish Catholic family in Warsaw, some sixty-five miles north of Radom.

In 1945, when Russian tanks beat back the Nazis, my parents returned to reclaim their then three-year-old child. In my mother's version of our reunion, the one I heard growing up, I ran to my mother as if guided by instinct. It was not until I was fifty years old that Hela Spus, the woman who had hidden my parents, told me the truth: Alexandra Szczepanski, Jan's wife, had to push me toward my birth mother as I clung desperately to the only mother I had ever known. And so, in what was supposed to be a period of gradual reacquaintance, my parents abruptly snatched me back. For them, it was a blessed natural reunion; for me it was a rupture.

Andrew, age three, in Krakow, a few days after being reunited with his Jewish parents.

We fled through Czechoslovakia to a

displaced persons (DP) camp established by the Allies in Stuttgart, Germany. We ended up, like so many immigrants before us, in New York's Lower East Side. Though settled, the sense of being displaced never left me. In America, I felt at home; in my own family, less so. One thing I did feel part of, however, was the special time in history when a Jewish homeland was at last a reality. In 1968, I traveled to Israel for a year of postgraduate study, knowing neither that my decision would be a fateful one, nor that this pilgrimage would mark the beginning of nearly sixty years of personal wandering—of never, definitively, calling one place home. Since then, I have lived a total of twenty-seven years in Israel. But these years have been interspersed, in more than fifty moves, with nearly equal time spent in New York and Washington, DC.

In Israel, I met Anita, who was also there to study. We fell in love. We married, returned to the States for two years to help my mother and sister relocate after my father died, and then, in 1971, we decided to make a life together in Israel. At the age of thirty-five, I served in the Israeli Army and managed to put behind me some of the sense of victimhood that had hung over my childhood.

In 1979, Anita and I adopted a newborn baby whom we named Tali. Five years later, I moved back to Washington to take a job at a prestigious international economic consulting firm. This was a professional opportunity I could not pass up. I knew I had to leave Israel. Just as firmly, Anita knew she wanted to stay. What we might call clarity has eluded me for the better part of my life. The long shadow cast by my earliest years, something I now struggle with consciously, was, until my forties, an unconscious fight played out in self-doubt, wavering commitments, and poorly defined goals.

Clarity finally found me, minutes after midnight on my forty-third birthday, after a phone call from Jerusalem that would change my life forever. In 1985, the tranquil Sinai beach resort of Ras Burka was under Egyptian sovereignty but accessible to Israeli tourists due to the 1978 Camp David Accords. Anita had planned to camp there with Tali and a couple of other families over the Succoth holiday. One night, Anita and the other parents sipped Turkish coffee with the local detail of Egyptian soldiers while their children played on the sand dunes; the next day, one of those soldiers opened fire on the group. Two boys escaped by running down the dune back to the Israeli encampment. The only other survivor was six-year-old Tali. When the shooting started, Anita shielded our daughter beneath her body. Anita was hit and bleeding to death, but she found the strength to whisper words of comfort to Tali until she drew her last breath.

Less than twenty-four hours after that phone call, I was the first person off the plane when it landed at Ben Gurion airport, the first through customs and, running quickly, the first to get to the waiting area outside. There was Tali, in the arms of a close friend, a big smile radiating from her face when she saw me. Something clicked deep inside me, a certainty that, somehow, I would find the emotional wherewithal to help my daughter deal with what she had just endured.

Tali's physical wounds were minor—scratches and scrapes. Her psychological wounds, however, were unknowable and my primary concern. She had given clear and precise testimony to the Israeli police; she seemed to remember the incident in full. From the moment I arrived back in Israel, I received well-meaning and often conflicting advice from psychologists and social workers. "Do not take Tali to the funeral," said some. "Yes, take her to the funeral," counseled others. "Do not send her back to school immediately; Yes, send her back to school. Keep her in Israel; Take her out of Israel." The instincts I had felt when I first saw her at the airport—paternal, protective, loving—were clear and powerful, so I put my trust in them above all.

When I look back at that time, especially the first year after the shooting, I can't fathom how I held it all together. Tali had witnessed the murder of her mother and six other people close to her and had narrowly escaped death herself. I was contending with the grief of losing my wife. Yet, I faced our lives with a confidence felt in innumerable moments, both quiet and fraught, through decisions big and small. This was altogether new to me. It's not that I always made the right decisions; I made plenty of mistakes. But for the first time in my life, when it mattered most, I had the strength of conviction.

I had never felt such certainty before, a feeling that endured throughout Tali's childhood and adolescence. From where did it come? I felt that I had somehow been prepared for this awesome responsibility. Perhaps my pain had prepared me, the accumulated residue of my own separations and displacements, and of having been raised by parents with their own emotional scars. Where my parents had inculcated in me a sense of victimhood, I vowed to do the opposite with Tali.

In contrast to the silence that had surrounded the source and subject of my family's grief, I was determined to let Tali know, by word and example, that it was okay to let it all out. I wanted to spare her from what I had experienced in my own childhood—the sense that my emotions, however strong, had to be pushed deep down.

As it turned out, my efforts to help Tali bore unexpected fruit. During the years when my focus was squarely on her well-being, feelings that I had suppressed since childhood started to surface. Shortly after my fiftieth birthday, I resolved to try to find the part of my past that had been lost. And so, I made my first trip to Radom.

My search for the first mother and father I had known began at the Radom city registry, where a young archivist had one word for my story: "Impossible! You cannot be who you think you are," he told me through my translator. "No Jewish baby born in Radom in October 1942 could have survived the liquidation of the ghetto. No Jewish baby could have lived undetected by the Nazis or their many Polish informers."

He took out the old records that, to my amazement, had come through the war intact. Yes, there was a leather factory named Elgold owned by Israel Werchaizer and located at 9 Czarna Street. Yes, Israel Werchaizer and his wife Leah gave birth to Pola Sura Perl and twelve other children. No, there was no record of Sura Perl marrying Henryk Griffel, no record of the birth of a son. I asked the archivist to look in the Radom phone directory for Jan and Alexandra Szczepanski. He chuckled as he told me the name Szczepanski is one of the most common names in Poland—"Like Smith or Jones in America," the translator added. He reluctantly agreed to go through the list of twenty-two

Szczepanskis in the Radom directory and began calling. On perhaps the thirteenth or fourteenth call, a woman answered. Her parents Jan and Alexandra had died five years ago, and she was living in their apartment. Yes, her father had been a chemical engineer in a leather factory—Elgold sounded familiar. Yes, her parents had taken in a newborn Jewish infant, born in secret at the factory to the factory owner's daughter. Helena had been nineteen months old at the time. The infant's name? Andrzej-Marek.

"What happened to him?"

"His biological parents came and took him away at the end of the war."

Would she agree to meet this fifty-year-old American man who claims he was born in secret in a leather factory in Radom in 1942 and was immediately handed over to a young man who worked there? "Come now, quickly," she told the archivist. "I have the child's birth certificate. I have pictures."

As I stood waiting for Helena Szczepanski to come to the door of her apartment, I reached into my coat pocket for a crumpled photograph my mother had given me long ago: me at three months. Helena opened the door with one hand; in her other was a picture of a baby boy. We were holding the same picture!

Ten years later, I took Tali to the city registry where the young archivist had helped me find Helena the first time. He was still there, now the director and chief archivist. He remembered me and extended an enthusiastic greeting. In halting English, he told Tali how, when I came to him ten years before, he refused to believe I had survived the Nazis' purge of all the Jews in the city. "I am happy," he said, "that your father convinced me I was wrong."

Where does the story go from here? It is a question that has plagued me since I first attempted this account. During that return trip to Poland, I went for an early morning run in Krakow. As I passed through the city's Jewish quarter, I found myself spontaneously yelling out, "Fuck you, Hitler! You didn't win!" On reflection, I was struck by how my uncharacteristic emotional outburst contrasted with my mother's resigned and oft-expressed view that "Hitler won." It seemed a fitting way to end this tale.

With time, however, I've come to see the emotional truth as existing between these poles of triumph and despair. There is, on the one hand, the enormous satisfaction and relief of having helped Tali overcome her trauma. I was able to be there for her in a way that my father and mother had not been for me. And there is the knowledge, tinged with gratitude, that through committing myself to raising my daughter, I was able to consciously confront what had been tormenting me unconsciously for years. I managed to reclaim some measure of what had been hidden from me.

I am a survivor of the Holocaust; yet I do not feel like a Holocaust survivor. It is the contradiction within, still unresolved.

Andrew Griffel *has extensive experience as an international lawyer and economic consultant to multinational corporations, and was the head of an international development agency working in Africa, Latin America, Asia, and the former Soviet Union. He advises companies on creating business-nonprofit partnerships, institution building and restructuring, board leadership training, and corporate social responsibility.*

PART IV

The Teenagers

“I Would Rather Have the Pain of Memory than to Forget”

By Dasha Werdygier Rittenberg

(Excerpted from The Hidden Child, *Volume XXV, 2017.)*

I was born in 1928 in Bendzin, Poland, into a tightly knit family consisting of parents, three sons, and three daughters. I was the middle daughter. My father was a great Chasid and scholar, and in my parents' home, Shabbos was a major event. On Fridays, my three brothers would come home earlier from their place of learning to prepare themselves. My job, among others, was to shine their shoes until I could see my face in them. The kitchen was the busiest place in our house—with cooking and baking, scrubbing the floor, washing hair, boiling water, and ironing. Each Friday, at noon, a white damask tablecloth was placed on the table, along with a silver tray and candlesticks that had been used by my grandparents. Thus, the spirit of holiness seeped into our home and our hearts.

Life as we knew it came crashing down on us in 1939 when Hitler's army invaded Poland. Our family, now including my married brothers' spouses and their children, were all forced to spend the next two and a half years in the ghetto of Bedzin. In 1942, even this came to an end. I remember vividly a cold winter evening that year, with biting frost outside and not much more warmth inside. The Gestapo had already confiscated warm clothing from all Jewish homes and sent it to Germany for their women and children. Wood or coal for heating was unobtainable. So, we had nothing to heat our home with and insufficient clothing to warm our bodies.

Prewar photo of the Werdygier sisters.

That day, placards had been posted all over town ordering all Jewish men to register for work brigades the next morning. Anyone failing to register would be severely punished. We all knew what that meant, and we also knew from other towns that anyone taken to a work brigade was never seen again.

That evening, there was crying and mourning in every Jewish home. Our house was no exception. Because of the blackout rules, we could not have any light. My father was pacing back and forth, lifting his arms to the sky from time to time, and moaning deeply. My three older brothers stood in a corner and spoke to one another quietly. Every so often, they raised their voices, and my sisters and I, sitting in the next room, heard words like "let's fight against being led to the slaughter." My mother, sitting in the corner of the room, was deep in her own thoughts. Every now and then she would look at either my father or my brothers and would cry quietly.

My two sisters and I sat stunned. We understood that a terrible misfortune had befallen our family even though we could not absorb all its implications. Tears were choking us, but we controlled ourselves. We sat this way for many hours until sleep finally overcame us.

At about one o'clock in the morning, a terrible banging on the door awakened us. We surmised that the Gestapo had come, and we three sisters hugged one another tightly. On her way to open the door, my mother yelled for us to hide. My two sisters climbed into a big box of old clothes and covered themselves with the contents. I, however, did not hide. I was curious to know what these brutes wanted so late at night. I did not have to wait very long to find out. They had come for my twenty-year-old sister, Chana.

One of the Gestapo men took out a list and yelled at me, "Where are your two sisters?" Of course, I said I did not know. Pushing my mother aside, they searched the house for them. Luckily, it did not occur to them to look in the box of old clothes. After they had ransacked the house, they shouted at me to "Come with us." My mother then arose like a giant between the Gestapo and myself and screamed out, "She will not go with you. Take me in her place."

When he met such firm opposition, the leader of the group seemed confused, and he explained to her that he had an order to gather all the Jewish girls of working age so they could be sent away to work. My mother answered that she could carry out the work better than I, a young girl, could. Then the leader struck my mother, shoving her aside, grabbed my hand, and pulled me after him. My mother fainted from the blow, and I, half asleep, with glaring eyes and chattering teeth, witnessed this man's brutality against my mother. Everything in me cried out to pounce upon the beast, but his firm grip upon my hand made me realize my helplessness. All I could express was my contempt. One phrase tore itself out of my throat, "Why did you strike my mother?" The bloody hand of the guard closed my mouth.

My father looked as if he'd been stricken. Tears streamed from his eyes. It was the first time in my life that I had ever seen him cry. As we walked out of the house, the leader of the Gestapo thugs shouted to my father that he should not forget to come early in the morning with his sons to register for work. This seemed to rouse my father from his shock. He jumped up, ran to the bookcase, grabbed a little *Siddur*, and taking off his coat, he ran after me on the stairs. He put the coat over me, kissed me, and said to me, "Put it on my child. You shouldn't catch a cold, G-d forbid. In the pocket, you will find a little Siddur. Let it guard you against all evil."

Walking after me on the stairs, he spoke to me with a strange voice. "Remember my child, that you are a Jewish daughter and as a Jew you may have to suffer. Bear it bravely. Fight to uphold the Jewish tradition. If necessary, die a martyr's death. The one who watches over Israel should save you from evil."

Long after I had left my parents' home, the words "Jewish daughter," "be brave," "be martyred," and "the one who watches over Israel" followed me wherever I went. My father died a martyr's death, but his words are with me still.

It is difficult for me to relate what happened to me after I left my home—a real Jewish home where every Sabbath was dedicated to G-d. Instead, a volcano of hate erupted in our midst and gradually destroyed us, taking me one day, another the next. I wondered if we could ever be united again, if our broken home would ever become whole again.

Most of my family members were killed in Auschwitz, and of traveling on foot or in carts from one camp to another. The crematoria at Auschwitz were not fast enough to incinerate all Jews, so some of us were dispersed to be worked to death in other camps. I was first sent to a *Durchgaangslager* in Sosnowiec, Poland, then to Blechammer, a horrific concentration camp for men (women were there only in transit). Finally, I arrived at Schatzlar, a concentration camp in a little town in the Sudetenland, Czechoslovakia. I remained there, working in a textile mill, along with 120 other Jewish girls of various ages.

We worked fourteen hours a day on a hungry stomach, washing floors or soldiers' laundry. Until then, I had never even washed a handkerchief for myself. I lost my name and acquired a number, 22944.

A respite from my tragic existence is the love and devotion that five girls and I felt for one another. Whenever we had a chance, we were together. We tried to help each other and keep up each other's spirits. If one of us was sick, we did her work and helped her with whatever we could. Together, we also dreamed of a time when our suffering would end and we would be free. This friendship made our unbearable life more tolerable.

It is hard for me to describe the two and a half years I spent in that gloomy camp where everything was carried out under a strict disciplinarian. The outside world was mostly closed to us. Each day felt infinite. We wondered how long it could last.

Still, our young minds imagined that someday soon we would be reunited with our loved ones and be free to enjoy the world again. The cruel reality of our lives depressed us, robbed us of our dreams, and destroyed our spirits until we lost all semblance of normalcy. All we girls could feel was the existing moment. That was our past and our future.

One girl, Rifka, was a Hungarian from a religious home. I bonded with her. She was desperate not to do hard labor on Shabbos. I also wanted to lead an observant life and tried with all my will to do so in the camp. I didn't let our oppressors touch my soul.

There was another girl who spoke French but knew no German or Polish. Her bunk was next to mine; she was a poet. She wrote lines of hope. She was the only one who could read French. In the village, French POWs would sometimes throw rocks, with notes attached, to encourage us. We would hide the notes until the night and then gather around to hear them read. The notes would have news: the Nazis were losing the war. There is no calculating how such news renewed my spirits to celebrate Shabbos.

Our method of supporting one another sounds simple, but in a place where one day was made to bleed into another without difference, where routines were repeated endlessly, it was not simple. Certain repetitions helped us mark the time. For example, on Saturdays, the toilets were to be cleaned in the camp; on Sundays, we would be sent to clean the Nazis' barracks and houses.

We counted the days to Shabbos. And we counted, or tried to count, the days to the holidays. On Passover, we would trade bread for potatoes, so as not to eat leavened bread. Once, on Yom Kippur, we fasted on the wrong day, so we created another fast day. But we few girls who tried to be observant were not alone. The older girls, twenty and above, were not observant, but they helped us. They would trade workdays with us (at great risk to themselves). They would work on Saturdays so that we could work on Sundays. And if it were unavoidable, if we were found out or forced to work, we would work the minimum of what was demanded.

We girls in Schatzlar wanted the world to know there were such people. Throughout the camps, many of us never forgot our responsibility to retain their Jewish identity.

Why did I do it? The obvious answer is that observance was a part of who I was, and to preserve my identity I had no choice. But I often wonder, would I have taken the risks and made the sacrifices if, for a moment, I had known my parents and my brothers and sister were no longer alive? If I had known the truth, that they had all been murdered, that I would never reunite with them and be able to assure them that I had not been touched—that I had remained a Jew and that they would be proud of me, proud to say this child is my child, who kept the wishes of her mother and her father? At the end of the war, there was no mother, no father, no brothers.

I mention this not only to affirm that Judaism is a religion of laws and observance, but also to affirm that Judaism is a family, one's own and others'. As I look back, it was my mother who was concerned with my observance, my father only wanted me to survive and come home. If bonds of loyalty and of steadfast faith are not broken, this Jewish family survives.

During the last six months, we noticed certain changes in the camp. The SS guards started putting us on long marches from our camp to another camp called Bernsdorf, which was several miles away. This was in the winter of 1944 and the weather in the mountains of the Sudetenland was very severe. I remember marching in deep snow, wearing wooden shoes that made it impossible to walk without tripping and falling. If any prisoners fell out of line, the SS dogs attacked viciously. One of the dogs lunged at me and ripped at my foot. I do not remember the pain of the actual bite. I do remember the beautiful white snow turning red as I hurried forward, trying not to be left behind.

That March brought a change in the weather and a marked change in the camp's atmosphere. The SS, once so imperious, began behaving nervously. The French POWs' notes, thrown over the fence, spread the word that the war would soon be over. One of the notes also passed on the news that President Roosevelt had died.

For almost two weeks, our "elders" assigned a night watch in each bunk. We slept in our clothing, and someone watched at the window. Near dawn on May 6, the guards of the camp forced us out of the bunks into a nearby forest where they lined us up. The woods were filled with the sounds of horses and shouting men. Through the trees, we could glimpse Nazi soldiers on horseback racing furiously in all directions. Smoke poured into the forest, and we thought we would all be burned to death. (Later, we found out that the director of the factory in which we had labored, knowing that the end was near, had shot his wife, his two small children, set his villa in flames, and then shot himself. I remember how pretty his wife was and how blond and Aryan-looking the children were.)

We stood in line in the forest, not knowing how the day would end. We did not know that the Russians were encircling the village and that this was the reason the SS guards were panicking. Finally, the SS guards herded us all back into the bunks. We were all shivering and praying. I still had my Siddur and read a lot of Psalms. We kept hearing shots, but we didn't know if it would be our end or theirs.

Some days before our liberation, camp discipline became stricter. The nervousness of the guards became very noticeable. Their shouts, and very often blows, became a common occurrence. Wild rumors traveled throughout the camp that some girls who showed a smile disappeared and were not seen again. We were not allowed to show we understood our liberation was near. Still, depression hung over us: we were on the threshold of liberation, yet we wondered if we would live long enough to see that day or would we also be among the disappeared.

One day, at dawn, when we rose for our usual lineup to get our daily work assignments, we found that the guards had disappeared. The firing of artillery sounded very close, a sign that our liberators were close by. Now, we were restricted to our barracks, and we remained full of fear.

The day of liberation was Tuesday, May 8, 1945. Toward evening, we heard tanks driving into the camp's valley. Finally, we knew these were not Nazis but our liberators.

Suddenly the gate opened and a few tired-looking Russian soldiers, with dust and dirt all over their faces, entered. With much energy, they screamed, "*My vas vysvobodil!*" (We are here to liberate you!)

We were free to go wherever we wanted. But now that freedom had come, we were stunned. Where should we go? One of the Russian officers identified himself as a Jewish partisan (an underground fighter) from Poland. He understood our dilemma and spoke to us in Yiddish. He told us we were free, that the enemy had been beaten, and that we could travel wherever we wanted to. Then he asked us to sit down; he had something to tell us. We sat around him, and in a firm voice, he said:

> Dear sisters, your liberation has come. Each one of you surely plans now to go back home to be reunited with your parents and brothers and sisters. Well, I have just come from Poland. I also went to look for my dear ones. Instead, I found ruin and desolation. The cities are destroyed. The Jewish population has been annihilated. No Jewish family can be found. Polish Jewry does not exist anymore. I have wandered in dozens of Jewish towns and cities and have found nothing but desolation. No doubt your dear ones met the same fate. The only thing to do now is to start life anew and the only place you can do it is in the Land of Israel. Don't depend upon the justice of the world. After such destruction of our people, they will feed you with high-sounding phrases. But nothing can compensate us for the sacrifices we made in this war. Take fate into your own hands. Join underground movements with the purpose of going to Palestine and start to build a new life.

The words of the Jewish Russian officer were like a thunderclap upon us. The moment when we should have celebrated and danced for joy had turned to mourning. We cried bitterly on one another's shoulders, calling to our mothers and fathers, when we realized that liberation was not the end of our suffering. It was only the start of facing the reality of the tragedies and the loneliness.

I remember that the Jewish officer stayed up all night with us to make sure that no harm would be done to us by the young soldiers. He told us we were free to go into the village the next day and see that the SS women had their heads shaved and were put in open windows where they could be spit upon and beaten before they were taken away. Even though we had suffered a lot from their sadistic behavior, we didn't go there to seek revenge.

Slowly, the bitterness of liberation fell upon us. In spite of the words of the Russian officer, we all decided to go back to our hometowns. Perhaps we would be the lucky ones and meet a relative or a friend.

Right after the war, survivors ran from one local concentration camp to another, looking for family members. Out of my whole family, I found only my older sister, Chana, who had been in a nearby camp. We fell into each other's arms and remained together for about another week. Then we began preparation for a different journey. After two and a half years, it was time to say goodbye to the other girls. We hoped that what the Russian officer had told us was not true. Maybe some of our loved ones would be waiting for us.

The village had a train station, and soldiers were being transported east. They took Chana and me with them. We traveled in open cattle trains for four weeks, with no shelter from the rain and dirt. We didn't know where the trains were going; we just stayed on. At last, we reached our hometown, Bendzin.

No one was waiting there; they had all perished—my parents, my three brothers and their families, and my sister. That is how the liberation from tyranny began.

When Chana and I arrived, we headed for our apartment, where we had lived before going to the ghetto. The present tenant didn't allow us to enter, even to take a mere look.

Due to severe malnutrition during all those war years, I became gravely ill. My body was covered with boils, and I required a lot of medical care. When I began to recover, I would run to the train station every day, always looking, always waiting…maybe they would come back on this train…or maybe on the next one…maybe tomorrow. Eventually, I realized that nobody would be coming back…nobody!

After many struggles and trepidations, I wound up in a DP camp in Innsbruck, a beautiful Austrian town. I was still sick and depleted, physically and emotionally. One day, while taking a stroll, I passed an old monastery. The gates were wide open, and

I glimpsed inside. It was a quiet and serene island of tranquility. At that very moment a thought struck me, that the best thing for me would be to become a nun. It would have been a life away from the cruel world, a solitude I craved for, and peace for the rest of my existence. However, I was moved from the DP camp and onto the road that took me to Palestine and then to the USA.

My sister and I joined an underground movement that took people illegally to Palestine and, after wandering through many countries—Germany, Czechoslovakia, Austria, and Italy—we finally boarded a ship, the Dov Hos, that sailed toward the shores of Palestine. But the British caught us and sent us back to Italy. A few weeks later, after a seventy-two-hour fast, we were allowed to board the *Eliahu Golomb*, this time as legal passengers.

It is difficult to describe the reception the Yishuv gave us. An ambulance was waiting to take me to Rambam Hospital. (During the voyage, I had caught diphtheria, a contagious disease.) We started life anew in our land, a life that gave us back human dignity and Jewish worthiness. This life slowly healed our wounds, though the scars have remained with us always. I felt I had come back home—not the home of graves but the home of Jewish life and its upbuilding—the home my parents had envisioned for themselves, for their children, and for their children's children.

Dasha Rittenberg *(1925–2021) was a self-taught, warm, and personable woman with many friends in all walks of life. She was young in spirit, wise in life, and she had a great sense of humor. Her son, Moshe, lives in Jerusalem with his wife, nine children, and many grandchildren. He is a very observant Jew and a Talmudic scholar. Dasha was a proud great-grandmother who visited her family in Israel twice a year.*

My First Kaddish

By Alexander Kimel

(From Children of the Holocaust Discussion Guide *© 2015 Anti-Defamation League.)*

On March 19, 1942, I was sent by the *Judenrat* (the Jewish Council) to build underground storage facilities. Our group was led to a bleak, desolate place outside the city where a tall Nazi with a red, square face told us that, if we worked hard, we would get extra food rations.

After a long day of digging, breaking up large boulders, and carting away the dirt in wheelbarrows, I went home with a coupon for an extra half pound of bread, and, with some pride, I gave it to my father. But I was disappointed when he said, "I've arranged a new job for you. You'll be a carpenter for the Nazi army." I was upset. I did not know carpentry and I did not want to lose the extra bread rations. Anxious and worried, I left for my new job the next morning. It was still dark outside and lights shone through the small windows. The ramshackle streets were covered with a blanket of white snow. The ghetto seemed quiet and peaceful.

I was assigned to help a Nazi soldier named Hans. He turned out to be a friendly fellow who laughed heartily at my clumsy handling of the saw. "To make a straight cut, you have to pull the saw gently. Don't jerk it. Don't use force."

I was so absorbed in my work that I took no note of the sporadic shooting that erupted at midday. At lunchtime, I sat at the roadside with Willy, the other Jewish carpenter. A passing Ukrainian peasant warned, "They are killing the Jews in town. Why aren't you boys hiding?"

"Killing Jews? What are you saying?" I asked in disbelief.

"Look, there," he said, "see for yourself."

When I followed the old peasant's pointing finger, I saw, about five hundred yards away, heavy Nazi trucks unloading groups of people who were then forced to walk uphill. The shooting persisted, intermittently, but I could not believe it.

I did not know what to do, but before I could decide, Willy took off running in the direction of the railroad station. After a moment's hesitation, I bolted after him. We found shelter in a storage room and hid in a far corner under a mound of cement. The shootings grew louder and louder, soon a continuous barrage. I leaned against Willy and felt his heart racing.

We sat there for what seemed to be forever. At five o'clock, the shootings stopped. Covered with cement dust, we crawled out of our hideout, and, still dazed, we walked back to the ghetto.

On the way home, I saw a horse-drawn wagon heaped with stained clothing. The driver walked alongside, whip in hand, and behind were five Jews. I heard someone call out, "Al, come help us. We are taking the bodies for burial." It was our neighbor, Jankel.

"For burial?" It made no sense. Nobody buries stained clothing. As I looked more closely, my heart skipped a beat. The wagon did not haul bloodstained clothing—these were dead bodies.

I wanted to run home to find out what happened to my family. But how could I refuse? I joined the other Jews behind the wagon.

Overloaded with the corpses, the buggy swayed. The horses slowed. "Let's push," yelled the driver. Grabbing the wooden railing, I saw, to my horror, the face of a classmate. "Oh my God! It's Arnoldek." A tremor passed through my body.

Arnold Rek, or Arnoldek as we used to call him, was a plump, good-natured boy. We shared the same bench at school. He loved candy and his rustling of crushed wrappers used to drive me crazy. Just yesterday, I'd kidded around with him. Now he lay dead, his head piercing through the wagon's side spindles.

We arrived to a hideous scene: in a tremendous pit, bodies floated in a sea of blood. The Nazis were gone but the pit was guarded by the Ukrainian militia. They told us to dump the bodies into the pit and to collect those of the victims who had been shot trying to escape. After we finished our ghastly task, the shoemaker called out, "Jews, let us say *Kaddish*."

We lined up at the edge of the pit and began to recite the age-old prayer. "*Yisgaddal w'yiskadash Shmej Rabu*" (And the name of the Lord be sanctified and extolled). But standing before this mass grave of innocent victims, praising God seemed sacrilegious, blasphemous! I couldn't do it.

I glanced at the mourners, these broken people who, with rhythmic motions, repeated the sacred prayer as their forefathers had for a thousand years. In them, I had a glimpse of the indestructible Jewish soul, the source of our strength and our weakness.

After the Kaddish, the group moved slowly and silently toward the ghetto. Some passersby glanced at us in shock, others laughed.

As we approached the boundaries of the ghetto, my heart pounded wildly. I jumped over the border stream and ran to our house. No one was in the kitchen. A pot of blackened potatoes, soaking in water, was on the table. My poor mother would never leave potatoes like that. I was certain she was dead.

I ran out of the house and, to my great relief, found my parents in the alley. "Mom," I screamed, "you're alive." I embraced my parents and burst into tears. But when I didn't see my sister, I cried out, "Where is Luba?" My mother broke down, sobbing.

I had to find Luba! Running through the ghetto in search of my sister, I saw doors ajar, furniture in disarray, feathers, torn from bedding, floating in the air. But I will never forget the people—moaning, numb shadows—moving about forlornly.

At one house, a little boy, about four years old, was crying for his mother. His sister, Rachel, a six-year-old, was trying to comfort him. "Don't cry, Mottel. Mommy will come back." She pulled him up and with her small hand, she wiped away his tears.

At another, an ashen-faced neighbor was weeping quietly for his wife and three children. Esterka, one of his daughters, was my age. She had red hair, a freckled face, and was always neatly dressed in a black school uniform with an immaculate white collar. Her main concerns in life were her freckles and her grades. Now she was gone. I did not know what to do or what to say. Silently, I left the crying man and continued my search for my sister. When it grew dark, I returned home.

My mother was still standing in the alley, waiting. "Did you find out what happened to Luba? Where were you all this time? I'm so scared."

I turned my head in pain and spotted my sister walking with Mr. Baczynski, the Commandant of the Ukrainian Police. Luba had been working as a cook for his outfit. Not knowing what to do or where to run, she had spent the whole day cooking.

Seeing her alive and well, I felt euphoric. "We made it! We're all alive!" Amid all the human devastation in the ghetto, I was unable to suppress my exhilaration. But at the same time, I felt ashamed of my good fortune. I repeated many times, "You are a selfish bastard."

This feeling of shame has stayed with me throughout my adult life. It is only recently that I came to understand the precariousness and limitations of the human existence. A man can't control his feelings and, in times of danger, he rarely controls his deeds.

I often think of my friend Willy with whom I survived this dreadful day. Willy the indestructible, with his raspy voice and charming smile, was a fighter. In December 1942, Willy was caught, stripped naked, and sent to the gas chambers. With bleeding fingernails, he pried open the planks of the cattle car and jumped off the train.

After the liquidation of the ghetto, Willy survived the raids, the hunger, and the cold of the forest. He was drafted into the Russian Army, and on May 9, 1945, one day before the signing of the Armistice, Willy Bloch died in the Battle for Berlin.

For Willy, Esterka, Rachel, Mottel, and all the other victims, I do recite Kaddish now.

Alexander Kimel *(1926–2018) survived mostly in the Rohatyn ghetto. After the war, he studied at Wroclaw's Polytechnic Institute and earned a bachelor's and master's degrees in electrical engineering. After marrying in 1956, he and Mrs. Kimel went to Israel, and later, in 1959, to the US. He founded his own consulting engineering firm, which he ran until his retirement. Mr. Kimel was known for his vitality, intellect, and poetry.*

Clara Haras Strahl Tells Her Story to Her Grandchildren

Transcribed from the videotape by her daughters, Joanne Ashe and Pepi Strahl

(Excerpted from My Story, *February 2023, Volume XXIX.)*

I was born in 1924, on January 16, in Tarnopol, Poland. I had two sisters and two brothers. We were all two years apart. My sister, Regina, was two years younger than me. She was very sweet. Issua didn't want to study. Hannale was younger, and Shulum was the youngest. We lived in one house together with my grandparents, my aunt and uncle, and their children. It was a beautiful life. My other grandma and grandpa lived a few houses down the street. I had a lot of aunts, uncles, and cousins throughout the city. Tarnopol was beautiful, and our family life was rich—we celebrated all the Jewish Holidays.

My father, Asher Haras, was tall, dark, and handsome. He was not a serious man; he was fun-loving. He used to take me to

Clara Haras Strahl, during a videotaping session with her grandchildren.

the club to play dominoes. When I went into the third grade, I was very worried about the teachers being strict and mean, so I stopped eating. My father would take me to the store before school and buy me *halvah* so that I would have something in my stomach. He was warm and loving and not as religious as my mother. He had a fabric store and I helped him, even though I was only ten or eleven years old. Once a week, my parents went by horse and buggy to a flea market to sell their fabrics. They would travel all night to be there in the morning, and I would stay behind to look after the store, which was really a little stand.

My mother would do a lot of preparation for Shabbat, baking rugelach, challah, cookies with poppy seeds, potato kugel, gefilte fish, and chicken soup with noodles. We invited a poor person to eat with us each Shabbat, even though we were poor ourselves. We had no electricity, and there was only a coal stove for heat. Winters were so severe and frozen that we often could not see out the windows. The toilet was outside, and it was always frozen. The water was also brought in from a well.

Photo of the Lindeman-Haras family, retrieved from distant American cousins after the war.

Every Saturday in the summer, my father took the family for a walk to the river. It was very beautiful and one of life's simple pleasures. At night, when I got a little older, I would go walking on the boardwalk with a girlfriend. We would watch the most beautiful and stylish girls. I was fifteen and very pretty.

There was a lot of antisemitism at this time, and my father would get beaten up a lot. In 1939, when I was fifteen, the war broke out in Poland, and Tarnopol was occupied by Russian forces. In 1941, the Nazis occupied our part of Poland, and life became a living hell. Every day a member of our family was taken away and we never saw them again. One day, there was knocking at the door, and we knew it was the Gestapo, so my parents hid with my brother and sister. I had working papers, so I stayed in the house with my grandparents because they were too old to run. The Gestapo kept knocking and I had to open the gate. They came in and ran through the house looking for people. They went upstairs to where my grandparents were still in bed, and they told me to get them out. They were pushed down the stairs, still in their nightclothes. I still remember my grandfather saying, "Let me say goodbye to my children." They were just kicked, beaten, and taken away.

My mother's father, Aron Lindeman, lived with us, and the Jewish Police (*Judenrat*) said they wanted to take the elderly to a nursing home, so they should get dressed in their nicest clothing and be ready to go. As it happened, the next morning when we went to the synagogue, we saw elderly people on big trucks covered in blankets. On top were machine guns. They took them to the woods where they were shot.

When I was about seventeen, the Nazis rounded up a lot of young people for work. I had to work for the German Army, cleaning their apartments. One day, I was sent to a big warehouse at a railroad station. There were hundreds of people working in that place. A Nazi officer was walking around with a very mean look on his face. He called me to come to him. I started to shake, and I didn't know what he wanted. He asked me, "Do you know German?" I told him yes. "Okay, then you are going to work in an office." To tell you the truth, I was relieved. His name was Kurt Dietrich. I was the only Jewish girl working in the office.

There was no money exchanged, only paperwork. The office was located at the railroad station where they had big warehouses of goods—blankets, towels, salt, sugar, etc.—for the army.

At that time, my parents were in the ghetto. I still had my mother, father, two sisters, and little brother, and one brother worked with me at the railroad station. Once a week, every Sunday, we were allowed to go to the ghetto to visit our parents. At that time, we didn't have any telephones, so we didn't know who was still there or who had been taken away and killed that week.

During Purim of 1943, "the butcher" of the region, named Rokita, who used to walk around randomly shooting at people, came to our camp and told everybody to line up on the platform, separating women from men. After looking at everyone, he chose three girls. He pointed to me and to two of my friends, and he told us to come to his quarters in the ghetto. I didn't know what this was all about. When I got there, it was unbelievable. Somebody was playing the piano and there was so much food that I couldn't believe it.

Everywhere people were starving, and in his quarters, there was everything—meat, fruits, vegetables. You name it, they had it. This was the most frightening thing I went through during the war—spending an evening in the house of this butcher. He occupied the nicest apartment in the city of Tarnopol where a Jewish family used to live. He thought he would have a lot of fun with us. He poured different kinds of liquor, and every time he drank, he poured a glass for me and the other two women. I was sitting near a plant, and each time he poured a drink for me, I poured it into the plant when he wasn't looking. And that was very smart, you know....

But then he said, "We all have to go to different rooms, and each of you will stay here overnight." I thought, "My G-d, what is this? I'll never get out from this place alive!" I was really afraid this would be the end of me. I was sent to a bedroom and told to undress. Lying on top of the bed, still in my clothes, I waited for a man responsible for tens of thousands of murders and shook when I heard him enter the room. When he approached me, I told him, "I am sorry, but I just got my period." He left the room, thank G-d.

One time I came into the ghetto, and people were saying, "They are going to round up the Jews again. Why don't we go into hiding?" They built a bunker underground in the house we lived in. And we all walked in there. It was a very narrow passage. There was no air to breathe, and I remember how crowded it was. It was like going into a chicken coop. My little brother was holding onto me, and that time, the Gestapo didn't find us. We survived, but we could hear them walking all through the house, banging on doors and shouting, but they didn't find us.

A few weeks later, when I came back to the ghetto, my father said, "They took away your mom, your little brother, and your sister." It was a Sunday. Only my father and one of my sisters were still in the ghetto. Shortly after that, there was talk that the Nazis were going to liquidate all the Jews in the city. I decided to escape.

I was working—it was June 9, 1943—and my boyfriend came to see me. He had taken his star off. It was lunchtime, and another man had taken my new boss' place. He was not too dangerous. A train had stopped, and Russian people were coming out onto the platform for water. One of my friends came over to me. "Do you have a coat?" I said yes but asked her why. "Because I want to escape—I want to run on the train together with those Russian women." I said, "Okay, here is my coat. You can take it." A few minutes later, she came to me and gave me my coat back. "I don't want to go."

"Well, if you don't want to go," I said, "then I will." Just like that—in the spur of the moment, I decided to go on the train with the Russian women. I joined them and walked onto a cattle car. I had nothing to lose. I thought, sooner or later, we all would be killed or sent to a concentration camp. I was wearing a summer dress, a raincoat, and my yellow star.

My brother was standing near me on the platform, so I gave him some jewelry that my father had given me in case I needed to save myself. I gave him everything except for my mother's watch. He gave me a loaf of bread. That was the last time I saw him.

What did I do? I wondered. Where am I going? I don't have any papers or anything. But it was too late to get off the train because the Nazi SS was standing on the platform. The Russian women all looked different. They all wore long dresses, and their hair was braided. So, I took off my dress and I pulled it down to look like a long skirt. I wore my raincoat over it and tied it with a belt. The train started moving and I realized that I had to think of a different name, one that sounded Ukrainian. I looked out of the window and saw a goat, which is *kuzi* in Ukrainian. I named myself Julia Kusira. I was determined not to be a Pole but to be Ukrainian because the Polish girls are mostly blonde, and I was a brunette. I remember going through the city of Lvov (now Lviv) and on to the town of Przemysl, where everybody had to get out and be strip-searched and examined. I was given a number.

We got back onto the train, and I saw that many of the Russian women had discarded their clothing. I picked up some clothes and dressed myself as a Ukrainian. I looked like a beggar. In Przemysl, there were other Jewish girls I knew from the camp who had also escaped. One of them had been a good friend of mine, but nobody wanted to talk to each other. They didn't want to be conspicuous. I also didn't know where the train would stop. After a few days, it stopped in Linz, Austria. They put us all into a big camp. There were thousands of people from all over Europe—from Greece, Yugoslavia, Romania, Hungary, and Czechoslovakia. It was from here that people were assigned places to work. I didn't have any identification papers, so I was taken to the Gestapo. I had to make up a story for why I was on the train with Russian women. So, I told them that I was on the street when they were rounding up the Russian women for work in Germany. I was just caught in the crowd of women and pushed onto the train. That's why I don't have any documents. I begged them not to send me back because all my life I wanted to come to "beautiful Austria!" I told them I would write home to my parents and ask them to send me my documents.

I was standing in line to get food when I saw a young man staring at me. Aha, I thought, he can see that I'm Jewish! He came over to me and he asked, "What are you doing in this group of Russian women?" He knows, I thought. But I said, "Why, what do you mean?" And he said, "Well, you look just like typical Polish aristocracy." I said that I was, and then I told him that my father was a Polish officer and when the Russians occupied this part of Poland, he was sent to Russia. "Well, I'll have to see you a lot now since you're here. Get away from the other Russian women, you don't belong with them. You're a typical Pole." He wanted me to go meet his sisters. I thought, oh, my G-d, that's all I need now is to get involved with a Polish guy. I couldn't get rid of him, so I decided to go.

When I came into the house, his two sisters were both kneeling and praying. I had no idea about anything having to do with the Christian religion. I didn't even go to a school where any Christians were enrolled. I went to an all-Jewish school. But I kneeled and I pretended to pray like them. Luckily for me, the very next morning, they shipped him out somewhere, and that was how I got rid of him.

I was eventually sent to work in a huge factory called Hermann Goering Reichswerke. There were a lot of people from Europe working there, mostly from Poland. I was afraid that someone would come in and recognize me. I thought I would never survive there! It was impossible among Polish people! I frequently used the excuse of having headaches, and I would go to the infirmary, where I would say, "I can't stand the noise in this factory." They would give me pills for the pain. One time, while I was examined by a doctor in the hospital, he said to me, "Why don't you work here in the hospital?" I said, "Well, I can't choose. I have to go where they send me." I was always worrying someone might recognize I was Jewish at the factory.

I was moved to the hospital, which was very lucky. I felt much safer. We lived in barracks, and I was free to go in and out whenever I wanted. I was not in a camp. I lived with ten women. They were from all parts of Europe. As it happened, there were two girls from Poland, actually from my hometown, but they didn't know me. They were typical Polish peasant girls, and they asked me why I spoke so differently. "Well, I'm from a big city. You're from a village." They respected me. They never let me even wash the floor.

Every minute of the day, I had to be somebody else. Whenever somebody spoke to me in Polish, I pretended that I was Ukrainian. When they wanted to train me to be a nurse, I said, "Oh no, I'm too stupid. I just don't understand anything. I'd better stay and clean." I just didn't want to get involved. I felt that the less I showed myself, the less I would be involved with people, the better off I'd be.

I did everything possible to avoid talking to people. An Austrian woman told me her husband was in the army. "Why don't you come and live with us?" I thought, "Oh my G-d, how lucky to be staying with an Austrian woman?" I went to the police and registered. I told them I didn't have any papers and made up another story. I pretended that I had been caught on the street, but they asked me how I could speak German so well. So I told them, "My mother was a German teacher. She taught me German."

From then on, I lived with this Austrian woman in her house. I felt so secure because she didn't know the difference between Jews and non-Jews. We used to go to the opera and to the theater. Imagine this! I was sitting in the opera house. Next to me were German Nazis, and I thought, "If only they knew that I am Jewish!" Later, I received a summons to come to the Gestapo, who were the Austrian police. They asked me about my papers. I had to make up a story. I told them I was caught on the street, and

G 19 617

Nr. G 19617

Name Kusira

Julia

in Linz/Donau.

Lager Str. Nr. 44

geb. 16.1.1924

Eigenhändige Unterschrift:

Kusira Jul

Julia Kusira's ID card.

I had no papers. The officer in charge said, "Why don't you write home?" I said, "Okay, I will do that." I wrote a letter, and I sent it to an unknown address because I didn't have an address. But I had to send it by registered mail just to have a receipt that I sent a letter to my parents. Each time, I received another summons to the Gestapo. I would say, "Look, I wrote to my parents, I don't know what happened. Maybe the war is…maybe the Russians are back there. Who knows what's going on there?

Diese Arbeitskarte berechtigt nur zur Arbeit bei dem genannten Betriebsführer und wird beim Verlassen dieses Arbeitsplatzes ungültig

Herkunftsland: Sowjetruss. 3081 Nr. 2

ARBEITSKARTE

LAA. Oberdonau Auftrags-Nr. XVI/379

Familienname: Kusira Rufname: Julia

(bei Frauen auch Geburtsname) led.,

Geburtstag: 1924 Wird die deutsche Sprache beherrscht? ja/nein *) weiblich *)

Heimatort: Mischkowize Kreis: Tarnopol

Staatsangehörigkeit: Sowjetruss.

Beruf und Berufsgruppe: Landarbeiterin

Arbeitsbuch (Ersatzkarte) Nr.

Unternehmer (Betriebsführer): H. G. K. Linz / D.

Arbeitsstelle (Ort): Linz/Donau Kreis:

Ausgestellt am 22.6.1943 194 Gültig bis zum auf weiteres 194

Wenden! Tourner! Vedi a tergo! Zie ommezijde! Vend! Fordíts! Intoarceţi! Okreni! Obrátif! Обърни! Обернуть!

*) (Nichtzutreffendes streichen)

Laa Od. mf. grau schreib 60 g/qm. ausl. 230 x 235 mm. 10.000/12 Garn. IV. 42. 1435. Q/0550

Julia Kusira's work permit.

"Look," I'd say, "you are worried about my stupid papers, and I don't even have a winter coat to wear!" After six months, the Gestapo officer decided he was tired of me. They gave me official papers with my photo attached. "We are writing that you are a Russian." At that moment, I was so happy and relieved. I started to cry, but he didn't know why I was crying. I said, "Russian! How can you insult me like that? I will show you who I really am when the war is over!"

Eventually, I had to go back to the camp with the ten women. They were all antisemitic. I used to come from work, go straight to bed, and pull the covers over my head because they were reading letters from home about what people were doing to the Jews. One time, two of the girls approached me: "Oh, you look like you're a Jew and you're trying to be someone else." I laughed at them, and I said, "Oh, no, are you crazy?" But at the same time, I was afraid they would go to the Gestapo and tell. I had to leave the hospital. I decided to get on a train again and go to Vienna.

After the train had traveled a few miles away, two Gestapo asked everybody for papers and passports. Naturally, I didn't have a passport. They asked me where I was going, and I said Vienna. They sat down and pointed their guns at me. Upon arrival, they took me away from the train station to the police in Vienna. There, I convinced them that I was on leave from work, although I did not have papers to prove it. There I was. I didn't have a place to stay. I didn't have a place to work. I didn't have money, just a few shillings. The first night, I slept outside in a telephone booth. When you step in the center of the booth, the light goes on. I had to stay with my legs apart the whole night long. In the distance, I could see the police. I was lucky they didn't come to make a telephone call.

There I was, without a job, without a place to sleep. In the morning, I went to a coffee house, and I said to the woman, "Would you know a place where I can sleep? I don't have money to go to a hotel." She told me to go next door where a janitor and his wife might let me stay. They were an elderly Austrian couple with a nice apartment in the basement. They said I could sleep there. During the day, I was assigned different jobs.

After seven days, I was sent to clean an apartment belonging to a Viennese woman. On her nightstand, I saw a Jewish prayer book. I panicked and decided that I had to return to Linz. I also had a bad infection on my finger, but I couldn't go to a hospital in Vienna.

At Christmastime, I didn't know what to do. The Polish girls in the camp wanted me to spend Christmas with them, but I was afraid I didn't know the music and customs. So, I told them that I was invited to an Austrian family with my boyfriend. And when the Austrian people asked me to spend Christmas, I said, I'm invited to a party with my friends. Instead, I bought a streetcar ticket, and I was riding from eight in the evening to midnight from one end of the city to the other. There were two guys on the streetcar, and they were saying to each other, "Look what happened to our beautiful Vienna! We have all the nationalities here now, even Spanish people." One asked me if I was Spanish. I said, "*Si, si, señor*," and I jumped out of the streetcar. Every minute, I had to think of something.

Those two years—from seventeen to nineteen—were a living hell. I was afraid every minute of every day that I would be discovered. One day, I came into the dining room and a Ukrainian woman said to me, "You know, you look just like a Jew." I said, "If I look like one Jew, you look like ten." But my legs were shaking. I always had to be prepared. I could have been anyone, a Polish aristocrat, a Ukrainian peasant, a Volksdeutscher, a Spaniard, yet I was a frightened nineteen-year-old Jewish girl from Eastern Europe playing the game of "Aryan," acting a role without a script or even lessons. The truth was that I had never left my home, and I had never traveled anywhere. I had only attended a Jewish school and had lived in a Jewish neighborhood. I didn't know anything about being Christian. But I knew how to speak several languages and that helped me to survive!

In May 1945, the American Army came to Linz. The war was over. It was a very sad day in my life because I knew I had no one. But I stayed in the hospital, and I didn't go back to the camp. I went back to the same Gestapo policeman who used to question me, because I wanted to get my name back. And I said, "Mr. Prakowski, you were always wondering who I am. Now I can tell you I'm Jewish." And he said, "What? But why didn't you tell me? I would have helped you!" Can you imagine? He would have sent me to Auschwitz!

A survivor from Mauthausen, Maurice Strahl, came to the hospital with sick people from that concentration camp. He was assisting at the hospital. A Polish doctor said to him, "Here, come meet my little Polish girl." Maurice took one look at me and said, "You're Jewish." I said, "No, I'm not." I was still afraid to tell anyone I was Jewish. But then I turned around. "Oh yes, I am."

"You don't have to be afraid," he said. "The war is over."

I told him which of the nurses were the worst, and he put them all to work in the typhus wards. They were screaming and crying that they had children at home, and he told them, "I had a family once, too." I ended up marrying Maurice a few months later. I always said that Hitler was the biggest matchmaker in history because, after the war, we gravitated to whoever was left to begin our lives again and start new families.

After the war, **Clara Strahl** *heard that every Jew who remained in Tarnopol was gassed on June 20, 1943. She had escaped just eleven days before. Clara and Maurice eventually immigrated to the United States and raised a family in Beverly, Massachusetts. After their grown children moved to New Mexico, they followed, and spent their last years with their children and grandchildren in Albuquerque.*

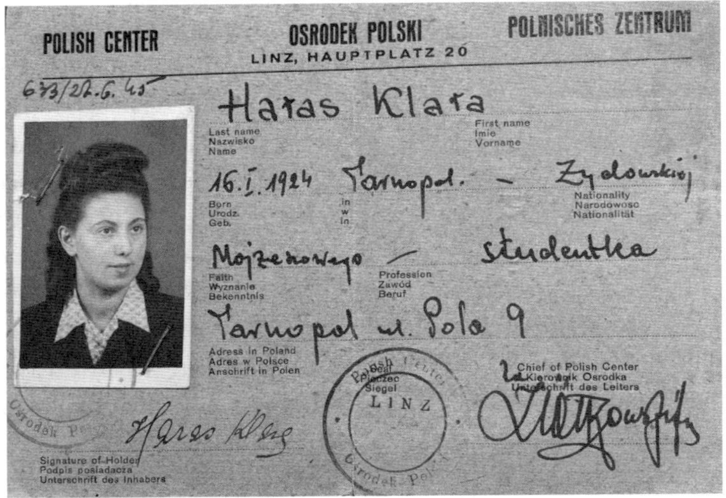

POLISH CENTER OSRODEK POLSKI POLNISCHES ZENTRUM
LINZ, HAUPTPLATZ 20

Haras Klara
Last name / Nazwisko / Name — First name / Imie / Vorname

16.I.1924 Tarnopol.
Born / Urodz. / Geb. — in / w / in — Nationality / Narodowosc / Nationalität

studentka
Faith / Wyznanie / Bekenntnis — Profession / Zawód / Beruf

Tarnopol ul. Pola 9
Adress in Poland / Adres w Polsce / Anschrift in Polen

Seal / Pieczec / Siegel — LINZ

Chief of Polish Center / Kierownik Osrodka / Unterschrift des Leiters

Signature of Holder / Podpis posiadacza / Unterschrift des Inhabers

Hidden in Berlin

By Manfred Segal

(From The Hidden Child, *Volume XV, 2007)*

I heard the story of my birth over and over. It was 1926, and my sister, Gerda, and brother, Hugo, were thrilled. As I grew, I adored Hugo, who watched over me through all my "firsts"—my first tooth, my first step—it was Hugo who ran alongside my bicycle the first time I rode it.

Starting at about eight years old, I spent all my free time riding that bike through Berlin, streaking past the buildings that told the story of our family's life in this city. The grocery store across the street was where Mama always shopped. The shoe store down the street was where Hugo got his first summer job. The beauty shop around the corner was where Gerda had her hair done. The row of buildings in the heart of the city was where Papa worked, and the huge park at the end of the business district was where I went after school with my friends. Each corner, street, or structure represented our past or present.

In 1935, after laws were passed that separated Jewish people from their non-Jewish neighbors, I became aware of a growing tension at home. I noticed the first change in my mother's eyes. Although she still smiled at me, her eyes seemed worried. At night, from my bed, I could hear strain and fear in my parents' voices. I was only ten years old when I understood that neighbors were avoiding eye contact with me because I was Jewish. Eventually, my mother could no longer go to her usual grocery store because Jews were not allowed to shop there. She had to travel an hour away.

One afternoon, as I walked to the park with my friends after school, I was shocked by a sign declaring that Jews were not allowed to enter the park. My classmates and I stared in confusion, realizing that I was the only one affected by this change. I looked at my friends for support or comfort, but they didn't know what to say. They just looked at me as if I had suddenly become a stranger.

The situation continually worsened. On my eleventh birthday, my schoolteacher praised the Nazi army for their strength and pride. She told the class that Adolf Hitler and the army were elevating the quality of life for Germans and making them a superior race. The class listened when she said that Jews were the enemy of the army and of all Germans. My body froze as she spoke. I could not look at anyone, and my breathing became shallow. The damage was done. After that day, I could never walk home again, I had to run.

Despite the growing antagonism around me, I tried to live a normal life. When Adolf Hitler and his government demanded that all Jews wear an identifying star on their arm, separating them even more from society, I slipped the star on my arm. When it became illegal for a Jew to attend public school, I transferred to a Jewish school. When the government said I could no longer play outside because of my religion, I played at home. But when the government ordered all Jewish schools shut down, I cried.

Instead of going to school, I was forced to work in a place called Wannsee. I dug in the gardens and lifted heavy bags over my shoulders to transport material from building to building. I remember being surprised that I could still stand under such a heavy burden. I was also ordered to pull concrete away from a wall using hand tools. It was brutal. Once, a Nazi soldier slapped me so intensely on the face that I reeled.

One evening, when it came time to go home, the soldiers threw me in the back of their truck without revealing their intentions. Fearing that I would never see my family again, I jumped out of the moving vehicle as we neared Alexanderplatz. In midair, while the truck zoomed ahead, I leaned my upper body back just enough to compensate for the speed of the vehicle and jumped, landing on my feet. I heard gasps from the pedestrians around me. I ran the rest of the way home, avoiding eye contact with anyone who might have seen me jump.

I never returned to Wannsee. A couple of days later, the Nazi government announced formally that Jews were no longer allowed to live in Berlin. We were told trains were waiting to relocate us to another city. The thought of getting onto a train without any control or knowledge of a destination was terrifying. A family decision was made. We would not report to the trains as ordered. We would stay in Berlin and hide.

At nineteen, Hugo could make his own decisions, and he decided to try to get out of Germany. He said goodbye to us and headed for France. My parents, Gerda, and I went into hiding. But four people hiding together would attract too much attention, so we had to hide individually. It was deemed safer for me not to know where either Gerda or my parents were hiding in case I was found out. We arranged for the family to meet monthly on a crowded platform of a subway station. At the end of each encounter, we'd agree on the time and place of the next one.

My first hiding place was with a tenant in a building that used to belong to my father before it became illegal for Jews to own property. This tenant risked his own life to hide me, and I was very grateful. I would leave his apartment only when he asked me to run an errand for him or to meet my family. But the exposure proved to be very dangerous. Once, on a bus, my eyes met those of a soldier I had seen at Wannsee. This man knew I was Jewish. I could see his eyes widen in recognition as he spotted me. I felt the blood drain from my face and my heart pounded. Understanding the danger of hesitation, I flew past the soldier's seat just as he was about to rise and made my way to the back exit of the bus. I jumped out as it began moving, running as fast as I could, not looking back, praying that the bus would not come to an abrupt stop.

One day, my protector approached me with a troubled look on his face. It was the same look I had seen in my mother's eyes when the anti-Jewish laws were first passed. Now, in 1943, I could no longer react as a child. I needed to protect myself. I was told that a neighbor had spotted me and was asking questions. The neighbor was curious as to my identity because I reminded him of a boy named Hugo. I understood immediately that an association with my brother placed me in danger.

I left the building as soon as I could arrange for another hiding place. I was taken in by a Catholic priest, and I became an altar boy. I learned what was expected of me and worked hard to respect the religion and person that I owed so much to. At church, I received subtle messages that the priest was interested in converting me. I sent not-so-subtle messages back that I never would. Eventually, the priest informed me that many people around him were asking questions about me. He said I could remain in the church, but I needed to pray to God for more protection. I prayed as hard as I could, but I also asked my mother to help me find another hiding place. I left the church and hid with my father in an empty and abandoned warehouse. At night, we heard and saw bombs exploding all around us. Because my father and I couldn't risk exposure in a bomb shelter, we remained in the warehouse, taking a chance on the bombings instead.

I looked for fear in my father's face, but he was still and expressionless. In my desire to measure up to my father's bravery, I tried to be as well, but I crumbled inside. I understood that I could cease to exist at any moment. My family and I lived in hiding for the duration of the war. We continued to meet every month, and I continued to have close calls. We had lost touch with Hugo altogether. We waited and waited and prayed and hoped to hear any news about him. I was so desperate to see him that everyone on the street started to look like him. Our hopes and prayers turned to tears and anguish as the months passed without any news. We learned later that Hugo had been caught in France and deported to Auschwitz where, like millions of other Jews, he was killed. When I heard the news, I wept convulsively.

In 1945, the Nazis were defeated and surviving Jews could come out of hiding. My family and I had the enormous task of restarting our lives. We needed to discover our postwar identities, both as individuals and as a family unit now consisting of only four members instead of five. My priority became my physical well-being. While climbing a flight of stairs, I collapsed.

Manfred Segal with his sister Gerda Weiss at Manfred's daughter's wedding.

The doctor who examined me said that although I was just nineteen years old, I had extremely high blood pressure. He remarked how thin and undernourished I was and suggested that if I wanted to be healthy, I had better live a very quiet, stress-free life. No easy task for a nineteen-year-old, robbed of a proper education, needing to find a life, a livelihood, and a way to cope with the killing of a beloved brother. If I was an adult, what had happened to my childhood?

It was now normal to see the occupying Russian Army everywhere. As I encountered these uniformed men, I became even more aware of the loss of my childhood, and I struggled with a seething anger. Once, while in a friend's store, a soldier started to help himself to all he wanted. This was not an unusual occurrence. It had become customary for these men to obtain supplies without paying. As I watched him, I felt my temper rise to a new, uncontrollable level, and I attacked him. In my mind, I was fighting someone who had contributed to my very painful experience. He had participated in a war that had caused me so much fear and grief. It did not take long for him to draw his gun and point it in my face. Everyone was suddenly very quiet. I could not help but think of the irony and tragedy of surviving the Nazis' death sentence only to die like this. But this man was not a Nazi, he was a Russian. He put his gun away and walked out.

Clearly, I could no longer stay in Berlin, in the land that held so many painful memories. We arrived in New York in 1949, where we concentrated on healing and building a life. Throughout the years, there have been weddings and births. Today, between the two of us, Gerda and I have six children, sixteen grandchildren, three great-grandchildren, and counting. We laugh, cry, cheer, shout, but most importantly, we live.

Manfred Segal *resided in Colorado until his death in 2010. He and his wife had three daughters and six grandchildren. Gerda and her husband moved to Maryland where they raised three children. Later, Gerda made aliyah and lived in Jerusalem near her son, grandchildren, and great-grandchildren.*

The Magic School

By Salomea Kape-Jay, MD

(Excerpted from The Hidden Child, *Volume XXI, 2013.)*

Although there was no reason to be high-spirited in the summer of 1939, I was then a happy thirteen-year-old girl looking forward to September. I would attend my first classes at Maria Konopnicka Gymnasium and Lyceum, named after a noted Polish poet. I heard but did not listen to Hitler's thundering voice resonating on all radio stations, warning and threatening Poland that Gdansk is *uhr-Deutch* and must be returned to the *Vaterland.* I looked at, but didn't see, Hitler's face, distorted by hatred. Instead, I viewed him as a comic figure. Detached from reality, basking in the glory of having passed the gymnasium's entrance exams, I continued my carefree life.

The streets of Lodz seemed to bend under the heavy load of Nazi tanks entering the city on September 8, 1939. In a matter of days, our invaders began staging bloody spectacles on the streets, torturing, degrading, and killing Jews. The sadism and cruelty matched Nazi doctrine, but what to make of observers who enjoyed the scenes? They were our neighbors, our coworkers, our fellow countrymen.

To my surprise, all Lodz schools opened their doors at the end of September, and I started classes in my dream *gymnasium* (an advanced German school), meeting new classmates and teachers in an atmosphere of grave uncertainty. Two months later, the Nazis instituted racial segregation, sending Jewish students to Jewish schools. Soon new orders followed, reducing all the Jewish *gymnasia* to one with separate classes for girls and boys.

Director Stella Rein with a group of children.

The schools in Lodz were rarely co-ed. The mammoth, nameless Jewish school with its five thousand students was assigned to a prewar school building in the newly formed ghetto in the winter of 1940. Mrs. Stella Rein, a well-known and respected person in Lodz and the former director of Ab's Gymnasium and Lyceum for Girls, obtained the same position in the ghetto school.

The school was functioning well in the ghetto, but the lives of students and teachers were already dysfunctional because of constant deportations and hunger. My father was jobless and living in fear of deportation; my mother, a nurse, worked abnormally long hours in the hospital and was practically absent at home; my old grandmother vegetated in a restless state of dementia. The small room where we lived exacerbated our misery. Our suffering wasn't unique. A few classmates were already orphans. Others took care of sick, bedridden family members. In the delirium of hunger and stress, some parents lost their parenting ability and followed only the hungry voice in their heads.

The school remained an oasis of tranquility, a diversion from harsh reality. What's more, the blessed school gave all students a powerful magnet: hot soup for lunch. We were hungry teenagers, jailed in an ugly place, deprived of the guidance and warmth of a normal family. Our teachers partially assumed the nurturing role, with Mrs. Rein as "*materfamilias*." A tall, slim woman, dressed always in black, she walked in fast, long strides on the school grounds. Her piercing gray eyes looked at us as if they were able to read every single thought crossing our minds.

The ghetto was full of paradoxes: one of them being that our school probably became the last bastion of Polish culture in the Nazi-occupied city of Lodz, which the Nazis had renamed Litzmannstadt. The ghetto chairman, Chaim Rumkowski, who barely and rarely spoke Polish, and the Nazi Commandant, Hans Biebow, failed to notice the school's Polish cultural structure. Mrs. Rein introduced foreign languages, such as Latin, German, Hebrew, and later Yiddish and Bible studies to camouflage the heavy dose of Polish.

Our favorite teacher was Irene Wolfeld. She was not much older than her pupils, and the ghetto gymnasium was her first assignment. Her round, open face and sparkling, large, brown eyes were not yet dimmed by the hopelessness of ghetto life. She put all her youthful energy into teaching, reminding us, "There's always a tomorrow, and tomorrow you may need Latin. Latin is *sesame* (sesamum) to other languages you'll learn in the future. *Disce puella Latine* (Learn Latin, girl)." Irene repeated the phrase, adding, "Hunger is a physical sign of food deprivation, and I can't help you too much, but in a more sublime way, hunger for knowledge can be satisfied here, in school."

Mrs. Zofia Prechner had been my mother's Polish teacher. When I met her, old age and harsh ghetto life had left visible marks. Although Mrs. Prechner was slowly fading away, she demanded knowledge of Polish writing and literature in her quivering, hardly audible voice. Because her vision was limited, she couldn't move much, but she could always identify a gifted student, and Yola Potashnik—tall, slim, blond, and multitalented—was her favorite. Yola wrote the best essays and poetry, made little figurines from clay, sang beautifully, moved like a ballet dancer, and was the object of our admiration. One couldn't compete with her. Mrs. Prechner was too old to conquer our hearts, too stiff to evoke warm feelings, too lonely to reach us, but she remained a superb teacher who taught us how to read, understand, and love books. She made poetry reading sound like music and helped us to comprehend and master the difficult grammar of Polish.

Mom asked me about school and Mrs. Prechner, adding, "I owe her so much. She taught me how to express myself clearly in spoken and written Polish, and my perfect spelling is the result of her endless dictates. I passed the entrance exams to nursing school with flying colors and graduated with the highest honors because of her. She was also the *grande dame* of Lodz's high society, the elegantly dressed wife of a well-known physician." I couldn't tell my mom that the stylish dresses had become filthy rags and that I had been horrified to see lice crawling on her mentor's neck. I hated to see tears in Mom's eyes. "She is still an excellent teacher," I said.

Nobody could compete with Mrs. Rubinstein. Tall, in a long dress that seemed to belong in the last century, she walked briskly, keeping her back straight and head high, and carrying a black cane. Mrs. Rubinstein had the difficult task of teaching us German, a language we detested. To our ears, it sounded like the barking of a hundred wild dogs. "*Raus, raus, schnell, Jude*," and the hated new Nazi idioms: Gestapo, *Kripo*, SS, *Sonderkomando* caused abhorrence and fear. Here she was, a woman who seemed to have walked out of an old painting, strict and not maternal, teaching the language of our oppressors, yet making it sound melodious, interesting, human, and poetic. How did she do it?

Under the nose of the Nazi commandant, a Jewish teacher taught Jewish children German culture and history with clarity, sincerity, and beauty. Mrs. Rubinstein taught us that the German language had nothing to do with Hitler and his followers. We learned that Germany had given the world glorious poets whose works we had to read and remember by heart, great writers whose books we had to study in their original beauty, and splendid composers whose music we would hear one day in a symphony hall. We read the poetry of Heine and Goethe. Later, Mrs. Rubinstein introduced us to the musical settings of their poems and from these *lieder* (songs), the hated German tongue emerged soothing and relaxing. She sang the lieder because all musical instruments, radios, and gramophones had been confiscated from the Jews as soon as the Nazis established their presence in Lodz. After the war, thanks to my great teacher, who never identified Hitler with

Germany, I understood the slogan, "Hitlers come and go, but the nation remains." Her legacy helped to remove the dark forest of hatred from my heart.

Mr. Cender, our handsome and young music teacher, one of the rare male teachers in the girls' school, was a highly popular figure. His only musical device was an old piano in need of repair, but he was able to squeeze out melodic tunes from this malfunctioning instrument. We attended his classes with joy. Our chorus, with its soloists, entertained the Chairman, who liked mostly Jewish folk songs.

Solo singing came into my life when I was deeply depressed after my grandmother's death. I had witnessed her physical and mental decline and her slow agony. Her body was quickly removed from our room, and nobody could participate in the burial. School was my refuge, but with all the sadness in our personal lives, nobody talked about problems. I couldn't cry or talk of my loss. Instead, I began to sing a popular song. Soon, other girls joined me. An unknown and unexpected singing talent was discovered, forcing me to nurture and improve the untapped gift. My career as a singer of prewar popular songs was not an easy task because I have an imperfect pitch. I sang off-key quite often, but nobody cared.

Soon, I realized that the old, sweet lyrics had to reflect our current situation and a grand finale of optimistic lines needed to be added. "*Sursum corda*" (lift up your heart) rhymes were needed, and the Latin saying found its application. The makeover songs entertained the audience and even Mr. Cender, blinded by my popularity, selected me as a soloist of Jewish songs at the performance attended by Chairman Rumkowski. The Chairman liked children's concerts. (The children literally sang for their soup.) After my solo, Rumkowski kissed my forehead, thanking me for the song that had brought tears to his eyes. My name was recorded by his ever-present secretary, a photo was taken by his photographer, and my fame exploded. Recognition was a splendid feeling, but I would have preferred instead a thicker soup or maybe a second one. That kiss from an old man was my only gratification. Singing was a cheap commodity while a bowl of soup had the value of gold.

My audience demanded more songs, and I delivered, sensing that my singing career was due to a weird stroke of luck, not talent. Mrs. Rein would sometimes come to our classroom and ask me to sing as if to rest and forget the constant nagging of the Chairman. He disliked the Polish-ness that emanated from our school.

In the fall of 1941, the school was moved to the wooden shacks of Marysin, the nicest section of the ghetto where, in the summer, the ghetto elite had their "dachas" and agricultural plots. We had to walk one mile or more to the school. The penetrating cold of the fall made teaching impossible. Dressed in heavy coats, warm shawls on our heads, gloves on our shivering hands, we couldn't sit still on the benches. Mrs. Rein gathered several classes in one room so the heat generated by our bodies could warm it up. To forget the cold and the rumbling in our stomachs, we sang and danced, shaking the wooden shack on its base. But dancing and singing provided only a one-day remedy for the harsh Polish fall and oncoming winter.

Rumkowski sometimes visited the school. Mrs. Rein's thin silhouette towered over his short, stocky, well-fed figure, and her silence said more than his complaints delivered in a raised voice. He didn't like the curriculum—too much Polish, too little Yiddish, and not enough religious studies. "After all, there is a God in the ghetto, Mrs. Rein," he reprimanded her, lifting his hand to the sky. Additional Jewish studies were introduced promptly, but Mrs. Rein did not receive more soup for her students and teachers. Among her rare pleasures, she issued baccalaureates to the students. (A few diplomas were found in the rubble of the ghetto after the war.)

The school in Marysin, without warning or goodbyes, suddenly ceased to exist. With our schooldays at an end, we had to join the workers in shops, factories, and offices. The ghetto was a small, restricted, and dangerous to walk in, and the long work hours plus the curfew made home visits difficult, if not impossible. I never saw most of my teachers or schoolmates again. The majority died in the ghetto or in Auschwitz. I accepted the closing of the school without visible pain for I had to preserve my strength for more tragic goodbyes and events to come. As young as I was, I knew subconsciously that we were marching on a road to destruction, paved with hunger, disease, and deportations. I knew that my young years were over and that I had to gird my heart with steel for days to come. I began to doubt the education I had acquired: literature and poetry shall never dull my hunger...Latin shall never remove the fear of deportation or separation from my parents...trigonometry will not help me in everyday survival. And the songs? Will they brighten my days in the workshops?

The hope, the value of education our teachers tried to instill in me, became useless, empty slogans and promises of a life I shall never taste. The school became an illusion.

I looked for a job, fearing that, deprived of a daily soup and food rations, I would not survive another week. The photo taken with Rumkowski was my best chance, but the chairman was unreachable. His lowest ranking secretary stopped me in her cubicle, looked at the picture, and ordered, "Now sing for me." I sang till my voice, reduced to a whisper and an acute pain in my throat, put an end to my "recital." She sent me home, almost kicking my posterior with a stern warning: "Don't dare to come again."

My mom found the best way through a patient whose husband was the head of a factory producing coats for the German Navy. The next day, I joined three hundred workers in so-called Gummi Resort. My happiness was complete when I spotted my classmate, Ania Szymkiewicz, who embraced me saying, "Sally, come and join our group." I knew that I would now share good and bad days with a friend, and even bad days would not be as bad with Ania around me. "Friendship" was a widely used word in our school's lexicon.

After the war, I met some of my classmates in Poland, Israel, and the United States. One of them was Halinka, who discussed her obsession with our Latin teacher. "My parents died early in the ghetto and in my mind, I adopted Irene as my mother," Halinka recalled. "I saw her in Auschwitz and barely recognized her, for she was in rags and her head was shaved. I was in transition to another camp, but I called her name. She turned her head to tell me, 'Halinka, don't give up. Have hope against hope.' The alchemy of her words gave me strength and her mere presence reminded me of who I was." Hope, a word widely used in the ghetto school, echoed in Auschwitz.

Dr. **Salomea Kape-Jay** *was an anesthesiologist whose stories and essays were published in* JAMA, Lilith, Anesthesiology Journal, Short Story International, Together, *and* Medical News.

PART V

Survival

Notes from the Holocaust

By Susan Thumin Silk

(Excerpted from The Hidden Child*, Volume XV, 2007.)*

Escape from the Workcamp

Father and I fled the Tarnopol *Arbeitslager* (a work camp also known as a "*lager*") at daybreak at the end of June 1943. The camp was being liquidated of the last few hundred Jews. It seems that Rokita, the camp commander, left the lager after telling his Jewish girlfriend that he would no longer be able to protect her. The word spread like wildfire. No curfew was enforced. Nobody slept that night. People were milling around on the streets of the camp. Those who thought they had somewhere safe to go, left. Some, who had money, purchased food and hiding places in the sewer canals under the streets of the lager.

At one point in the night, Father and I lifted a manhole cover and scrambled down an iron ladder into brightly lit sewer canals beneath the streets. There, underground, people were scurrying back and forth. Small chambers, filled with frightened people, were located off the main arteries of the canals. We ran back and forth, bent over, anxiously looking for a hiding place for ourselves. After what seemed like an interminable amount of time, Father felt as if he were suffocating, and we left the way we had entered.

Emerging from the canals, we met a young man and his fiancée, who were hoping to leave the city that night. He was the son of good friends of my parents. His parents were "gone." This was a euphemism used for those who were killed. He told us that during one of the actions, when Jews were being rounded up, his parents' hiding place had been betrayed by his older brother. His brother worked for the Jewish police. He knew about the hiding place but did not know that his parents were there. To his horror, he discovered that, in order to save his own life, he had inadvertently betrayed them. He then took off his police armband and joined them in the death march. Thus, the young man lost all three members of his immediate family. This was not an unusual story for those times.

Toward daybreak, Father and I stood next to the barbed wire fence separating the camp from the now-deserted ghetto. There were no more Jews in the ghetto, and soon there would be none left in the lager. Suddenly, the large wooden gate that closed off the camp from the rest of the city burst open and black-clad SS men ran down the street, guns at the ready. At that very moment, without another thought, as if we had planned it all along, Father lifted some of the barbed wire and commanded me to slide under. On the other side, I did the same for Father and we began running away from the fence. The buildings around us were one- and two-storied structures, all abandoned, all in shambles. I noticed a man running into one of them. He seemed to know where he was going, so we ran in after him. He stood there in one of the rooms, pointing a flash-

Front: Susan in center, flanked by cousins Zenek (left) and Emil (right). Back: Susan's sister Bella (right) and Cousin Gisela (left). Zenek, the youngest child, did not survive.

light at a hole in the floor. Some people were disappearing down it. When he saw us, he beckoned us to enter and quickly jumped in after us. Then he covered the entry with a wooden crate.

There were several people in what appeared to be a long and narrow, downward-sloping rabbit hole. We could see nothing. We huddled together for three days and three nights. Several times we heard German and Ukrainian voices in the room above us as we held our breath. They were searching for runaway Jews. Miraculously, no one stumbled over the camouflaging box.

When all was quiet, we left our hiding place and scattered in different directions. It was still dark. None of us had eaten anything for three days and three nights. Father decided to make our way out of the city toward a forest located near the village of Draganówka. We crouched as we ran through the streets of the abandoned ghetto. There was a Nazi sentry standing at a brightly lit fence. What was he guarding in this dead place? Crouching, we waited until he turned his back on us, and we ran quickly across the street. He did not hear us. We made our way to the edge of town toward a river that we needed to cross. Father wanted to swim. Maybe we could have waded, but I was afraid. I did not feel strong enough to swim even a few yards.

Slowly and cautiously, we made our way to the bridge, the same that the Tarnopol Jews slated for extermination had been walked. Among them, on April 9 of that year, had been my mother. On the other side of the river, over open graves, the helpless people had been machine-gunned. Was it because the general population had no apparent objections to the mass murder of Jews that the Nazis decided to kill them locally rather than ship them to the Belzec gas chambers as they did the year before?

As luck would have it, the bridge was not guarded, and we crossed over into a wheat field where we rested.

At dawn, smoke from a nearby house rose upward. People were getting ready to meet another day. No one could tell from this bucolic scene that in the last seventy-two hours, hundreds of people had been murdered—just because they were Jews.

Years later, we learned that all those who had hidden in the town sewers had been rounded up and killed the day of our escape. It seems that the Nazi and Ukrainian police always knew about the sewers as hiding places. Luck had been with us. Each extra day that we lived was because of luck and not because we were smart, or brave, or cunning.

We needed to move on. But first we had to eat. With very little strength left, we took our chances with the people in the nearby farmhouse. Although the city of Tarnopol was predominantly Polish, the surrounding villages were mostly Ukrainian. Most Ukrainians collaborated with the Nazis and were virulently antisemitic. We had no way of predicting the reception that we would get. Father knocked on the farmhouse door and we entered.

In a large kitchen, three men who appeared to be father and sons were sitting, eating soup. There was no bread on the table. They were poor. Without a word from us, the mother motioned for us to sit at the table. They seemed to know who we were: people running for our lives. She placed two bowls of beet and lima bean soup before us. We ate greedily. I don't recall if anyone talked. After we ate, we thanked our hosts and left. Soon after, I became violently ill. We had to rest in the fields for quite some time, until my stomach cramps subsided. Then, in broad daylight, we made our way to the Draganówka forest, some ten to twelve miles from Tarnopol.

Pierogi for Dinner

Draganówka was a Polish village of some five hundred houses in a Ukrainian area. My father knew some people there. Summer in the forest was a time of plenty. There were berries to be picked. Hazelnuts were ripening. The nearby fields of Draganówka were full of potatoes and corn. We helped ourselves to all these foods. The Polish peasants knew that at dawn my father, in his white linen pants, was picking potatoes and corn. They understood how desperate we were. In the forest, we met other Jews, equally desperate to stay alive, and equally poor. Eventually, there were sixteen of us. As fall arrived, and then winter, we were reduced to going into the village, usually by twos, where we would knock on people's windows or doors, always late into the evening, sometimes even in the middle of the night. The village was poor, people had very little. We would sit in the villagers' warm one- or two-room houses, talk about the news from the front, sometimes get something to eat, usually some beans, potatoes, and beets, never any meat or cheese. These people had none for themselves.

Father and I kept going to the houses at the edge of the village, the ones closest to the forest. I think that Father was making sure we did not visit any one house too frequently. In one, a young couple with a baby was always happy to see us. We only went there for warmth and to get news. The man was very eager to discuss politics with Father. They never gave us anything, but we sat there on the clay floor and warmed up. We never actually asked anyone for anything. They gave if they had and didn't if they had nothing to give.

Whatever we got we shared with the rest of our fellow Jews. All the vegetables went into the only pot we had. It was a black cast-iron kettle, narrow at the bottom and wider at the top. It was meant to fit into a woodburning stove with a hole in the middle. The pot, placed against an open fire, would take hours to come to a boil. We all shared the soup. Occasionally, we got bread. At Christmastime, Father decided to venture deeper into the village to visit a wealthier peasant whom he had known as a young man. Leaving the forest was always traumatic. The forest felt warm; there was no wind. Snow would cover the branches, keeping the wind down. Exiting the forest into the open fields was like leaving a heated house and going into a howling gale.

We huddled as we trudged, and our feet bound with rags sank deep into the snow. We leaned forward, holding onto each other, rushing through the open fields toward the deserted road. It was easier to walk on the road where the snow was packed down by the horse-drawn sleds and foot traffic. We left early that evening, for the walk was long and we wanted to find our anticipated hosts awake. When we finally knocked on the door, we were let in and permitted to sit down. The household was busy with holiday preparations. There was a Christmas tree.

Everything was beautiful and warm. Some children stared at us, others snickered. We must have looked like apparitions from hell, covered in rags, unkempt and unwashed. The last time I had washed had been on an unusually warm day in late October. We sat there for hours, it seemed. When we finally left, having had nothing to eat or to contribute to the communal soup pot, we felt relieved to be out of there.

As we made our way to the main road, a woman bundled up in a warm shawl ran out from a small cottage, adjacent to the big farmhouse we had just left. It seemed she had been waiting for us to come out. In a hurried whisper she invited us to dinner for the following evening. Father said that we would come.

The next evening, the wind and snow were just as fierce as we made our way toward the distant cottage. We did not know what to expect. When the woman opened the door for us, there in a poorly lit room was a table full of potato pierogi, waiting to be cooked. She had no way of knowing when we would come, but she was ready. As soon as we entered, she asked us to sit, and she proceeded to drop the pierogi one by one into the boiling water. What a sight! Father and she talked about the old times when they knew each other, about the current situation, and about the war. We ate our fill. She did not eat with us. We felt like honored guests for the first time in many years.

Susan Thuman Silk, *PhD, is a retired biochemist.*

Memoirs of a Girl in Hiding

By Erna Stopper Bindelglas

(Excerpted from the January 2023 issue of My Story.*)*

November 13, 1941, was my birthday. I've had many birthdays since, yet this birthday remains in my memory over all the others—perhaps because that was the last birthday I would have in relative peace, and the last birthday I would have with my father. Life as I knew it was about to end.

I have fond memories of my father. He would walk me to school, take me shopping, and he taught me how to ride a bike. I

Erna with her mother and siblings, Amsterdam, January 1941.

can still remember him shouting to me as I pedaled and he ran next to me, "*Voor je kijken en doorrijden*" (Look ahead and keep pedaling).

Eisig (Isaac) Stopper

We lived in the center of Amsterdam. My parents' store was on the street level; our living quarters were above. While we were by no means wealthy, we led a comfortable life. I went to a secular Jewish school, had lots of friends, took piano lessons, enjoyed summers at the beach, and for the most part, got along well with my two older sisters, Henny and Tilly, and my little brother, Abbie.

Even as the war began, there was always a belief that Holland was different from Poland or Germany. Maybe it was naïveté. Maybe it was ignorance. But who could really have imagined the nightmare that would follow? If not for the courage and sacrifice of so many people, including my father, my uncle, and the countless strangers who for three years would risk their lives for me and my family, this story could never be told.

Amsterdam, May 1940

I'm nine and a half years old. The Nazi army, having already steamrolled through Poland, Denmark, and Norway, is at our border. Bombings start, and we go into shelters. In just a few days, the Dutch capitulated and the Nazis marched in. At first, we didn't know what to expect. We continued to go to school, adults kept working, and we remained close to our Jewish and non-Jewish friends and neighbors. But slowly, things began to change. First, we had to register at our local municipality to have our IDs stamped with a "J." Then Jewish ghettos were erected in the

The Stopper Family wearing the yellow star.

southern, eastern, and central parts of Amsterdam. There were large signs at each entry, "THIS IS A JEWISH STREET." Signs also appeared on the windows of shops and restaurants, stating "*JODEN VERBODEN*" (JEWS ARE FORBIDDEN).

The Nazi authorities established a Jewish Council, the *Joodsche Raad*, to mediate between the Nazi authorities and the Jewish community. Its stated purpose was to "ease" communications between the Jewish community and the governing authority. At first, the Joodsche Raad believed they were helping the Jews. But it was the exact opposite. The Joodsche Raad made it easier for the Nazis to keep track of, and ultimately round up, the Jews of Amsterdam. As in other parts of Europe, no one really fathomed the true intention of the Nazis. It was thought that appeasing them would make life easier on us. Might things have been different had we Jews not taken that first step of registering with the Nazi authorities?

Everyone in my family already had a yellow star with *Jood* printed on it—one of the early directives. Any Jew found without it faced stiff penalties, usually deportation to a concentration camp. As time went on, the restrictions became more onerous. We could not mingle with non-Jews. Upon meeting our non-Jewish neighbors in the street, we could only look at one another. They would nod that they understood. There was also a curfew, from eight p.m. to six a.m., when Jews were not allowed in the streets. Any soldier could arbitrarily arrest any Jew. Nazis commonly picked up Jews from their homes at night and seized young people in the streets to send to work camps. One day, my sister Tilly was arrested and sent to a prison for criminals. Fortunately, my uncle Shiye knew someone who knew someone in the occupied-Dutch government administration, and Tilly was released after several hours.

Despite the worsening situation, there was still some semblance of normalcy in our lives. We went to school. But if any of the pupils or teachers didn't show up, no one had to ask where they were. We knew.

By the end of 1941, the situation became worse and more desperate. Some Jews (who could afford it) hired guides to take them over a treacherous route, from Amsterdam through Belgium to France, and then over the Alps into Switzerland. Such a trip required circumventing Nazi troops who were everywhere. Some of my relatives chose this path and managed to reach safety. This option was not possible for us, not just because it was expensive, but for a family with young children, it seemed impossible. Also, we still were certain the Dutch people would never allow any slaughters. Even as more and more families disappeared, we clung to this belief.

Palacheschool, 1942. Fifth grade children wearing the obligatory Jewish star.

By late 1942, the situation in Amsterdam had deteriorated further. The Nazis continued their massive roundups, and deportations accelerated. All Jews were instructed to prepare a bag of possessions for an impending departure. But my father wasn't one to give in easily. While most Jews complied with all the edicts and were herded onto trains to their death, my father was determined to resist. He boarded up the store's front windows and doors to give a vacant appearance. Business was already non-existent now that interaction with non-Jews was forbidden and our Jewish customers were in no condition to shop.

One early morning at about six, loudspeakers in the street announced, "*Hallo, hallo*! All Jews have to stay in the house and get their backpacks ready." We waited with our backpacks in the kitchen as we heard screaming, shouting, and crying in the street. The Nazis were pounding on our front door with the butt of their rifles. The sounds were terrifying, but my father refused to open the door. Finally, after what seemed like an eternity but was probably only a minute or so, the Nazis moved on. We had evaded them!

The following days were filled with fear and uncertainty. Once, when my parents looked out the window, they saw our neighbor from across the street. That evening, when it was dark, she brought us bread and left it by the door. Slowly, we saw other Jewish families walking in the street. It was a relief to see that they too had escaped the roundup. But our ordeal was just beginning.

In the end, after a harrowing journey, my uncle and his family had made it to safety, and he was able to procure false Uruguayan identity papers for us sometime in late 1942 or early 1943. Since Uruguay was not at war with Nazi Germany, possession of Uruguayan papers provided a small shield. It was believed the Nazis treated citizens from allied or neutral countries more humanely. Of course, the process to get such forgeries was not easy or inexpensive.

My parents thought it would be safer to move to East Amsterdam. So, taking just a few items, we found an apartment that had been vacant, and were there only a few weeks when we heard the same loudspeakers telling all Jews to stay inside their homes with their packed bags. The same green trucks were outside, with the same yelling and screaming and crying, and the same rifles hitting the doors. And the same terror in our eyes.

Again, my steadfast father resolved not to comply. This time, rather than not answer the door, my parents decided that my father, sister Tilly, my little brother, and I would hide in the attic. My mother and older sister would remain in the apartment, pretending that my mother was having a miscarriage. Things didn't work out as we'd hoped. The Nazis came into our apartment and discovered my mother and sister. They then searched the whole house and found the rest of us in the attic. They placed us in large green trucks, and we were taken away. They told my mother and sister that they would be back with an ambulance.

We were dropped off at one of Amsterdam's train stations. The platform was chaotic with hundreds of screaming men, women, and children, all surrounded by armed soldiers. My father instructed my brother and me to wander off among the frenzied crowd and sneak away from the station. I covered my "yellow star" with something, and we walked away. When I saw that nobody was paying attention to us, we quickly ran home. After a while, my sister Tilly came. Unfortunately, my father never made it. The train came shortly after we left, and that was the last time we ever saw my father. A few days later, we received a postcard that he had tossed from the train. It was dated August 31, 1943. Father wrote,

> *Dear Sophie and children.*
>
> *Don't be upset. I am traveling to visit. Keep well. I will also. I am traveling with company, Mr. Mahler and his wife, and others. Definitely do not worry. You should try to get the papers from Osias. I am very hopeful. Stay well, also, the dear children.*
>
> *See you soon at home.*
>
> *Bye, Sophie, Henny, Tilly, Erna, and Abbie*

My mother now had to be the courageous one, and she too was determined not to be taken quietly, and to fight back in her own way. We knew the Nazis had an intense fear of contagious diseases that could infect their entire army. My mother figured, if we could fake the symptoms of scarlet fever, we might be able to fool the authorities. We were told that one of the symptoms is a very red and painful throat, and the incubation period is six weeks. So, if we could convince the Nazis that one of us had the disease, we could buy some time, almost thirty weeks of isolation, as the disease would "spread" to each member of the household.

To simulate the symptoms, my mother scraped the back of my throat with a long-handled spoon that had been dipped into mustard. It was very painful, but it created a desired irritation. We placed a large sign on the door, "This apartment is contaminated by an infectious disease."

There was a catch: we now had to report to the city's health department. Fortunately, my mother learned that the doctor in charge was very anti-Nazi. When we went to him to report the illness, he didn't ask what was wrong, or what hurt. He asked leading questions: "Does her throat hurt?" Still, the Nazis came to the door almost every day to see if I was getting better. A nurse also came, but the doctor from the Health Department sent a nurse who knew to ask the right questions and to tell us the answers. Each day, we also washed the floors with disinfectant to make the place smell like a hospital. We still believed that the Dutch wouldn't let the Nazis continue to round us up and deport us, and by stretching our ordeal for even a few weeks, we thought we were getting that much closer to the end of the war.

After the six weeks of "quarantine" were over, my sister also "contracted" the illness. But the Nazis grew tired of us and decided they'd had enough. They brought an ambulance for my sister and took all of us to the former Jewish theater, where people were taken before the concentration camps. The usual stay at the "theater" was two to four days. However, because my mother claimed that all five of us were contagious with scarlet fever, we were brought to the only Jewish hospital still in use. During our second or third night in the hospital, there was a lot of commotion. Nurses and doctors were going back and forth. Finally, we heard that the hospital was to be cleared out the following day.

During the previous weeks, my mother had contacted some of our Jewish friends who were connected to the Dutch underground, and we knew that we could go to them in an emergency. But we couldn't just walk out the front door. Plus, we had to retrieve the clothes that had been taken from us when we had first arrived.

We noticed a little window on the ground floor that seemed inconspicuous, and we decided to make that our escape. Once again, my little brother and I were to go first and run to the Resistance. Fortunately, there was a lot of commotion in the streets, and no one noticed us. Soon after, my sister Tilly came; but, unfortunately, the green trucks arrived before my sister Henny and my mother could leave. Everyone, including my mother and sister, was taken away.

On My Own

It is now September 1943, just two months before my thirteenth birthday. I am to be on my own on a farm in the province of Drente, where Johanna Koeling, a widow, lived with her two teenage boys, Willem and Jan. All were risking their lives to protect me! The boys worked in the fields, and I helped their mother. We had no electricity, just kerosene lanterns; no running water, but a water pump and a large barrel to collect rainwater for the laundry. The Koeling family treated me like the daughter or sister they didn't have. In the beginning, I even went with them to church and Sunday school. We would tell the neighbors that I was an acquaintance from the city. At that time, city people would often send their children to farms. I don't think any of the neighbors really believed us. I didn't look much like a typical Dutch girl.

My mother's last instructions to me and my siblings had been to "remember that you have to listen to these people all the time and you have to eat everything." She said that there is no such thing as "I don't like this or that." Of course, I had never experienced non-kosher food, such as bacon or ham. Now, I had to eat all the ham and bacon put in front of me. Since we were in a remote town, we had plenty to eat.

I was with the Koeling family from September 27, 1943, until June 18, 1944. It would be the longest period I would spend at any home. Though they were good to me, I always felt like a stranger. This feeling was exacerbated as I went through puberty. I didn't fully understand the changes going on with my body, and I felt I had no one to turn to. Although Johanna Koeling was only in her forties, she seemed "old" to me. And since she was a widow, and a bit severe looking dressed in black, it made it difficult for me to approach her with such sensitive issues. It was hard enough going through the war, being in hiding, but missing my family's closeness made my life even more challenging.

One day, while I was sitting in front of the kitchen window, two Dutchmen—Nazi collaborators—came toward the house. The boys and Mrs. Koeling quickly hid me in a small cabinet where they kept rags and pieces of fabric. Then, both boys ran out the back door since they were evading the Nazis' work camps. I could hear the two men talking to Mrs. Koeling and claiming that she was hiding a twelve-year-old Jewish girl. Of course, she kept denying it. Meanwhile, some of our neighbors organized themselves in front of the house. These two men knew that if they tried to take me or Mrs. Koeling, the neighbors would kill them. To mollify the men, Mrs. Koeling gave each some strips of bacon that were being cured in the kitchen. They left, saying they'd be back.

As soon as they left, one of the sons, Willem, and I went to a nearby forest where the Koelings had prepared a hiding place. We hid in the forest for five days and nights. I was petrified! I was mostly afraid of the animals. But without Willem there, I don't know what I would have done. Our hideout was a hole in the ground covered by leaves and plants. We were able to talk very quietly, but we couldn't make any noise during those five days. Each day, Mrs. Koeling brought us food.

Meanwhile, five armed men returned to the house for "the Jewish girl." Obviously, someone had denounced me. It was too dangerous to stay there. I became a nomad, going from one hideout to another, thirteen places in all.

After two short and risky stays on other farms, I ended up on the Fledderus family farm. Hilligie and Peter Fledderus were a very nice young couple with two small children. I helped, working in the field, collecting hay. I felt comfortable with them and their boys. I stayed with them about three months until it became too risky because Peter Fledderus was involved with the Dutch underground, and the British were dropping firearms behind his farm for him to store and bury. The last place I was in was in another province, Friesland, still close enough to be transported on the back of a bike, as usual. I remained here until liberation.

The Fledderus barn.

On June 3, 1945, Canadian soldiers rolled through our town, a sight I will never forget. People were elated and dancing in the streets. But liberation was a bittersweet moment for me. After three years of hiding in attics, in forests, in strangers' homes, barely escaping the Nazis, I was free. But I didn't know if I was alone—if anyone from my family had survived this nightmare.

The Aftermath of War

The people involved in the underground during the war helped to find and reunite families afterwards. I was looking for my little brother (Abbie/Avraham) who was eight years old, my sisters Tilly and Henny, and my mother, Sophie. Soon, they found my brother. He had registered in his town, and when the registrars met, one said, "I have a girl here by the name of Erna who is looking for her brother. Another said, "We have a boy looking for his sister, Erna." And since there were no phones, the next Sunday, Abbie's "par-

Johanna Koeling and Erna in 1988.

ents," Tante Marie and Oom Geert, brought Abbie to us on the back of their bike. His first words to me were, "*Je bent zo dik geworden en je haar is zo lelijk*" (You got so fat and your hair is so ugly).

Of course, we had both changed a lot over the two years, which accounted for my brother's unkind words. Truly, he was right. I got fat from all the potatoes and greasy food I was eating, and the "ugly" hair was from the attempts to dye my hair blonde. Abbie survived the war by staying in a small room "*op de zolder*" (in the attic) all day. At night, Oom Geert would take him out riding on the back of his bike to give him some fresh air. Abbie and I remained with Tante Marie and Oom Geert until our cousin, Gerzon, came from Switzerland to get us. Gerzon had heard from the Red Cross that we had survived. He brought us to his parents, our uncle and aunt, in Amsterdam.

Eventually, we were reunited with my mother and oldest sister. Both had been sent to Bergen-Belsen concentration

Erna's postwar visit with Hilligie and Peter Fledderus.

camp. As bad as my ordeal was, they had experienced much worse. But they survived! My other sister, Tilly, went through seven concentration camps. Upon her liberation, she was first taken to Malmo in Sweden where she was placed in quarantine. We never heard from my father again after receiving the postcard he threw out of the train. In 1949, our family immigrated to Israel.

Erna with Tante Marie and Oom Geert, April 29, 1994.

One of the Last to Tell About the Holocaust

By Leo Vogel

(Excerpted from The Hidden Child, *Volume XXVI, 2018.)*

I came into the world in 1940, shortly after Holland capitulated to the Nazi invasion. My first memories go back to the spring of 1943. My mother and I were sitting at the table eating our breakfast when the door burst open, and my father, in a swirl of panic and fear, rushed into the room. My father was a house painter, and as usual, he was wearing his overalls, which had paint blotches smeared in a mosaic of colors.

Sometimes he would come home in the middle of the day, sit me on his knee, and we would invent stories about those shapes and colors. Not this time. He shouted, "We have to leave immediately, the Nazis are blocking off the street!"

The dark clouds of doom, which had been gathering for some time over Amsterdam's Jewish community, finally settled on us. Suddenly, we were no longer able to escape the terror that had already come to so many others in Dutch communities. I was just a toddler. It came in gray faces, goose-steps, and a language I could not understand spoken by violent people. It came in shouts, in silences, in screams of fear, and in the terror on the faces of my mama and papa.

At that morning's breakfast table, my mother was no longer trying to coax me into eating. In that instant, the peace and love I had known until then was gone forever. Instead, there was confusion and apprehension. Why is Mama putting all these clothes on me? I am so warm. Why is she yelling at me to stop crying?

She is crying! Where are we rushing off to? Why are they crying and whispering in my ear that they love me? Why is Mama squeezing me so hard? How come my oma and opa haven't come to see me?

Maybe my mama and papa were bad, because I heard them talking once about being Jews. Papa said the Nazis say it is bad to be a Jew, that's why they have to wear that yellow star, so that the soldiers can see who is good and who is bad. I don't understand, because when I have done something bad, I try to be good again. So why can't Papa and Mama stop being Jews, then they won't be bad anymore?

With a deep, unselfish love, while experiencing unspeakable heartbreak, my parents—mustering what must have been superhuman courage—decided that, to save their baby's life, they had to place me into the care of the Dutch resistance movement.

They must have been aware that they were on the brink of being deported to the camps. Now, with my own children and grandchildren, I cannot ever come close to imagining the depth of their despair.

From that moment on, my parents had no knowledge of my whereabouts, nor would they ever know whether I lived or died. How they must have cried! How desperate they must have felt, worrying about me and about each other...while they endured, daily, the horrible suffering at Auschwitz.

These haunting thoughts, which I've carried with me my whole life, are deeply ingrained in my mind, and at times they resurface during unguarded moments...a legacy from which there is no escape. My parents would never know that through their own extreme sacrifice and the incredible heroism of the Dutch underground workers, I would eventually be hidden in a "safe" house with a Christian family in the south of Holland, far away from Amsterdam.

I have fragmented memories of the moment I was taken from my parents by a Dutch resistance worker, who, as prearranged, was dressed as a Nazi officer. Who is that man dressed like a soldier? Why is Mama saying that I must be good and go with him? I'm so scared! Is Mama coming with me? Is Papa? Don't leave me with this bad man! I promise I'll be good! I promise I won't be a Jew!

I didn't know then that I would never see them again. I was not yet three when I watched my parents stumble away, crumbling in their grief and misery while I was held back in the powerful arms of a resistance worker dressed as a Nazi. This brave man, who helped to find a hiding place for me, was later also murdered. He and his organization helped to save three hundred Jewish children.

The equally brave Christian family with whom I was eventually hidden protected and loved me. I was able to stay with them until I was nearly ten years old. Decades later, in 2000, I had the honor to have their names inscribed on the wall of the Righteous at Yad Vashem, the Holocaust Museum in Jerusalem.

When the war had already been over for five years and I was by then ten years old, it was decided by various bureaucrats and government organizations that I, like so many other orphaned children, had to be returned to my Jewish roots and that I could no longer live with my rescue family: the people I loved, who had cared for me for eight years, and who had endangered their own and their children's lives to save a little Jewish boy from death.

This family fought hard against losing me, but in 1950, it was sanctioned by the Dutch courts that I be moved to a Jewish orphanage in Amsterdam, hundreds of miles away from the Christian family who had loved and protected me.

For three years I lived in the orphanage, then, at age thirteen, I was finally placed with another foster family with whom I moved to Canada. Not long after settling in this country, it became obvious that this was not a good placement for me. Both foster parents were survivors of the camps. They too struggled with their own psychological and emotional demons and were not able to deal with the sadness of a displaced and abandoned orphan.

All my life, my only tangible connection with my parents was one small passport picture of each. Then, six months ago, in a box of memorabilia that had belonged to my cousin's deceased mother and that had been locked away since the end of the war, a letter was discovered, written by my father in May 1943 on what's now old and yellowed paper. All at once, I received a small glimpse of him as a person. Suddenly, it was as if he'd come alive…he was no longer just an image on a photo. Now, I feel even more intensely the agony they must have felt during those dark days in 1943, when we were still a little family.

He addressed the letter to "Dear Everyone." The content appears to be written in a code known only to the family, outlining events happening to various family members. It is not clear to me where this letter was written, who the recipient would have been, or what all the coded messages meant. There is a short reference about me that, as a two-year-old, I was good with words and that I had recovered from scarlet fever, and soon I would be playing with my new friends. This statement was probably meant to alert the family that I would be placed into hiding.

Leo at about age three, in front of his rescue family's home. In 1992, at the Dutch Hidden Children's conference in Amsterdam, Leo found this picture (one of only two of himself as a child) in a photo album belonging to the Dutch rescuer Semmy Riekerk, who, during the war, was married to Joop Woortman, the man in charge of the Naamloze Vennootschap (NV).

Leo Vogel, *now living in Canada, was one of about 250 children rescued by the Naamloze Vennootschap (NV), an underground cell in Holland run by Joop Woortman, who was arrested in July 1944 and died in Bergen-Belsen in March 1945.*

A Survivor's Affirmation of Life

By Eva Paula Nathanson

(Excerpted from The Hidden Child, *Volume XXVII, 2019.)*

Before the Holocaust reached Hungary, my maternal grandfather, Adolf Kohn, participated in the "underground railroad" that saved Jewish refugees from Nazi-occupied Czechoslovakia and Poland. Grandfather, a widower and father of six adult children, owned land, a manor house, and a kosher dairy farm near the Czechoslovakian border. He had his own *shul* in the manor house, and all neighboring Jews were welcomed. Each Shabbat, he opened his home to stranded travelers and Jewish soldiers. In 1939, my father, a friend of my mother's brother Miklos, was one of those soldiers.

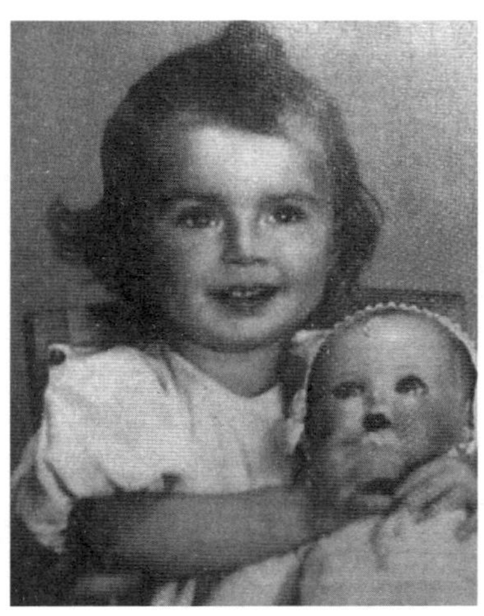

Eva at her first birthday, holding a doll given by her birth father.

My parents, Magdolna Kohn and Mozes Ádam, married shortly thereafter. I was born in Budapest on January 28, 1941. While Grandfather's sons and sons-in-law served in the army, his daughters and their children lived with him. Although my mother spent weekdays in Budapest running my father's furniture factory, I stayed with the family. Mother would arrive each

Magdolna and Mozes Ádam, Budapest, 1940.

Thursday evening and return to Budapest on Monday morning.

Grandfather had progressive views: he believed in equal rights and responsibilities for his two sons and four daughters. All had been equally educated and instructed in the management of the land and farm. He did not permit child labor, insisting that every child on his land attend school, and he treated his employees fairly. Grandfather was respected and admired by everyone.

One night in a local bar, in early 1943, a farmer who had had too much to drink unwittingly denounced Grandfather. The man bragged that his employer, Baron Kohn, was not only fair to everyone who worked for him, but that he also rescued Jews from Nazi-occupied countries. The Hungarian *Nyilas* (Nazis) set out to make an example of Grandfather and our family. All were arrested and immediately deported.

My earliest memory begins here. I was playing with my favorite doll upstairs in the children's quarters with my governess. My aunts, cousins, grandfather, and great-grandmother were downstairs in the day room. We heard trucks pull into the courtyard. This was followed by piercing shouts, screams, and firing bullets. My governess ran down to see what was going on. She returned, pale, trembling, and said in a terrified voice, "We are going to play hide-and-seek." Placing her index finger over her lips, she whispered, "Not a word, not a sound! If we run into anyone you do not know, pretend you cannot understand or speak." She took my hand into hers and led me through the rear corridors, out the back entrance, then onto the small path from the house to the service quarters. As we turned, I saw uniformed men shove my family onto the trucks. I turned to my governess for an explanation.

Young Eva with her mother, Magdolna Ádam.

Visibly shaken, she replied, "They are also playing a game." As I followed her into her parents' house, I felt frightened and confused. She dressed me in clothes belonging to one of her sisters. It was to be part of the game, a game I could not understand. On this fateful day, I escaped the horrific fate of my mother's three sisters, their children, my grandfather, and my great-grandmother. None were ever heard from again.

The next day, my governess took me to my mother in Budapest. Shortly thereafter, a family friend, Laszlo (Laci) Hantos, who was working with the underground, came and said to my mother, "Pack what you can carry; you and Eva have to leave immediately. They're coming for you both. I will try to get some of your valuables later. The underground and I are taking responsibility to make sure you will be safe. We owe that to your father."

Sometime later, Laci found a little girl crying by herself on the street. Vali was younger than I was. He brought her to my mother. "She seems to be all alone. I could not leave her; she needs to stay and hide with you." I was pleased to have a companion. The three of us were hidden by the underground, wherever and whenever good people were willing to take us in. Hiding two small children was a major risk, and each place proved to be temporary. We hid in pantries, attics, basements, closets, cellars, and in a hole dug under the floor of a room. In the end, we hid in empty, bombed-out buildings all over Budapest until April 1945.

Throughout our hiding period, we were petrified, confused, traumatized, afraid, hungry. We followed orders without question: we wanted to survive. We lived in discomfort, fear, dirt, hunger, and silence. When we had any normal activities, such as eating, speaking, crying, walking, moving about, washing, or using the bathroom, we felt grateful. Vali and I learned to cry in silence, speak in whispers, and be still most of the time. Mother tried to keep us clean with a washcloth, but most of the time, we felt grimy.

The money and valuables we escaped with did not last, and our rescuers needed cash to feed us. Mother, an amazing knitter, worked day and night to produce saleable or barterable items. Our job was to roll the yarn into balls and unwind it for her as she knitted. We stayed in windowless, confined places, and when we had to be moved, it was always at night. I could no longer remember the feeling of fresh air and sunshine, or of being among people.

Once, as we were transferred to another hiding place, we were discovered. Vali and I were separated from my mother and brutally shoved onto a truck. I pulled Vali into a corner next to me. Through a tiny gap, I saw four men in SS uniforms following us on horseback. Two climbed onto the truck as the others held the reins of their horses. I held my breath, petrified. Men in uniform scared me. They threw us into the arms of the other two men on horseback. I was so terrified that I threw up and soiled myself. I remember the shame, disgust, the paralyzing fear as the man held me. Without a word, they brought us to the cellar of a building where we were reunited with my mother. Those SS men were actually part of the underground.

I was immersed into a small wooden tub of warm water, and the filth was washed away. This was the first bath I'd had in a very long time. I stopped crying, and a sense of calm and safety came over me. That feeling of warmth and coziness had to last for a long time. Vali too was bathed, and we both got some hot milk. That is one of the few good memories I have from those years.

Cellar living was hard on our health. I was malnourished, and I contracted an infection that led to a constant low-grade fever. My mother hid my ailments from our rescuers, worried that if they learned I was sick, they would make us leave.

One time, while cramped together in a storage area, flat on a wooden shelf, with our faces nearly touching the shelf above, our building was hit by a bomb. This must have been toward the end of the war when Budapest was under attack. Vali and I were soundlessly crying, choking back our tears as everything rocked from the impact. My mother covered us with her body to save us from the falling jars, cans, and debris. I asked my mom, "Are we going to be all right?" Her response was, "Shush, just one more bomb and we'll never have to be afraid again." By this time, Mother had lost hope, was depressed, and felt weak. In her despair, she no longer believed in a future.

Someone from the underground had sent her a message from a man who had witnessed the murder of my father and my uncle Miklos. It seemed that my father and uncle were punished with hard labor and regular beatings because they had tried to escape. My uncle was tied to a tree and cold water was poured on him until he froze to death. The Nazis had ordered my father to dig his own grave; they shot him and buried him alive. The news of my father's and uncle's murders had shaken my mother's resolve. She was twenty-two years old and a widow. She told me later that the only reason she fought to live was to save us.

By then, the Hungarian Arrow Cross militiamen were doing all they could to dispose of those Jews who had escaped deportation. They dragged the remaining Jews to the bank of the Danube where they were tied together, shot, and tossed into the current. We too were discovered.

It was in the late afternoon of a dark, cold day in early 1945. I was too weak to walk, so my mother carried me in one arm while holding Vali's hand with the other. We got to the Danube and stood at the end of the line. I heard crying, begging, screaming, praying; then shots, followed by a splash, a thud, then gurgling.

The river was red with blood and full of floating bodies. We were shaking from the cold and the fear. Mother said to us, "Close your eyes and ears, you will feel warmer." By the time our turn came, only two Hungarian Arrow Cross men were left.

One wrapped a cord around us; the other aimed. Then, suddenly, the latter lowered his weapon and said to my mother,

"You dirty Jews, I recognize you. You lived in the same house as I did before the war. If you promise to testify for me when this is all over, I will save you and the brats." Of course, Mother agreed! Then, he said, "I will loosen the cord and shoot, but not to kill. Don't forget who saved your life. You will be found when you will be needed to testify." I was still clutching my doll. The cord was loosened, and he fired. Mother was grazed in her arm. We fell into the ice-cold water. There were some tree roots and other outcroppings that kept us from floating down the river. Mother told us to be very still, not to wiggle.

And then, a miracle! We were pulled out of the water and taken, soaking wet, to an apartment, where we were washed with warm water and given hot drinks and dry clothes. We were ushered into a dark room crowded with people. The windows were covered. I could only see their forms as they lay on the floor. We slid into an empty space and rested among them, Mother holding Vali and me in each of her very thin arms. There seemed to be some order in the care we received over the next few days. Food was distributed, and bathroom breaks to an outhouse were organized. Yet, people spoke in muted tones. The air was stale with the odor of unwashed, sweaty bodies and clothing. Thin, depressed people stared at one another with vacant eyes.

One morning, the door opened and two armed, uniformed men stood before us. I shrank with fear and burrowed into my mother's arm. Seeing me so agitated, Vali followed my lead. One soldier noticed and walked up to us. He reached into his pocket, took out something, broke it in half, stuck one piece into my mouth and the other into Vali's. For the first time in my memory, I savored the gift of chocolate. To this day, chocolate means all is okay in my life.

Meanwhile, the other soldier pulled down the window covers, letting the morning light stream in. Being blinded by the light was at once painful and pleasurable. We were told, "These two soldiers are part of the liberating forces of the Soviet Union. Budapest is under siege. The Russian and Nazi armies are fighting in the streets. The Soviets are taking the city, street by street. From now on, we are allowed to go into the yard in small groups. Mother took us out into the spring sun. I barely had enough strength to walk, but for the first time in years, I was sitting in the sunshine, seeing a world I barely remembered.

Eva Paula Nathanson*'s family fled Hungary in 1956 and immigrated to the United States in 1957. She raised two children and has two grandchildren and feels blessed to have a loving family, friends, and supportive community.*

The Irony and Mystery of Survival

By Henry R. Huttenbach, PhD

(Excerpted from The Hidden Child, *Volume XIII, 2005.)*

Escape from Nazi Germany

It all began for us on April 1, 1933, the day of the state-mandated boycott of all Jewish enterprises throughout Germany. Brown-uniformed SA thugs physically prevented customers from entering the family store. For my parents, this was incomprehensible: the family dated back to 1435 and the family business to 1810, to the time of the French occupation by Napoleon. Were we not Germans? Good neighbors? Had we not non-Jewish friends? That day in spring 1933 created doubt, but not enough to urge us to leave. One still hoped for better days. The fear was muffled.

Then, in 1934, came the repercussions of the Great Depression: to head off bankruptcy, my father was forced to sell the store to a large department store conglomerate in Berlin, which happened to be Jewish. The transaction left my father unemployed and, because he was Jewish, unemployable. Fortunately, in 1935, he found work with an American firm (NuEnamel) in a nearby city, Mannheim. We were financially solvent again and the future seemed rosier. Perhaps, it was reasoned, we could ride out the storm. But the storm struck mercilessly.

It came in several forms throughout 1935 and 1936. The first thunderbolt happened in September with the declaration of the Nuremberg Race Laws. In brief, all Jews were marginalized and expelled from mainstream society. I was prevented from entering kindergarten. My parents began to think of leaving Germany "for the duration." (There was always hope mixed with despair.) The frequency of calling us "dirty Jews" or similar epithets in public increased. But where to go?

The answer came out of the blue in the form of Boleslaw Huberman, a musician from Palestine. The Jewish Agency had entrusted him with the task of assembling one hundred Jewish musicians to form the Palestine Philharmonic. My mother, a professional violinist, passed the rigorous audition; my father, an amateur cellist, was not accepted. Huberman had one hundred certificates to hand out to musicians and their children under sixteen years. Spouses—in this case my father—were not included. In consolation, he was offered a job with the Jewish orchestra in Berlin. We were given the anguished choice: all stay in Nazi Germany or split the family between Palestine and the Third Reich. With hindsight, the Jewish Agency had made its own brand of "selection" which would give life to mother and son and death to the father. My parents chose to remain together and seek safety in another country.

Selecting a country that welcomed Jewish refugees was a form of running the gauntlet. Entering the US—my mother's dream from childhood—was its own obstacle course of filled quota numbers, consulate corruption (paying bribes) and finding sponsors willing to assume financial responsibility. The urgency was exacerbated by an incident on Fastnacht—the Purim-like carnival before Lent. That day my mother dressed me in a costume of a pink rabbit and sent me (age five) into the street to play with other children also wearing costumes. When they saw me, three boys dressed as cowboys chased after me shouting "Catch the rabbit." Delighted they would play with me, I let them catch me. Jubilantly they brought back their trophy and tied me to a lamppost outside our apartment. They placed crumpled newspaper at my feet and lit it. Joining hands, they chanted "*Brenn Judebub, brenn.*" (Burn Jewboy, burn.) Had my mother not looked out of the window at that very moment, there is little to be guessed. That night, my parents decided to leave Germany unconditionally. If any doubt remained, it was removed a few days later when a cello student of my father—a man in his mid-twenties—came by one evening and informed my father that he was about to be arrested. "How do you know?" my father asked him. He had learned it at Gestapo headquarters where he worked as a clerk. Within a week, we had packed and settled in Milan, Italy. We had been saved thanks to the intervention of a Gestapo; we had not been saved by the restrictive policies of the Jewish Agency. Is this not a sign of irony and mystery?

Escape from Fascist Italy

Crossing through Switzerland was a rude reawakening that danger lurked everywhere: Since our passports were emblazoned with a page-length "J"—an idea initiated by the Swiss government to which Nazi Germany readily consented—we were not allowed to leave the train while stopping in that country. Had we not had papers permitting us to enter Italy, the Swiss authorities would have "repatriated" us back to Germany where nothing but persecution awaited us. Safe in Italy along with other refugees from Nazi Germany, we were prepared to see the "Storm" back home burn itself out. True to what they had learned in high school, my parents waited for the *Thermidore* (the political thaw) to follow the terror. How could we know that the violence so far was but a preview of genocidal violence to come?

The Italian honeymoon did not last long. Disturbing news from Germany about my four grandparents' declining conditions marred each day. Then came the first rude intrusion. The two dictators—Mussolini and Hitler—signed a pact. One of its conditions was the recertification of German residents. This meant a passport revalidation by the Gestapo. All who failed to register or refused to comply or were turned down by the Nazi authorities would have to leave Italy within six months or be deported back to Germany. It was a cruel trap to catch Jews. So, again, where to go?

The United States, the first choice, was an impossible goal: limited quotas, corrupt consuls, lack of sponsors, insufficient hard currency made us prisoners. The only open door was that of President Chiang Kai-shek's China. For a fee, it offered visas. But how to get to Shanghai? As the deadline approached, only the Soviet Union offered a trans-Siberian train ride, but that meant crossing Austria (by then annexed to Nazi Germany). We were not ready to risk that itinerary. Anyway, by then, Shanghai had fallen into the hands of the Japanese. At the moment of total despair—many had committed suicide for failing to reach a safe asylum—rescue came from the most unexpected quarter, a relative in England, my father's brother, Alfred.

My uncle Alfred was a gifted sculptor; a rebel; the family black sheep; irresponsible, many said; a permanent bachelor; and a romantic; certainly not one to count on in times of turmoil and terror for Jews. While living in Berlin, enjoying prestigious commissions, his work caught the eye of England's most prominent sculptor who, in 1934, invited Alfred to join him. This coincidentally became the key link in our quest for a haven from Nazism in Italy. Thanks to Alfred, the entire family was saved, but we did not know that then.

Alfred procured visas for all three of us. He managed this miracle by taking advantage of a British law allowing workers into the country willing to do housework for the aristocracy: it was called the Domestic Servant Visa. Thanks to his English friends, they vouched for the suitability of my parents to become butler, cook, and maid. Documents in hand, we booked passage to England without difficulty. My parents raised the money by selling everything of value except their musical instruments. But there was one major hitch: the liner—coming from India via the Suez Canal and Genoa—was scheduled to arrive three weeks after the deadline for our mandated departure from Italy or face deportation to Germany. What to do?

We had tickets, but without legal papers, we were subject to instant arrest if we remained in Italy till the time to board a liner. First, we had to give the impression we were returning to Germany: my father resigned from his work, and we gave notice to the landlord. All possessions not sold were packed. When the day came, friends and neighbors saw us off at the train station, many in tears, fearing for our lives. Those German Jews who had preceded us disappeared at the Swiss-German border. The same awaited us had we not had another plan up our sleeves. Instead of staying on the train, we got off one stop before the Italian border and never turned back. Total strangers, friends of friends, took us—my mother and me, and my father separately—in hand, whisking us in their cars. (Later, we learned that our belongings were unloaded from the train and taken to close friends who lived in a nearby villa in Varese. We retrieved almost everything after the war. But at the time, our concern was not our property but our very lives.)

For the next three weeks, we lived underground, never sleeping in the same home twice. Good Samaritans housed and fed us, no questions asked. Not a single host asked for money. They were simple, small-town, decent people who knew right from wrong. Above all, they were shocked to hear that our plight was made worse by Mussolini's pro-Hitler policy. Each day, they arranged a phone call to my father who, like us, was whisked from home to home until the day to board the liner—the Llangibby Castle—in Genoa. On that day, my mother and I joined the passengers lined up to be processed by Italian and British officials. At the last table were a Gestapo agent and his Italian counterpart on the alert for refugees like us with invalid passports. Just as we came to them, all hope evaporated into despair. At that moment, we faced the abyss. We would be stopped, arrested, and deported. The spasms of fear remained with us forever. We could see my father who had boarded before us. We were about to be separated, he from us, our nightmare screaming at us, when suddenly, as the Gestapo agent was called away, seemingly to answer a phone call, strong hands violently pushed my mother up the ramp while I was picked up bodily and unceremoniously dumped on the ship's deck. We were safe, safe on British "territory" according to international law. At which point, both my parents collapsed, emotionally exhausted. But we were not fully out of the woods. Several weeks after our arrival in England, the country was at war with an aggressive Nazi Germany, and the war enveloped us with the gnawing fear of a Nazi invasion.

Surviving World War II in England

Fear of a Nazi invasion was not unfounded. Poland fell, and its Jews entered hell. France fell, and its Jews faced lethal antisemitism. The dire consequences to my family if the Nazis succeeded in conquering England were obvious. We had no idea of genocide, but we knew enough that, as Jewish prisoners of Nazi forces, terrible things would befall us. We did not know of death camps, but we were aware of concentration camps. We had heard tales of dozens of men who had been arrested and incarcerated in Dachau and not released until they obtained a visa to leave Germany. In possession of ships' manifolds, the Nazis knew the names of virtually every German Jewish refugee in England. The archives testify to these lists of names, which were tantamount to arrest warrants had the invasion gone as planned.

Meanwhile, my father was interned as an "enemy alien." British fears of spies planted among the tens of thousands of refugees entering the country led to mass arrests of foreigners, ironically the majority being Jewish. The family was divided for eighteen months. Again ironically, while my father was in relative security in his internment camp, my mother and I in London experienced the intense bombing campaign launched by Hermann Goering. Twice, we were bombed out, both times escaping by the skin of our teeth thanks to the courage of the air raid wardens who dug us out. Then there was the time my school was strafed by a Nazi bomber, which killed a schoolmate sitting next to me. And always, the fear of a Nazi invasion. Not till the Battle of Stalingrad in January 1943 did we breathe easily, though not entirely until the war in Europe was over in May 1945, for till the end, Hitler rained flying bombs and rockets onto London, where we resided.

What do our experiences mean? Are they worth remembering? Are the questions our special legacy? Do they celebrate life over death? Should my children (all five of them) be told? Do these anecdotes warrant retelling to my grandchildren (all twelve of them) or to my great-grandchildren (all four of them at last count)?

And what about the debts owed to those who wittingly provided help and assistance to a grateful family of three over a dangerous decade? The young Gestapo clerk? The anonymous Italians? My Bohemian uncle? And what of those who did not help? The Jewish Agency? The United States? There is enough irony and mystery here to go around. There are enough questions here to satisfy even the most indifferent. For example: who taught the little children in Mannheim to set fire to a Jewish child? The parents? Their cruel inclinations?

After all, this morality tale could easily have been otherwise. In the middle of the nineteenth century, there were two Jewish brothers—my ancestors. One converted to Christianity, while the other remained Jewish; I descended from the latter. In 1942, one member from the Jewish side of the family was incarcerated with his wife and child in the Riga ghetto where he was sentenced to die for having smuggled food for his family. The SS officer in charge of the execution turned out to be a member of the Christian branch of the family. The young SS officer and his two brothers did not survive the war; yet most of the Jewish branch, including myself, survived genocidal death and lived to see three more generations.

What lessons can we draw from this multiplicity of perplexing ironies? I do not pretend to resolve them. All too often in life we pursue imperfect answers rather than nurturing the questions and the mysteries they hold. To survive is life. To try to answer why is to diminish the gift of survival.

Henry R. Huttenbach *(1930–2024) was a professor at the City College of New York (CCNY). As a specialist on Russia and Eastern Europe, he focused on national minorities, ethnic conflict, and genocide. He was founder and editor-in-chief of* The Journal of Genocide Research *and* The Genocide Forum. *He was also the director of the Center for the Study of Ethnopolitics and Ethnonationalism and a contributing editor of* Soviet Nationality Policies. *He published works in over half a dozen countries.*

The Rescue of a Jewish Family in Greece

By Yolanda Avram Willis

(From The Hidden Child, *Volume VI, Number 1, fall/winter 1996.)*

My family had lived in Greece for centuries. Immediately after Nazi Germany attacked Greece in April 1941, we attempted to leave for Egypt via Crete. My father listened to the BBC and, knowing how the Nazis treated Jews elsewhere, anticipated the Jewish persecution. On our escape from the mainland, my parents had brought along my grandmother, two of my aunts, and a young housemaid. I brought along my doll. I was six years old; my brother was two. Three days before our planned escape, the Nazis made their surprise attack on Crete. With the dawn of May 20, 1941, came a massive bombing of the small town of Kastelli where we had rented a small house across from a military installation. As the sky turned black with planes spewing fire and

Yolanda, right, with her mother and younger brother.

windows shattered, we cowered, defenseless. When we tried to leave, we found the house surrounded by craters. We thought this would be our end.

And then a miracle happened. The Xirouhakis family, recent acquaintances, asked us to join them in their escape to the mountains. My father had sought out Mr. Stilianos Xirouhakis, a very prominent citizen of the area, seeking his support for our efforts to flee to Egypt. As the two got better acquainted, Father confided our secret identity to him.

In the early morning of May 20, my father appeared at the Xirouhakis home as the family was preparing to flee, and asked his new friend, "What will become of us?" It was an unanswerable question.

Father looked Mr. Xirouhakis in the eye and uttered, "Now I have but you and God." Mr. Xirouhakis replied, "We are going to the mountains. It will not be easy," and offered at once to include us in their flight to Tyliphos.

My eighty-year-old diabetic grandmother, my baby brother, and the women were the first to go, riding on donkeys bearing supplies. I was sent with the men. My father was given a dark mule to share with me. Mr. Xirouhakis, an impressive-looking patriarch, wearing the traditional Cretan baggy trousers, wide sash, and boots, rode on a white horse.

Late at night, we reached a small mountain chapel, Our Lady of Tyliphos. I was shown a spot to sleep on the stone floor. My parents spent the night under the small church portico, desperately trying to quiet my brother who was suffering from dysentery. In the morning, the Xirouhakises led us to a clearing. They made a sleeping enclosure out of green branches, leaves, and blankets and surrounded it with thorny branches to keep animals away. They taught us to use garlic to repel snakes. They found water and introduced us to snails for dinner. After dinner one night, I crept away and wept in secret, longing for our home, our routine, my school, my friends—all lost, along with our sense of safety.

One night, I was dragged out of my makeshift bed to move to the other side of Mount Tyliphos. We had to avoid making any sound, lest the Cretans or Allies mistake us for Nazis—and lest the Nazis discover us.

Later, when things quieted down in the towns, the Xirouhakis family took us to Messoghia, where they had relatives and life was less arduous.

Fifty-five years ago, we went to Crete as strangers. The Xirouhakises sheltered us, risking their lives while saving ours. During the darkest hours of the Nazi occupation and the Jewish persecution, the Xirouhakis family, in their humble and quiet way, helped sustain our faith in human decency.

My plea for help in finding the Xirouhakis family was heard and taken to heart by many of the members of the Pan-Cretan Association of America attending the 55th Anniversary of the Battle of Crete in Washington DC on May 17–19, 1996. The most effective results came from Dr. Yannis Nathenas, who after numerous transatlantic phone calls, located the two surviving Xirouhakis sons, Stratis and Manolis. It was not easy, as I had the town wrong and had forgotten their first names. Within four days, he had us speaking on a three-way conference call. What an emotional and joyous experience!

We have been speaking since then and we had a reunion in September. There are many questions answered, some misconceptions corrected, and amazing new information imparted every time we speak. And so, I learned how the miracle happened.

Yolanda Avram Willis *has also written a more complete biography,* A Hidden Child in Greece.

PART VI

The Liberation

Waiting for Liberation in Poland

By Alexander Kimel

(From The Hidden Child, *Volume V, Number 1, spring 1995.)*

We were hidden on a small farm in the village of Lopushna. One day, my sister, Luba, who stayed in the main house, appeared in our bunker. "What happened, Luba? Are we in danger?" asked our father. "No," replied Luba, "the Russians are about twenty miles away, and Koenisberg, our host, ran away. He is afraid of the Russians."

Our spirits rose. We would be liberated within a week! Afterward, I sat for hours at the ventilation pipe, our only connection with the outside world, waiting for the Russians.

A few days later, I heard loud voices and the roar of motors. "The Russians are here. Let's go," I cried out. My father approached the vent, listened for a while, and said: "Those are Nazis. The military police have taken the farm. The Russian offensive is broken. We are lost."

Our excitement quickly turned to despair. We had only a three-week supply of bread and water. To preserve our precious resources, we agreed on half a glass of water and a piece of bread daily.

One day, I heard a familiar voice, pleading with the Nazis: "I am a Jew. Please give me a bowl of soup and a shower and kill me later." I still don't know if the Nazis wasted a bowl of soup on the dead Jew, but with their bullets, they were generous.

A few days later, I was awakened by loud shouts: "Stop! Stop!" Then two piercing shots, followed by the screams of a wounded child. It was Cesia, the neighbor's daughter. She had run away when the Nazis came to arrest her Jewish father.

As the days passed, I rapidly lost weight. The skin on my cheekbones had become thin and I had trouble sleeping. Worst of all was the thirst, the ever-nagging thirst. Dozing most of the time, I began to lose all sense of time and place.

Once, I awakened and saw my father and sister crouching restlessly on a bundle of straw. In the flickering light of the oil lamp, the underground vault seemed like an Egyptian tomb. My poor father had aged. My sister had developed protruding cheekbones; the luster of her black hair and her beauty were gone. I thought we might die here.

"Oh God," I cried out, "What is going to happen to us? Let me die first." After all those years of running, hiding, fighting, were we now destined to die a slow death? We considered breaking out, but where could we run? The farm was swarming with Nazis and the barking of the vicious neighborhood dogs would certainly alert them. Our best chance for survival was to remain in our bunker.

I dreamed of liberation, of going from well to well, drinking cool, delicious water, only to awaken to the pain of my parched lips.

A few days later, I heard loud voices. Slowly, I crawled to the vent pipe. These were Russian voices! I jumped up, yelling, "Father, Luba, we made it. We are liberated!"

We sprang up, amazed by our renewed strength, embraced and kissed one another, and swiftly emerged into the bright, blinding sunshine. I felt dazed. My eyes opened to the miracle of creation: the big oak tree was green, a dark vivid green. The flock of white geese with their orange beaks looked so peaceful, so alive. Even the gray sparrows chirping on the thatched roofs were wonders of nature.

Suddenly, I saw Stepan, the field hand, carrying a pail of water. Oh my God! Water, life-giving water! I ran toward him and sank my head into the pail.

When I got up, my sister was talking with a Russian soldier. What a sight! I ran toward the road and yelled to a Russian riding a horse: "I am a Jew. I survived. Thank you for the liberation."

"*Paschol prokliatyj narod*—go away, you cursed people. Get away from me," he screamed.

Nevertheless, the first month of our liberation was the most exciting time of my life. I met other survivors and immediately felt a strong bond and kinship. It was wonderful to experience closeness and trust again after all those harsh years.

Still, liberation was not all that I expected. Two weeks later, I was summoned to the mayor's office where I was told: "You are being sent to work in the coal mines of Donbas."

"I am seventeen years old, undernourished, sick with diarrhea, and I weigh exactly eighty pounds. How can I work in coal mines?" I protested.

"Never mind, you will manage. We Russians don't differentiate between Ukrainians, Poles, and Jews. Everybody has equal rights and obligations," answered the mayor.

At this moment, I realized that my struggle for survival was not over. It merely entered a new, more subtle phase. The next day, I enrolled in high school, claiming that I was only fifteen years old. I simply deducted the years in hiding.

Alexander Kimel, *(1926–2018) was born in Podhajce, Poland (today Pidhaitsi in western Ukraine). When the Nazi army invaded eastern Poland, and Rohatyn was occupied, Kimel was forced into the ghetto with his family and all other Jews of the town. Kimel wrote about his wartime experiences on his award-winning website, where he shared his insights about genocide and antisemitism. His poems about the Holocaust have been widely reprinted and cited.*

Yom Kippur: After the Liberation

By Leon Wells

(From The Hidden Child, *Volume III, Number 1, spring 1993.)*

It was about two months after liberation. We were still walking in a daze...bewildered. In the streets, when recognizing another survivor by his ashen face, skeleton-like body, and listless tread, we would say *Amchu* (our people) in Hebrew, and if the response was the same, we would begin a conversation. Somehow, in this manner, word spread among the survivors that we would meet on Yom Kippur at the empty "big synagogue," the last surviving temple in the city.

When I came out of hiding from the basement of a Polish home in Lvov, I didn't know where to go or what to do. For a time, I walked without a destination. I felt as if I were in an uncharted land, a sort of purgatory. In my concealment, I had eagerly awaited the day of liberation. There was a future; I lived with hope. Now, the future was gone. As I walked for hours without aim or purpose, I became weak and ravenously hungry. My feet began to bleed because of the shoes I was wearing after spending so many months in a cramped basement without them. Finally, I sat on the sidewalk curb, unable to walk another step, and took off my shoes. My feet were covered with blood. I sat...my head in a whirl.

Yom Kippur approached. We were to assemble in the only remaining synagogue, one that had recently been abandoned by the Nazis who had used it as a stable.

Who would be there? Meeting others who had known our families "before" was extremely important to us. "They knew them" was an expression of achievement. Our families were not unknown entities. They had existed, they had been, and, as such, we too were beings, coming from somewhere.

At the service, we were fewer than two hundred people. There were no benches; it was completely destitute of furniture. Someone had obtained a simple wooden Ark, a Torah scroll, and a stand where the Torah was to be read.

The chaplain, who was originally from Poland, conducted the service in a subdued and depressed tone as if bashful, not wanting to disturb people's thoughts or moods. He prayed as if not knowing how to handle this kind of situation, or to whom he should offer his prayers.

He started with these words: "On this day, we used to come to ask for forgiveness for our sins. Today, we, the remnant of the large Jewish community, are gathered here waiting for you to beg us for forgiveness." He did not say these words melodically as befitting a Yom Kippur prayer. He stopped, heaved a deep sigh, and looked sorrowfully at his congregation.

Leon Wells *was seventeen years old in 1943 when he was forced by the Nazis to dig up and burn the bodies of hundreds of thousands of Jews murdered in the Janowska camp. This was done to hide the truth about the Nazi death camps from the approaching Allies. Wells, the only member of his family of seventy-six to survive the Holocaust, testified at the Eichmann trial in Israel in 1961. Among those killed were his parents and six siblings. His memoir,* The Death Brigade, *is considered a classic of Holocaust literature.*

The Liberation in Belgium

By Rudy Rosenberg

(From The Hidden Child, *Volume V, Number 1, 1995.)*

At the end of August 1944, we heard that Paris had been liberated by the US Army. After hiding for more than two years in a Brussels basement, my mother and I felt a mixture of hope for our liberation, but also despair: we could not really believe that a day would come when we could freely go outside again without fear for our lives.

By September 1, we saw signs that liberation was imminent. Through a small window of our basement, we could see Nazis looting the house next door—occupied by units of the Gestapo and SS—and piling their booty onto three large trucks.

The next day, the Nazis made their final preparations for departure. They were able to obtain some gasoline which they poured from jerry cans into the trucks' fuel tanks. In the process, much gasoline spilled on the ground, to the great anger and frustration of the officer in charge who was verbally abusing the private for not using a funnel to save the precious liquid.

That evening, the Nazis were able to start two trucks while the third stubbornly refused to budge. Finally, they tossed a hand grenade into the truck, creating a very brief fire. Several Belgian civilians were watching these happenings from a distance and as soon as the fire went out, they rushed the truck and ransacked whatever they could. A Nazi corporal, caught in the throng, fired his pistol in the air, dispersing the group just long enough for him to escape.

When the truck was completely emptied, the mob turned its anger toward the house that the Nazis had just vacated and even though the house belonged to Belgians—it had been seized by the Nazis in the spring of 1940—they proceeded to vandalize it.

The morning of September 3 was relatively calm, although we could hear sporadic shooting from various parts of the city. Nazis were fleeing on foot, carrying bundles, pushing carts loaded with their belongings, riding in horse-drawn wagons.

That afternoon, my mother and I were bold enough to leave our basement and go to the first floor of the house where we joined Mr. and Mrs. De Knibber, the people who had been hiding us since 1942. They opened the doors to their balcony and my mother and I lay on the floor, trying to get a better view of what was happening without actually revealing our presence.

As evening came, we could hear rumbles swelling from other parts of the city, the sound of cheering crowds mixed with gunfire. A member of the FI (Interior Forces) drove by on a small motorbike yelling, "The British are coming, put out the flags!" Instantly, from almost every house on the street, Allied flags began to flutter from the windows and balconies. There were Belgian flags, French flags, British flags, American flags—flags that people had sewn together from bits of colored cloth.

The sound of a company of soldiers could be heard coming from the south and we all rose in anticipation. A man came rushing on a bicycle, yelling, "Pull back the flags. The Nazis are coming!" Then came four squads of Nazi troops carrying their rifles at port arms, double-timing up the street, their hobnailed boots rhythmically crushing the pavement. They passed as quickly as they could, looking neither left nor right, never seeing the people frantically pulling back the flags.

After the Nazis and their echoes disappeared around the corner, the flags returned, and, in the dusk, the cheering grew louder and louder. The time of our liberation had come. We embraced the De Knibbers. My mother and I were in each other's arms, crying with joy.

That night was the last in our basement. We chose not to leave the house because we did not want to chance catching a stray bullet. Outside, we could hear members of the FI rounding up suspected collaborators. One collaborator was complaining loudly that he could not move faster because his leg was hurting. I heard a shot and another voice exclaimed, "Now your leg is hurting. Move!"

The morning of September 4, I got dressed for the first time in almost two years. I had always been in my nightshirt, robe, and slippers. I had no shoes to wear. I went out into the sunshine and felt dizzy; the houses and the sky seemed to spin around me. I steadied myself against the wall of the house which, for so long, had been my tomb and my protector. The street was swirling through my tears. We were free.

Rudy Rosenberg, *now deceased, ran a small biotech company in Westbury, Long Island.*

Circa 1946, Austria. Polish Jewish orphans brought to Austria by teachers and nurses, and being cared for temporarily by the Joint Distribution Committee.

PART VII

The Postwar Orphans

Remembrances of 1945 in Poland

By Jakub Gutenbaum

(Excerpted from The Hidden Child, *Volume V, Number 1, spring 1995.)*

We were tired, sick, and despondent. Warsaw was in ruins; our apartments had been taken. The new owners refused to talk to us and were often hostile. After two and a half years in the Warsaw ghetto and more than two years in concentration camps, I came back, hoping to find my father who had escaped to Russia in the winter of 1940. I knew my mother and my younger brother were gassed in the ovens of Majdanek and the rest of my family were killed in Treblinka. With the Stalin regime now reaping the harvest, my hopes to find my father evaporated.

The entire ghetto was a desert of stones. I met people returning from concentration camps and traveled to Lodz with them. A Jewish Committee directed me to the "Children's House" in Helenowku, one of a few such homes financed by the Joint Distribution Committee.

There, I found heartsick, orphaned Jewish children who had been wandering in the woods, begging in the villages, or used by the Poles as free laborers. Regina, an old-looking fourteen-year-old, had hidden for two years in an underground hiding place built secretly and quickly by a neighboring farmer. She recalled the days of her liberation: "The Russians liberated the village. The entire village was jubilant—dancing, singing, drinking. I stood on the side, crying. I was alone, probably the only living Jew in the whole world."

A few of the older children were survivors of concentration camps. These children were already so grown-up and knew what they wanted—to study, to catch up for the lost years. Maria Falkowska, the former director of the home, said, "The most startling characteristic of this group was their thirst for knowledge. They studied late into the night and, even in the worst snowstorms, when they had to trudge many miles to the nearest tramway and would not return till dark, it was impossible to keep them home, away from their goal."

Zosia K., now a known radiologist at Uppsala (Sweden), who was shot in the leg during the evacuation of Auschwitz, was indignant when it was suggested she stay home and skip school. "I survived Auschwitz under greater hardships," she protested.

It was different with the younger children. Many did not understand why they were separated from the only people they knew as their parents. Feeling abandoned to "Zydkow," Yids, who "killed our Pan Jesus and were murdered for it," they cried and tried to run away. A heavy woman, the wife of a baker, brought a Jewish boy to the home, asking for payment and stating that the money was for the years she nourished and clothed him. The next day, she returned, crying, "What did I do? I love him so much, give me back my child."

Two Jewish families fought over eight-year-old Halinka. Each claimed that the child, a small girl with light hair, was their beloved daughter. There were many other disputes over the fate of these children: The Zionist Organization wanted all children transported to Israel, claiming that only there could the orphans return to a normal life; and the Jewish Communists, the controlling power in the Jewish Committee, thought the children belonged in a world free of antisemitism and nationalism—the newly evolving socialist society. The pogrom in Kielce seriously damaged this belief and thus the majority of the orphans now live in Israel or in the United States.

There are, at this time (1995), 450 members of the Society of the Children of the Holocaust in Poland. Eighty percent have a higher education, and among them are known writers, doctors, and journalists. Many are looking for their roots. For them, the war still goes on. Yet, even now, there is hope of finding living members of our families. Through our organization's contacts with people outside the Polish borders, there are sensational happenings at every meeting of the association: one found a brother in London, another a father in Canada.

1995 should be a year of celebration, but fifty years after the end of WWII, fifty years after Auschwitz, there can be little joy.

Prof. **Jakub Gutenbaum**, *a leading theoretical mathematician in Poland, headed the Society of the Jewish Children of the Holocaust in Warsaw. Translation by Leon Wells.*

To Palestine: August 8, 1947

By Ruth Lavie-Jourgrau

(Excerpted from The Hidden Child, *Volume X, summer 2001.)*

Bewildered, I'm standing at Lod Airport, a girl almost thirteen with a big suitcase. I feel the heat and humidity around me, and I can barely breathe. Is my face covered with sweat, or is it tears? I feel my clothes moistening. It's close to midnight. Outside, it's dark. Inside, people are running about noisily. Hearing a language I can't understand, I feel like a little island in a rapid current. What am I doing here? I feel sick. I've vomited all day, and my legs are shaky.

Ruth with her father, Dov Jourgrau, c. 1939.

Suddenly, two men are covering my face with kisses. Their faces too are damp. I try to wipe my face without their noticing. They are talking to me, but I don't understand a word. My language is Dutch, not Hebrew. Though I know some Yiddish words, it's not enough to understand these men who remind me vaguely of my father. Their strange attire baffles me. They're not wearing suits and ties. One is wearing shorts with socks up to his knees! Hesitating, I follow them to the door.

One of the pilots from the KLM Dakota airplane calls out to

me: "You are coming with us to Tel Aviv. The Arabs shoot at cars, but they might not if they see our uniforms." So, I'm back in a Dutch environment, and although there is some shooting and my head is pressed between my knees, I am comfortable and unafraid with these young men and women who have been so nice during the long flight.

It had been almost two years since one of my parents' friends found me on a farm in the north of Holland where I had been hidden for the last few months of the war. I can remember fifteen other places, but there were more. I knew my parents had been taken to the camps, but I was still waiting for them to come and take me home—as they promised. Four months had passed since the Canadian Army had liberated us. Every day, I stood at the fence next to the boy who had been hiding with the neighbors, where we could see the road between the green fields. His mother came and took him away, and I continued waiting—alone.

I wasn't really happy when I was taken to Amsterdam, where I was born, to begin a new life with my parents' friends. That cold feeling gripping my heart didn't leave me and I had difficulties adjusting to my new "parents" and their little girl. Nothing interested me. In the fourth grade at school, older than most of the others, I was a good student. But I did little more than what was asked of me. It was my former school where, if not for the war, I would have entered first grade. I recognized children from my nursery school—now one grade above me. It was only through books that I could forget for a moment. I read a lot. Once, on my way to school, I met another boy who had been in hiding with me. After he told me that his parents had returned, I lost all interest in him.

Ruth, center, with her two "sisters" during her "happy time," c. 1947.

If they could only have left me alone,

those people with their questions: "Do you remember me?" "Do you know who I am?" They must have thought I was dumb. My mother's only living sister came to see me from Paris; another aunt—the wife of my beloved uncle, my mother's brother—lived in Amsterdam. But no thanks; I didn't want to go with either of them.

One day I had a visitor, my mother's close friend, whom I had always loved. When I saw her broad smile and chestnut hair, I thought for a moment—Mama! After two or three visits, I agreed to move in with her and her family: her husband and two girls, one of them my age. They lived in a little apartment. I had to sleep in the same bed with the older girl, but I had a loving "real" family again and I began to flourish. I skipped the fifth grade and rejoined my former friends. Although I had to take two tramways to get to school, I didn't care. I went to music school, and I began to paint. All one had to do to please me was to bring me pencils, brushes, paint, or books. But I also played outside, getting into mischief with the other children and teasing my younger "sister."

On Sundays, we'd go on outings on our bicycles. We'd sing Yiddish songs with "Papa," and he taught us to dance. More and more I became a "regular" child. I felt the love of Mama and Papa, and my wounds began to heal.

Then comes the shock! I have family in Palestine—my father's two brothers who want me, the child of their older brother, with them. They threaten to take my foster parents to court. Having only returned a short time ago from hiding and still struggling after having lost everything, my foster parents do not have the money or strength to fight them. It is decided. I must go. My foster mother finds the money and coupons to buy me some summer clothes and sandals.

"Please, don't send me away," I want to plead, but once more, I am the damaged package sent from place to place. Can't they see I'm falling to pieces? But blood is blood. Some lies are told, some promises made. Thus, I stood early this morning at Schiphol Airport. Everybody was pale and quiet. I was angry and sad. The nightmare in the old and shuddering Dakota began at seven this morning. Now, it's nearly midnight. And my new life begins.

Promises weren't kept. The uncle who was to be my guardian suddenly had regrets. The other uncle took me in—very much against his wife's will. He was kind and caring, but he could not oppose his wife. And she had no love for me at all. The War of Independence in the new State of Israel was another war I had to cope with. I was not allowed to have contact with my former family. "You have to learn Hebrew now and not speak Dutch." I had to assimilate quickly with the Sabras who laughed at my clothes and talked about "sheep taken to slaughter"—insulting the memory of my parents. All this has had a disastrous impact on my entire life.

Years later, I would say, "Those years were worse than the war—then I had hope."

Ruth Lavie-Jourgrau *was born in Amsterdam in October 1934. She married, had three children and six grandchildren. Her parents were murdered in Auschwitz and Sobibor.*

Letting Go of Hate

By Pinchas Zajonc

(From The Hidden Child*, Volume XXIV, 2016.)*

In May 1946, my good friend Yaakov and I were in Germany on our long road to Israel. I was fourteen, Yaakov was twelve. We were studying in a school where older members of Hashomer Hatzair served as teachers and counselors. Our teacher, Hedva, was teaching Hebrew, which I already knew, and I must have felt bored. It is likely I disturbed the class and was asked to leave. At first, I felt hurt, but when Yaakov joined me, I was happy. We set out in the direction of a German village, about four miles away. As we neared, we heard some wonderful music coming from a small café.

We peeked through the window and saw three musicians, one of whom was playing an accordion. Its sounds captivated us. We could not break away, and each day we skipped class to return to the café. We'd sit by the window for hours, mesmerized by the joyful tunes.

One day, we decided to buy an accordion. But we had no way to achieve this. There is no denying that at the time we were filled with a terrible hatred toward Germans. "*Nemt nekume*," in Yiddish, meaning "take revenge," was the message of all the survivors we'd met in Poland after the war. Now was the time to implement our vengeance.

We returned to the village the next day looking for a football field or playground. We found one, and it even had a bicycle path. We hid in the bushes, awaiting a child that might come riding by, ready to knock him down, steal his bicycle, sell it, and

Left: Pinchas Zajonc. Right: Yaakov Kuperblum (now Jack Kuper). Jordanbad, Germany, 1946.

with the money, buy an accordion. We didn't find our victim, but we didn't despair. The next day, we returned to the same field. This time, we saw a young, unaccompanied girl, maybe eleven or twelve years old, pedaling by. We decided that when she approached, we'd spring forward, knock her down, and snatch her bicycle. But with each round, we recoiled. We decided to marshal our courage with her next advance. This time, we'd do it without hesitation. Still, even then, we lacked the nerve to rob her.

Suddenly, we heard her screaming and crying. As we emerged, we were shocked, though we really didn't fathom what we were witnessing. The girl was lying on the ground; an older youth was bending over her. When he saw us, he ran away. Filled with compassion and pity, we ran to the girl. We lifted her up, calmed her down, wiped away her tears, caressed her, and asked her where her parents lived. I took her hand and Yaakov took her bicycle, and we brought her to her parents. They thanked us, and in our broken German, we mumbled something.

The idea of stealing a bicycle faded away. We returned home wordlessly, somewhat shaken and depressed. But something substantive had changed in our souls, and we never had such thoughts again. In retrospect, it had been a fundamental event for me. At once, I lost my desire for revenge against Germans, despite what could have been deemed as a justified action.

About a month later, in June 1946, to Yaakov's good fortune, his father's brother, who had survived in Belgium, was able to locate his nephew with the aid of the Red Cross. He came to visit Yaakov and brought him a present, a new pair of shoes. The shoes, however, didn't fit him at all. We intended to sell them to purchase an accordion, but no store agreed to buy them. Then we found a shop that sold "antiques" and second-hand goods. The old owner told us to go up to the second floor, and there we found a small accordion with only eight bases. After a month, we both learned to play.

When our group met on Friday evenings, we accompanied the singing of Yiddish and Hebrew songs, making these more cheerful. Ever since this incident occurred, I haven't been able to hate anyone. I learned then that hatred is destructive, and I was happy to have cured myself forever of this terrible disease. I have tried to bequeath this to my three sons, my seven grandchildren, and to anyone else who will listen.

Pinchas Zajonc *is now deceased. Yaakov Kuperblum, now Jack Kuper, lives in Toronto, Canada.*

Bits and Pieces of Our Lives

By Mechel Jamenfeld

(Excerpted from The Hidden Child, *Volume XXII, 2014.)*

Life in prewar Amsterdam with my parents and baby sister had been very good. By war's end, only my sister and I were left to pick up and rebuild the shattered bits and pieces of our lives. To the outsider, I appear emotionally mended, but I know better. The damage to our bodies and souls cannot be totally repaired—our pain and our memories are still with us. In itself, our resilience is quite remarkable. Indeed, our achievements seem quite ordinary, but many of us are aware that such "normalcy" requires inordinate effort. I hesitated a long time before setting down my story. My daughter calls me a "survivor," but I cannot proudly proclaim that I overcame adversity. For me, surviving has been a continuous struggle.

I was born in Amsterdam to Moshe and Rachel Jamenfeld on December 24, 1934. We were a religious family of *Ostjiden*, Jews from the East, who, like many others, had fled Poland for the promise of the West. We, Polish Jews, were different from Dutch Jews, who had lived in Holland for generations. We spoke Yiddish; our Dutch was not the best, we had our own Hassidic *shuls*, our *shtiblech*, and in many ways, we lived a separate life.

I was named after my grandfather, Mechel Jamenfeld, who died half a year before my birth. My grandfather had dedicated much of his time to the care of Polish immigrants coming to Amsterdam.

In 1937, my brother Benjamin Hirsch was born, who, to our sorrow, died at the very young age of four from a heart defect.

Then, in September 1942, almost in the middle of the war, my sister Miriam came into the world.

My family worked hard for a living. Grandfather Mechel had been a milkman; my father worked for a Jewish bakery, delivering bread and *hallot*, first by tricycle, but later with his new blue Ford, which made me very proud. The days he took me with him on his rounds were happy days.

Not all Dutch homes had a shower or bathroom before the war. A weekly pleasure was Friday afternoon visits to the public bath with my father. As my father showered, I'd marvel at his enjoyment of steaming hot water.

In May 1940, in spite of their repeated assurances that Dutch neutrality would be honored, the Nazis invaded Holland, which was no match for the highly modernized Nazi forces and surrendered within days. A small number of Jews escaped, but the great majority stayed, awaiting their fate. To everyone's surprise, not much happened after the invasion. Life seemed to go on as usual. Nevertheless, all lived in fear. The harassment of the Jews began slowly, but their measures accelerated, culminating with the mandatory wearing of the yellow star in the spring of 1942. The real danger came in July, with the summonses for the *Arbeitseinsatz*, physical labor in Nazi Germany. Many of the addressees accepted these orders. Annihilation was simply unthinkable, and it was believed that hard work in Nazi Germany would not hurt anybody. Jews were rounded up in the streets or taken from their homes. A large transition camp was erected in Westerbork, and weekly train "transports" were sent to concentration camps.

I was very much aware of the gloom at home. We were afraid, living in suspense, expecting something terrible to happen. One day, my father was arrested, sent to the Nazi prison in Scheveningen, and set free a few days later. Why? In those days, all reason was suspended; he just came home. There was more. We corresponded regularly with our relatives in Poland. In reply to our last letter, we received a postcard, bearing the Nazi Eagle stamp with the puzzling message, "Left no forwarding address."

In March 1943, my parents decided to place my sister, then only six months old, in the hands of the Dutch Resistance. It still hurts me to dwell on what they must have felt the moment they gave their baby away so soon after having buried one of their sons. Strangely enough, I remember glancing often at her empty crib.

Our turn came in July or August 1943. Hiding was not easy. One had to have Dutch friends or connections willing to hide a Jewish child or family. I remember my father telling my mother that he could probably arrange a hiding place for our family, but he would add, he did not want to "trouble" other people. So, we waited for the inevitable.

When the Nazis came for us, my sister, at least, was in safe hands. It is possible my parents planned to hide me as well but were unable to do so in time. That summer morning, a police car stopped before our house. Nazi policemen knocked on our door. My aunt and grandmother happened to be with us. In anticipation, my father had prepared a hideout below the living room floor, closed by a trapdoor and hidden under a carpet. When the knocking on the door persisted, my father ordered us to hide, adding that he would return in a minute. My mother, aunt, and grandmother went in first. I was last, holding the trapdoor open, waiting for my father. It took a very long time, but after interminable minutes, my father appeared in the room with the Nazis. One of them ordered me and the others to come out. I probably felt betrayed by my father, but above all, I felt guilty for having failed my family. I was the last one, and I should have closed the trapdoor.

The Prozdor Children's Home, run by Nathan Dasberg, Hilversum, Holland, 1946.

We were taken to the Dutch Theater in Amsterdam, a waystation for Jews pending their transport to Westerbork. I was allowed to remain a few hours with my parents. Toward evening, I was sent to the *crèche*, a former daycare center across the street where young children were kept separately to be reunited with their parents on the day of their transport. That was the last time I saw my parents. My mother died in the gas chambers of Auschwitz on August 27, 1943, at the age of thirty-six; my father died in the same camp on January 21, 1945, at the age of forty. My father had lasted through all the hard labor and died only six days before Auschwitz was liberated by the Russian Army, on January 27, 1945.

The Dutch Theater had been a preview of what was to come. As instructions blared from loudspeakers in a hot, overcrowded, and unsanitary theater, fear permeated the air. The atmosphere in the crèche, however, was very different. Here, horror wore a different face. The crèche was managed by a Jewish staff that cooperated with the Dutch Resistance, and together they managed to rescue about one thousand children. The Nazi command was sure the children would not escape since the parents were already in Nazi hands. Therefore, no measures were taken to guard them. As a result, they managed to smuggle a thousand out.

A Jewish member of the resistance, Walter Süskind, befriended the Nazi commander of the theater, who happened to like good whiskey, which at the time was hard to come by. When his "friend," the commander, was drunk, Süskind changed the registration lists of Jewish families already in Nazi hands so that the hidden children would not be missed on the day of transport. Toward the end, Süskind was also sent to his death together with the Jewish staff of the theater and the crèche. Upon Nazi orders, the crèche was closed in September 1943. It was reopened in October of the same year for a short time, but by then, the deportations had ended and the Nazis had declared Holland *Judenrein*. Out of the 140,000 Jews living in Holland before the war, only 24,000 survived.

Measured against the thousands who passed through the crèche during the war years, one thousand children is far too few. I do not know by what measure these children were chosen, but I know about the anguish of the Jewish nurses who had to prepare the not-so-lucky children for each transport. A few years ago, at a meeting of former "crèche children" organized by a friend and by me, one of the participating nurses mentioned the heartbreaking duty they had to fulfill. I do not know whether my father arranged for my rescue before being arrested or if I owe my life to a simple coincidence. The parents in the Dutch Theater had to give their consent to hide their children; without it, they would have asked for them on the day of transport. *Zakdoekje leggen* is the name of a children's game, "Drop your handkerchief," which we played endlessly in the crèche. With such games, the nurses tried to distract us. The crèche children were not allowed to go to school, and there was little else to do other than the daily walk in the neighborhood. There was something unreal about it all. While we were playing and singing, our parents were held prisoners on the other side of the road, awaiting their transport to Nazi Germany. As far as I knew, I was about to share the same fate. Nobody had yet told me that I had been singled out for the *onderduik*. This word was used by the Dutch people to denote the period of hiding, meaning literally, "to dive under the water."

By summer 1943, the persecution had reached its apex, and the crèche children were frightened and nervous. The games we played and the songs we sang kept us busy, but they could not make us forget our fears and the terrible reality outside.

One afternoon, one of the nurses told me my parents had left with the morning transport. I sat on the floor and cried for hours. It was the only shiva I ever sat for them. Not long afterwards, I was told that the next day, during our daily walk, I would be smuggled out and hidden. I was to wear two shirts, two pairs of underwear, and at a certain point, I was to ask for permission to "pee" behind the bushes. The other children would keep walking, but I had to wait for a young man who would pick me up. All went as planned. The young man took me to the entrance of a large church opposite the Central Railway Station, where I was met by a young woman. She had another Jewish girl of about my age with her. We got new names, I became Kees, and, as I recall, the girl became Flora. We were admonished to behave quietly during the train ride, and after many hours, we arrived safely in Limburg, in the south of Holland.

Many years later, I learned that I had been saved by the "NV group," a part of the Dutch resistance that specialized in the saving of Jewish children. Many of their members were young university students. Their task was to move each child over the next hour or day. I remember one move particularly well. Two members of the resistance came by and drove me to my new address. The events followed each other too quickly; disaster upon disaster, move upon move, with no respite in between. I remember a big farm where I played with a bow and arrow fashioned by my new brothers. My "aunt" there knitted me a woolen undershirt for the cold winter—warm, but terribly scratchy. Situated near Holland's broad rivers, this location enabled me to take long walks and to spend hours studying the water's flow. I was lucky. I was well-treated; I was allowed to play outside, go to church and school, and to lead an almost normal life. Except for the last family, which was a very special "address," and where I was able to stay for a long time, I do not remember the names of the others.

By the time I arrived at the last family, I was a "hardened" war veteran, unable, or unwilling, to attach myself again to more strangers, because I knew my stay would be brief. This time, however, I was able to remain for more than one year until the end of the war in May 1945. Thus, I began to feel quite at home with this new aunt and uncle, and my friendship with their son and daughter has lasted until today. After the liberation, my onderduik father told me that my sister was alive and well. When my onderduik aunt passed away in 1991, my name appeared on the announcement of her death together with the names of her own children. I flew from Israel to Holland for her funeral.

After the liberation, I was sent to a children's home, *Prozdor*, literally a "corridor" to Israel. Prozdor was managed like a large family, not like an orphanage. Both managers had been teachers before the war, and both had a natural pedagogical instinct. Their own children lived with us and were treated like us. About thirty children were educated at the Prozdor home. Most had lost their parents during the war; some had come back from concentration camps or from onderduik families. All were children that "had seen too much" during their short lives.

In 1952, I was finally able to leave Holland for Israel. I would have left much earlier, but for my sister Miriam, whose onderduik family refused to return her to Jewish hands after the war. The Jewish community went to court. It was felt that my presence was needed as a "living reminder" to the court: "The brother is waiting for his sister to take her with him to Palestine." The case, however, dragged on and on, and after several years, it became clear that this argument had no influence whatsoever upon the case. The court decided in favor of the foster parents, and I understood that my prolonged stay in Holland had been quite useless.

My sister's onderduik parents claimed that she would have been returned to her own parents, had they survived the war, but since this was not the case, it would be irresponsible to send a little child to aunts in Palestine, a country at war, or to place her in a children's home in Holland. It was obviously in her best interest to leave her with her foster parents where she had found a loving home. This point of view, supported by psychological opinion, was accepted by the court and could not be changed by further appeals.

My sister's story was part of a greater tragedy, being played out in Holland after the war, the story of the OPK children (*Oorlogs Pleegkinderen*), hidden children, who were placed under the jurisdiction of a Dutch commission, deciding their fate. In most cases, it was accepted that the "best interest of the child" was to be found with the foster parents. In 1946, Rabbi Herzog, the Chief Rabbi of Palestine, wrote to the Dutch government: "Every child is to us, after our massive losses, like a thousand!" His letter, like other Jewish protestations, and even his subsequent visit to Holland, had no influence whatsoever upon the Dutch government or upon Dutch public opinion. At the time, I had no doubt that our point of view, requiring that all Jewish children be returned to Jewish hands, was justified.

Later on, I understood that this solution could not be applied to all children alike. Miriam did indeed love her onderduik parents. To have taken her away would have been very painful to her. I realized that a tragic situation had been created. Eventually, my sister remained with her foster parents until maturity; she married a Dutch boy and is living with her two sons in the south of Holland.

In 1956, I left Holland for good. I was not alone in my new country. I had relatives in Israel who received me with open arms; they offered me a home where I was always welcome. Many years have elapsed since 1945. The past has receded, but its inheritance has not easily been shaken off. As with many survivors, I've felt guilty about surviving. I've felt powerless to prevent the loss of my parents. I've felt guilty about endangering my war parents by my presence alone. I tried to behave like a perfect child, but I always knew that there was no possible way to repay them for their kindness. Though they never suggested gratitude was required, and I know they acted out of conviction, I could never shake my feeling of being a guest—and a dangerous one at that—in their home. The people who cared for me during the war had no obligation to me. It may sound paradoxical, but being thankful is sometimes a heavy burden.

Mechel Jamenfeld *spent his career at the Israel Discount Bank in Tel Aviv where he met his wife, Narcissa. Together, they raised a daughter and became doting grandparents.*

Uncovering My Past

By Richard Ned Lebow

(Excerpted from My Story, *Volume XXIII, August 2022.)*

I was born sometime in 1941, probably in Paris. I believe I was hidden in the summer of 1942, first in a Paris suburb and then in a village in the south of France. With other Jewish children, we crossed the Pyrenees into Spain, made our way to Lisbon, and then sailed to New York City, where we arrived in the autumn of 1942. We were offloaded at night with the immigration officials looking the other way. I was sent to an orphanage and, not long afterward, was adopted by an American Jewish couple. Ruth (née Newman) and Joe Lebow were married in 1926, and childless. They were wonderful parents to me and another baby boy they adopted at the end of the war. My first memories, maybe from early 1944, are of family—including an uncle in uniform—neighbors, and other kids on our tightknit block of terraced houses in Queens.

My first vivid political memories are all war-related: blackouts—Dad was a block warden—armed allied merchant vessels in the harbor flying different flags, President Roosevelt's death in April 1945, and VE day a month later. I dreamt for a while in another language, which then disappeared.

My parents told me about my adoption at a very early age and I cannot remember a time when I did not know. It was an interesting piece of information, but not really central to my identity until my teenage years. My parents were loving and very engaged in my life. They never gave me any reason to doubt they cared very deeply for me.

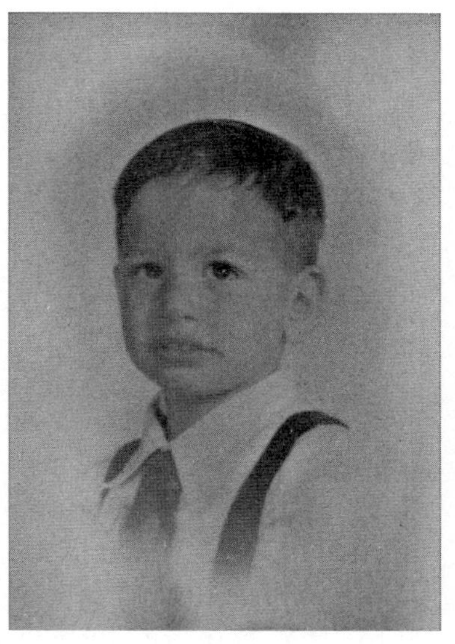

Richard Ned Lebow as a young boy.

In 1949, we moved to East Rockaway, Long Island. I felt isolated in suburbia. At about age thirteen, a few of my friends began to think they too were adopted, which they were not. Their queries provoked uncomfortable thoughts about my origins. I began to imagine a birth family of scientists or musicians—my heroes at the time were Bruno Walter and Toscanini—and several baseball players. I was learning French, and I fantasized being the scion of French Rothschilds, separated from my family by the war, but soon to be liberated from my tedious suburban life to assume my rightful patrimony.

What I know about my infancy I learned very late in my life. By sheer coincidence, my friend Janice encountered Paulette Fink, who had helped to save hundreds of Jewish children in France during the war. Janice learned that the first group of children Madame Fink helped were those who had escaped the July 1942 *rafle du Vel d'Hiv*, the first significant mass arrest and deportation to Auschwitz of foreign Jews in France. Madame Fink described receiving a baby from a French policeman who had smuggled the infant out of the bicycle stadium, the Vélodrome d'Hiver, commonly known as the Vel d'Hiv. His name was David, and she in turn handed him to a priest, who resided somewhere outside of Paris and who promised to find a parishioner to look after him in the short-term. In 1990, Janice arranged for me to meet Paulette in Palm Springs, where I learned many details of how these groups of kids got out of France. The Jewish resistance organized their departure south into Vichy France. One group traveled to Bordeaux, Biarritz, over the border to Spain, and then to Lisbon. The other group went to Marseille, crossed

Ruth and Joe Lebow, c. 1927.

the Mediterranean to Oran, went by train to Tangier, by ferry to Algeciras, and then up the Peninsula to Lisbon. A group of Jewish women in New York City arranged for a cargo ship to transport the lot of them to New York.

I subsequently established contact with a woman who had been a social worker at my New York adoption agency in 1942. She told me about children they brought into the country illegally during the war, many by train from Montreal, and others who arrived on a ship that docked in New York harbor. She remembered a ship from Lisbon in 1942 with about one-hundred French Jewish children. There was one baby who was looked after by a young girl in the group who was very unhappy at having to hand him over to her.

My parents were now in their eighties. They had left New York City for Seattle, where my younger brother was living. I told my parents what I had learned and asked if they could shed any light on it. Previously, they had denied any knowledge of my past but had encouraged me as a teenager to write to the adoption agency to see what information they could provide. I learned then that my birth mother was Jewish, from Budapest, and from a long line of greengrocers.

Now, my parents were surprisingly forthcoming. I suppose the combination of age and security in our long-standing and close relationship made them more confident and open. They had been trying to adopt for some time but there were no Jewish children available. Then they received a telephone call telling them to meet a man on a street corner in Manhattan. They were even given a password to exchange. They went to this rendezvous and were escorted to an orphanage in the Bronx where there was a gaggle of kids, all speaking languages other than English. My parents were told they could adopt any one of the children, and they chose the youngest. They named me Richard Ned—Ned was after my mother's late father, and his grandfather. Both were actually named Nedham, after the town outside of Boston where the Newmans first settled in 1806.

One piece of the puzzle fell into place. Then came another. As executor of our parents' estate, my younger brother, Rob, found our original birth certificates in their safety deposit box. Rob said that our names appeared to have been written over something beneath. He took the documents to be X-rayed and excitedly telephoned to report that underneath mine was the name David Beck, which did not mean anything to me at the time.

Fast forward to 2017, to the age of the internet and inexpensive DNA testing. My children suggested that I have my DNA tested to see if it would tell me anything about my past. I waited until I thought enough people had done this to generate a database large enough to make it worthwhile. I chose 23andMe, and they identified several second cousins on the maternal side, all living in the greater New York area. They were open to contact, so I immediately sent them a message. Within hours, all three responded. Despite having different surnames, they were first cousins and, they explained, members of the Beck family. So, presumably, I was too. They had consulted among themselves and emailed their cousin Tibor—and mine, they suggested—who lived in Budapest. He was a genealogist and had put together a family tree based on his DNA research. I awoke the next morning to find an email from Tibor—"Tibi," as he insisted I call him—asking me to download my raw DNA from 23andMe and send it on to him.

The next day, an email arrived from Tibi with the heading "Mazel Tov." I was indeed an offshoot of the Solomon-Beck family, and Tibi had identified my birth mother. An hour later, an email arrived from the mother of one of the New York women. She is the daughter of my mother's sister, who immigrated to New Brunswick, New Jersey, in the 1920s. She and her husband—surprise—owned a vegetable stall. But this being America, they later went into wholesale and their children became professionals.

My new cousin Tina was delighted to welcome me as a first cousin once removed and enclosed photos of my family. This was a dramatic moment. I was not about to open these images on my own. My wife Carol sat alongside me, as did our elder son Eli, visiting from Berkeley. Francis, my birth mother, born in 1905, looked perfectly ordinary in an undated photo. The next photo, of my mother's sister, her husband, daughter, and two sons, made us gasp. Both young men were in American military uniforms because the picture was taken during the war. The younger one could pass as my twin. I looked exactly like him at the same age. All three men had the large Beck nose, which I share. Alas, everyone in both photos is deceased.

Tibi arranged a family reunion in Budapest, and I got to meet some of my new family. On the journey, Carol kept asking me how I was feeling. "Fine," I said, framing the get-together as yet another of life's adventures, if an unusual one. We entered a large, modern hotel, where Tibi was waiting in the lobby to greet me. We hugged, and then Tibi embraced Carol. "Come meet your family," Tibi said. We walked a few paces to the café where ten relatives were waiting. They all stood up to greet me, and I burst into tears. I was surprised by my reaction but should not have been. Here were three generations of people to whom I was biologically connected. Some of them looked like me. And all of them could not have been warmer and more welcoming. We talked at length about our lives and connections, none of them closer than second cousins. The oldest of my cousins was my age and had survived the war hidden by a Christian family in the countryside. The youngest were two bright, good-looking teenagers, both absolutely fluent English speakers. We communicated with the others in a mix of English and German.

It was thrilling to make this connection, and all the more so as everyone I encountered was happy to welcome me as a new family member. I already knew how lucky I was. I had survived the war, was adopted by wonderful parents, grew up in the land of opportunity during the great postwar economic boom, had a successful marriage, and wonderful children and grandchildren. My Hungarian family was much less fortunate. They were a remnant who then had to suffer decades of communism and now were under the heavy hand of an authoritarian regime. They lived in a country where antisemitism was still rife. The contrast between their world and mine was sobering.

Reflecting on what had brought me to Budapest, I realized how multiple independent pieces of information had come together. At the outset, there was the letter from the adoption agency identifying my mother as Budapest-born and from a family of greengrocers. This tallied with what I learned from Tina and Tibi. My mother's father and grandfather owned a vegetable stall in Budapest's central market. Her grandfather had moved to Budapest from Beregovo, a town in Ruthenia with a mixed population of Jews, Poles, and Ukrainians (called Ruthenes). Ruthenia belongs in the *Guinness World Records* for being part of more countries in the twentieth century than any other province. It started out as the most northeastern province of Austria-Hungary. After 1918, it became the easternmost part of the newly created Czechoslovakia. In 1940, Hitler awarded it to his ally Hungary. In 1945, it was annexed by Stalin for the Soviet Union. Today, it is part of Ukraine. The Solomons worked the land of a Polish countess named Beck. She was without issue, but the DNA record indicates that she had a child in the course of a liaison with one of her tenants. This may be why she promised to deed her land to the Solomons if they adopted her surname. Some did, including my great-great-grandfather.

Next came my brother's discovery of the name on my birth certificate, "David Beck." David was also the name of the baby smuggled out of the Vélodrome, hidden and escorted through France, and then into the US via Lisbon by my adoption agency. In this connection, I registered with the Hidden Child Foundation in New York and received a letter from the girl—now a retired psychiatrist—who fondly remembered having looked after baby David on the Atlantic crossing. She was delighted to hear from me and to learn I had prospered. The feeling was, of course, mutual.

Then there was my encounter with Madame Fink and subsequent talk with a former social worker from my adoption agency. They connected the David my parents adopted to the David on the boat, and thus to the escape saga told by Madame Fink and the policeman who handed David to her. Most compelling of all was the DNA test and Tibi's identification of me as Francis's son. Finally, there were the photos, which spoke for themselves. Perhaps my early dreams were in Hungarian or French?

There's another twist to the story. My birth mother, Francis, survived the war. Nobody seems to know how. Her sister tracked her down in 1946 and brought her to New Brunswick, where she lived until her death in 1987. Tina, who knew her, told me that she was withdrawn and perhaps not quite all there after reaching America. Francis never told anybody in the family about having a child. Maybe she thought I had died and found repression the best way of coping with her loss? Perhaps it was all for the best that we lived an hour away for so many years and never knew of the other's existence? Having her walk into my life when I was young would have been traumatic for me and more so for my parents.

I know nothing of my ancestry on the paternal side; 23andMe has turned up no contacts. The few that might be related paternally are at best third cousins, and without knowing a family name, it is impossible to establish a connection.

The Beck-Solomon family fared better during the war than most European Jews. My grandfather was one of ten children, many of whom emigrated before the war, and some much earlier. There are Becks and Solomons in the US, Canada, South America, Australia, a few in the Czech Republic and Germany, and most of all, in Israel. One-third of the family who remained in Hungary during the war survived, and some immigrated to Israel in its aftermath. We are a family of peasants, shopkeepers, and more recently, of lawyers, diplomats, and businesspeople.

What does this all mean? This is a difficult question to answer. It is important to have roots, but I was never without them. I had a loving nuclear family and a very small but equally warm and welcoming extended one. I was not missing something that reconnecting with my birth family suddenly supplied. I was in my mid-seventies when most of this happened and am now in my eighties. It was wonderful to meet new family, but as my son Eli pointed out, family are people you have been close to all your life, or at least a good part of it. We have Italian "family" in

Venice with whom we have no biological connection. Carol and I and our children were close with them for five decades. My new *mishpocha* will not achieve this status, nice as they are. It is too late in my life, and they are too far away.

The new knowledge and connections are very important in other ways. I have always felt as much European as American, and it is rewarding to have knowledge about my roots on both sides of the Atlantic. As an adult, I came to realize that I had benefited greatly from the lack of knowledge of my origins. I had exploited it, not only for my teenage fantasies, but more fundamentally. It made it easier for me to detach myself from my familial and social milieus. I was an insider in both but also an outsider. From an early age, I craved knowledge. I learned to read at three and devoured the morning newspaper by the war's end. In primary school, I quickly discovered that if I misbehaved in class, I would be sent to the principal's office and from there to the library where I could sit and read uninterrupted. When we moved to the suburbs, I enjoyed the open space but not the social environment. I did not belong here and was revolted by McCarthyism and how it enabled authoritarianism in my school and community.

By then, I was also partly alienated from my parents. They encouraged my education but found it difficult to relate to what it produced. They could not talk to me about matters of interest to me. They were socially conservative, politically conformist, and very conventional in other respects. My mother was also anti-Zionist, fearing that it would threaten the status of Jews as Americans. My growing identification as a Jewish intellectual and steeping myself in European history and culture, but also in science and science fiction, involved considerable separation from those around me. Fortunately, I had a couple of friends who shared some of these interests. I was inventing myself and being of unknown origins proved to be an asset. It created an open space that made self-fashioning easier and allowed the kind of fantasies that were supportive of my project.

Richard Ned Lebow *is Professor of International Political Theory in the War Studies Department of King's College*

London; Bye-Fellow of Pembroke College, University of Cambridge; and James O. Freedman Presidential Professor Emeritus at Dartmouth College. His most recent books are The Quest for Knowledge in International Relations: How Do We Know? *(Cambridge 2021), and with Feng Zhang, he co-authored* Justice and International Order: East and West *(Oxford, 2022). He also published* Rough Waters and Other Stories *(Ethics International) and* Obsession *(Pegasus), a classic English murder mystery with a twist. Ned is married to Carol Bohmer, a New Zealand lawyer and sociologist, whose parents fled Czechoslovakia in 1939.*

PART VIII

The Rescuers: Individuals & Organizations

The Righteous Among the Nations: The Courage to Care

By Mordecai Paldiel, PhD

The following is excerpted from Dr. Paldiel's keynote address at the UN Holocaust Memorial Ceremony, General Assembly Hall, in New York, on January 25, 2013.

It was a clear moonlit night as I, a six-year-old boy, trudged along an isolated, tree-covered field together with my parents, my grandmother, and five siblings, one of whom I carried in my arms. We made our way slowly toward the double-barbed wire fence that separated France from Switzerland. It was the evening of September 8, 1943, the day Italy surrendered to the Allies, and Nazi Germany was about to guard that section of the border that had, until then, been watched over by the Italians. With the help of two Frenchmen, we made it across safely only to be arrested by a Swiss border patrol. We were interned but were not turned back into France, now fully controlled by Nazi Germany.

Our wanderings had begun three years earlier, in May 1940, as we had fled from Belgium to France in advance of the Nazi invasion. We had roamed from one place to another until France came under full Nazi rule, and we found ourselves with nowhere to run. At that point, someone referred my mother to a man who lived in the town of Évian-les-Bains. The man, a French cleric named Abbé Simon Gallay, had met my mother only a few days earlier and promised to arrange our escape to Switzerland. Abbé Simon Gallay kept his word.

Many years later, when I headed the Righteous Among the Nations Department at Yad Vashem, I promised myself to look

Dr. Mordecai Paldiel

him up, hoping he was still alive. I wanted to thank him on behalf of my family and the institution I represented. From other documents made available to me, I had learned of his help to other fleeing Jews. I was lucky to find him in a Catholic retirement home in Annecy, and to travel there in 1990 to award him Yad Vashem's prestigious Righteous Among the Nations Medal and certificate of honor. This tribute, on behalf of the State of Israel, recognized that, to save us and others from the Nazis, he had risked his life. That same year, I planted a tree in his name in the Avenue of the Righteous at Yad Vashem. I had fulfilled a long self-imposed commitment and obligation to give thanks and show appreciation to my, and my family's, rescuer, Abbé Simon Gallay, the man who allowed us to live by keeping us out of the reach of those who wished us dead for the simple reason that we were born.

In my twenty-four-years' work as head of the Righteous Department at Yad Vashem, I was instrumental in identifying and honoring thousands of other non-Jewish rescuers of Jews. These were men and women from various countries and walks of life, who, in saving Jews from the Nazis, stood the risk of losing their own lives. The Nazis threatened retribution, warning that, if caught, rescuers of Jews would meet the same fate as the Jews they tried to save.

The beginnings of the Righteous program are linked to another dramatic event, the 1962 trial of SS senior officer Adolf Eichmann. As the trial ended, testimonies had revealed not just the grimmest details of the Final Solution but also the deeds of persons who had aided Jews to escape the Nazi dragnet. As a result, Yad Vashem decided to launch a program under which non-Jewish persons who risked their lives to save Jews would be publicly acknowledged and honored by the State of Israel.

It was also decided that each rescuer honored with the title of Righteous Among the Nations was entitled to a tree in his or her name in a specially constructed grove, named Avenue of the Righteous, at Yad Vashem. This avenue lines the approaches to the Holocaust Museum, which details the horrific events of the Final Solution.

The trees are there to remind visitors that the final word is to be left not to the perpetrators but to the rescuers. After some two thousand trees were planted, it was decided to construct a special site at Yad Vashem, the Garden of the Righteous, where each year the names of the honorees are etched in stone in perpetuity. Rescuers also receive a medal with their names on it and a certificate of honor.

The Commission's work is ongoing, with many names added annually to this unique roster of knights of the spirit. They represent a varied collection of men and women from different walks of life and education: blue- and white-collar workers; farmers and city dwellers; clerics and lay people; as well as diplomats, such as Raoul Wallenberg of Sweden and Aristides de Sousa Mendes of Portugal. The former handed out protective letters, and the latter, transit visas, making the rescue of thousands of Jews possible.

We have an obligation to pass on to future generations two legacies: first, on the horrors of the Holocaust and their perpetrators, and the second, on the goodness of the Righteous Among the Nations. We must impart the lesson that one individual can rouse within the spark of goodness that is an innate part of humanity, and that such goodness may start with but one small act.

Sometimes, those lucky enough to be rescued by total strangers were able to regain and reaffirm their own commitment to a universe guided by moral principles. Primo Levi wrote that through Lorenzo Perrone, an Italian civilian construction worker who helped him, he "managed not to forget that I myself was a man"—this, despite Auschwitz. Consider, the answer given by the Dutch rescuer Johtje Vos to her mother, who, one day, upon visiting her daughter, was stunned to find there a Jewish child. The mother said, "You shouldn't do it, even though I agree with what you're doing, because your first responsibility is to your children." To this, Johtje Vos responded, "That's exactly why I'm doing it!" She added in her testimony, "I thought we were doing the right thing, giving our children the right model to follow."

And thus, they all acted according to the dictum of that ancient Jewish sage, Hillel, who stated, "If I am only for myself, then what is my merit?" A later Talmudic passage underlines this point in even stronger ethical terms: "Whosoever saves one life is as though he has saved an entire world."

Dr. **Mordecai Paldiel** *was born in Antwerp, Belgium, in 1937. Upon the onset of WWII, he and his family fled to Switzerland. He was the director of the Righteous Among the Nations Department at Yad Vashem from 1982 until 2007. During that twenty-four-year period, some eighteen thousand non-Jewish persons were awarded the "Righteous Among the Nations" honor for saving Jews from the Nazis. Dr. Paldiel has authored fourteen books, numerous articles, and he lectures before various organizations and institutions on the rescue of Jews during the Holocaust.*

My Hidden Childhood in Vert Galant

**Today, Vert Galant is part of Villepinte, France.*

By René Lichtman

(Excerpted from My Story, *Volume XXVI, November 2022.)*

There were only the three of us plus our animals. Papa Paul was the head of our household, and he rarely spoke to me except to improve my manners or ways of doing things, especially at the dinner table. I was spoiled by Maman Nana, and Papa Paul was my disciplinarian. Maman Nana would say to me gently, "You do what Papa Paul says, and we'll discuss it later." They always maintained a "united front" toward me, yet I was never unhappy.

The garden and the animals kept us busy. I especially loved our cats and dogs, and the animals loved Maman Nana and always followed us around. Each day, life went on, devoid of playmates or any other adults. I do not think I noticed this lack of play since there was nothing to compare it to or with. I did not notice this abnormal solitude until after the war years. Later in my life, as a painter, artist, knowing how to be alone was a good thing.

I remember Maman Nana always wearing an old, large apron, which she used for gathering vegetables from our garden, or as a kitchen towel, or for drying her hands after washing something.

Sometimes, if my elbows were on the table, Papa Paul would take his fork and hit my elbow as a reminder that elbows on the table are rude (I never understood why). The food was always delicious, all from our garden, with many salads, but also our

René Lichtman's rescuers, Maman Nana and Papa Paul Lepage, wartime photo, Vert Galant, France.

rabbits and chickens. I also remember the Christmas periods when the upstairs formal areas were decorated with a small Christmas tree and a crèche with animals, and small statues that appeared so pretty to me. I would play gently with them. These were the only toys I can recall.

We had no visitors. If there were any, I was never present. I may have been sent upstairs with strict orders not to come down. Since I knew nothing about myself, there was nothing to give away, even by accident.

Maman Nana did tell me many stories late in her life. One that stayed with me showed the importance of us having our own source of food, being as self-reliant as possible, never arousing suspicion from neighbors who often exchanged gossip in stores. Once, she was shopping in a small local store when the store owner's wife asked Maman Nana about the child she kept in her home. Anne Lepage was told by the storekeeper's wife that if she kept Jewish children, she had to "register" them with the local authorities and get ID cards with the word "*Juif*" stamped on it. Maman Nana answered she had no such Jewish children. The lady's husband then told his wife not to ask any further questions.

Still, there were many collaborators around us, and my French family knew this. Fortunately, we lived in a very isolated corner of the village. Some people may have had suspicions, but most minded their own business. Papa Paul held a job in Paris, and he went to work each day. He frequented the local café, but we were a very private family, and there was no reason to explain anything to anyone.

Thanks to the present Villepinte archivist and research team, I know now there were many resisters and rescuers or "Righteous" people in Villepinte, and many children were saved. Yet, because of the local collaborators—including town politicians—there were indiscriminate roundups and arrests, that, over the course of three months, resulted in eighty Jews being arrested and deported to Auschwitz, where most were gassed upon arrival. Many families who resided in Villepinte part-time, but lived and worked in Paris, were caught and gassed at Auschwitz.

René Lichtman *(1937–2025) graduated from the Cooper Union Art School and was the recipient of a Fulbright Scholarship in painting. He held degrees in fine arts, mass communication, and a PhD in instructional technology from Wayne State University in Detroit, Michigan. As an artist, he held solo exhibits in Michigan. René was a founder of the local Hidden Children of Michigan and of the World Federation of Jewish Child Survivors. He spoke regularly at the Holocaust Memorial Museum in Farmington Hills, Michigan.*

A Beacon of Light

By Eva Kuper

(Excerpted from My Story, *June 2023, Volume XXXIII.)*

My parents, Fela and Abram Kupferblum, married in 1936 and moved to Warsaw, where my father eventually started a small business preparing dyes for furs. After my birth in 1940, they moved to a lovely apartment in Bielany, a suburb of Warsaw, where we settled comfortably into our new community. From time to time, my father would stop at a small neighborhood grocery store to pick up whatever was needed at home. He made friends with the owners, the Rondio family, who were ethnic Germans. Mr. Rondio was employed as a police officer and his wife ran the store. One day, when my father stopped by, he found some men removing the stock from the shelves. When he asked Mrs. Rondio what was happening, she tearfully explained that she had not been able to pay some debts and her wares were being taken as payment. My father quickly offered to give her the needed funds.

Baby Eva with her parents, c. early 1940.

Eva with Aunt Sophie (Father's sister), c. late 1940.

This generosity sealed what would become an important friendship.

When the Nazis forced us to move to the ghetto, my parents left their new furniture with the Rondios, believing the situation was temporary. We were fortunate to secure a whole room for our small family, which now comprised five people—the three of us and my mother's cousin with one of her daughters. The cousin's other daughter, Regina, was my mother's closest friend, and she worked as a guard in the ghetto prison. There was a phone in the cellar of our building that could be used to make calls but not to receive them. My father arranged with Regina that, should an emergency arise, he would alert her by phone at the prison. My father now worked as a chemist in one of the Nazi factories in the large ghetto, but we still had very little.

By the summer of 1942, the Nazis ordered the Jewish "authorities" to round up people for transport or "resettlement." One morning, all the men in our section of the ghetto were ordered to report to the yard of the Többens factory. My father had to go. The men were locked up for several hours. It was only upon his release and return to our room that my father found our entire area had been cleared of women and children.

Everyone was gone! My father phoned Regina to alert her, then he ran to *Umschlagplatz*, the loading platform where people were being herded by the hundreds onto cattle cars. If my mother and I were to be "resettled," he wanted to join us. But when he tried to find us, he was stopped by a Nazi guard who threatened him with a gun.

Meanwhile, Regina had raced to the loading yard where she arrived in time to see my mother and me herded into one of the cattle cars. The timing was crucial. Had she arrived a moment earlier or later, she would not have seen us. Regina screamed that I was her child, and maybe because she wore a uniform, or maybe because they still needed her at the prison, my mother was permitted to pass me (now two years old) hand-to-hand until I was thrown off the train into Regina's arms. A true miracle! My father found Regina in her room crying while holding me in her lap. Ultimately, Regina and others like her met the same fate as my mother when they, too, were deemed unworthy of life.

Cousin Regina Bankier and Mother. Both were murdered by the Nazis.

My mother's heroic decision to save me haunts me to this day. The natural inclination of mothers is to hold their children close when sensing danger. What did that decision cost her? How insightful of her to predict the horror that awaited those on the train, many of whom still believed the Nazi "resettlement" story. How broken her heart must have been as she handed me off, believing that even that small chance was better than what awaited her.

From then on, my father planned our escape from the ghetto. However, I became seriously ill with dysentery. I was dehydrated and lapsed into semiconsciousness. My father's friend Dr. Kalinowsky came to help. He said that, without a curative solution, I would die shortly. In desperation, my father turned to the manager of the Többens factory, begging him to get the solution. The manager, who was not Jewish, agreed, and when I was treated, I revived. Saved again! Now it was definitely time to escape.

Each time there was a roundup, people scurried about, searching for a place to hide. During one such incident, my father, with me in his arms, stood in the water-filled cellar of a factory building, along with a dozen others, while Jews were captured above. The people hiding with us warned my father that, should we all survive the night, he would not find shelter among them again. It was too dangerous to hide with a small child whose cries could jeopardize the lives of everyone. My father knew the dangers and always carried two cyanide pills in his pocket. He was determined to kill both of us rather than being taken alive by the Nazis.

Believing the sewers were our only chance, he arranged with his sister, Sophie, who lived under false IDs on the Aryan side, to have someone pick us up. When we surfaced, my aunt's friend took us to the home of the Rondios, who welcomed us warmly. Although he considered himself a Pole, Mr. Rondio had been badly treated by the Poles, who distrusted and hated anyone German. Thus, the Rondios had moved into a German section of the city. They felt they would not be suspected of hiding Jews, so they were not worried about having us there. They fed and helped us to catch our breath from our ordeals. They were distressed to hear about life in the ghetto and to learn the fate of my mother.

Despite the Rondios' willingness to offer us shelter, my father did not want to jeopardize their lives. He turned to Dr. Lande, the pediatrician who treated the children of the fur trade union members, begging him to find a safe place for me. Dr. Lande promised to be in touch in a few days, and true to his word, he placed me with Hanka Rembowska, an artist and illustrator of children's books. Hanka was already caring for a little girl, Zosia, who, although not Jewish, had been orphaned by the war. Hanka, who was suffering from tuberculosis, took care of us until she became too sick. One day, Hanka came upon a small group of nuns waiting at a train station. She recognized one of them and begged her to take her little girls. I spent the next three years in a convent in Zakopane, about three hundred miles away, in the Tatra Mountains.

My own somewhat vague memories begin in the convent, which was located on a hill overlooking the town. There were many nuns, one priest, and many blind children, all boys, except for Zosia and me. There was little food. Potatoes were our main staple. All the children sat in a large circle outside peeling potatoes. Since the boys could not see, they would peel as best they could then pass them to Zosia and me to remove the missed spots before putting them into the big pot of water in the middle of the circle.

There was a cow that I brought back from the pasture for milking at the end of each day. I would hold the thick cord around her neck and pat her soft fur. That milk and the bit of butter that came from it were the only wholesome parts of our diet. I also remember sitting around a long rectangular table at mealtimes with all the other children, the nuns, and the priest. The priest sat at the head of the table with me on his left. He was the only one to get a small pad of butter for his bread, which he cut in half and passed to me under the table. He did not have enough to go around. I was the lucky one.

When the Nazis came to plunder the village, someone would run up the hill to warn the nuns. Anything of value, such as food and supplies, would be hidden—and so was I. I remember vaguely being placed in a hole in the pasture that had been excavated for that purpose. I would go in, and a board covered with sod would be placed above. I sat quietly, and strangely enough, I don't remember being frightened. I was used to being quiet. Somehow, I felt safe, which seems unbelievable to me now. I lived in this convent for three years until the liberation.

After the war, my aunt Sophie found my name listed at one of the agencies that were compiling names of survivors. Unsure that it was really me, Sophie did not tell my father but came alone to get me. I do not remember my feelings at being spirited away by my aunt, whom I did not remember at all. I do recall not being eager to leave my familiar and safe life. Yet, I did not put up a fuss…hardly surprising, since I had long ago learned to be a quiet and accepting child. Oddly enough, I don't even remember reuniting with my father, which must have been very emotional.

After the war, we lived as non-Jews in a city called Bielsko, now known as Bielsko-Biala, as antisemitism was still so strong,

Eva with Father and Aunt Sophie, Bielsko, 1946.

it was not safe to live as Jews. My father was the director of a government fur dyeing plant. He had an important position, and, by the standards of the day, we were quite well off, having a housekeeper, a chauffeur, and other servants. Aunt Sophie, who had lost her husband during the war, lived with us in a lovely apartment. I remember that she was beautiful and lived life to the fullest, as did others who had survived the horrors of the war. There were frequent parties, card games, outings, holidays, and strong friendships.

I went to school where I learned catechism. I had my first communion at the age of six, went to weekly confession, and felt purified by the experience. My father never went to church, so I went with our housekeeper, whom I loved.

In 1948, my father met a woman named Barbara and remarried. He felt that life as Jews in Poland would continue to be difficult, and I am sure he was tired of the deception.

It was only on the ship crossing the Atlantic that my father told me I was Jewish. It would have been dangerous to share this secret with me before. I was taught in school that the Jews had crucified Jesus and they were evil. I was horrified to learn that I was one of "them." It took many years before I became comfortable with the idea, and many more before I felt pride in my heritage and in my people.

After the initial period of adjustment, I began to feel Canadian, just like all my friends. Since I was young and had an aptitude for languages, I learned to speak English without a Polish accent, and my life in Poland quickly faded from my memory.

My parents spoke little about the Holocaust and their experiences during the war. They wished for me to grow up without the horror of those memories. I was not terribly interested in the few stories they did tell. I knew that they suffered from sleeplessness and flashbacks whenever they spoke of their experiences.

Nevertheless, the Holocaust, the loss of my mother, and the deprivations of those years have had a profound effect on me and my family, even my children and grandchildren. My youngest daughter, Felisa, is named for my mother, and since childhood, she has had an abiding interest in that part of our past. When she reached young adulthood, Felisa was always keen to hear the stories even though they were very difficult to hear and to tell. She was eager for me to go to Poland with her to retrace our family's history. I had no interest in going back and researching the terror of those years.

Eva's First Communion certificate.

Eva and friend Hania at their First Communion.

Yet in 1998, I was approached by the Shoah Foundation to videotape my wartime experiences as part of the Living Testimony Project initiated by Steven Spielberg, a request that started my own return to these past events. To prepare for the taping, I listened to audiotapes that I had begged my father to make for me about six months before he died. With great pain, he speaks of the horrors of those times and tells the story of how I was saved. These tapes were the raw material from which this chronology emerged.

With the videotape, my interest in this part of my life was reborn, and I became involved in Holocaust education at the school of which I was the principal—the Jewish people's and Peretz School in Montreal—and subsequently at the Hebrew Foundation School. In 2003, at a family gathering, the idea of a trip back to Poland with my husband, my cousins, and my daughter Felisa arose. Felisa was very keen to make this trip with me, and eventually the plan evolved into spending two weeks tracing our roots with my husband and cousins, after which Felisa would join me for twelve days to continue our search for my and my family's past.

On August 23, 2005, I attended a meeting of the Auberge Shalom pour Femmes, where I am active on the board and the executive. I took a seat near a former colleague and commented that I hoped the meeting would not take long, since I was leaving the next day for a month-long trip to Prague, Budapest, and Poland. Surprised, she told me that she too would be visiting Poland in October. She gave me the name and phone number of an American, Yale Reisner, who was the director of the Jewish Historical Institute in Warsaw. I took it but did not think I would need his help since I had researched convents in Zakopane and had arranged an appointment with a nun in the one where I thought I had been hidden.

However, on arrival in Warsaw, I did call Yale and told him a little about my history. He was eager to meet with me, so we went to the Institute. When we met, I elaborated on my story, mentioning that there were blind children in the convent. He bolted out of his seat and took a book off his shelves. It was the Polish version of Ewa Kurek's published doctoral thesis, *Your Life is Worth Mine: How Polish Nuns Saved Hundreds of Jewish Children in German-Occupied Poland, 1939–1945*. Flipping through the pages, he came upon this paragraph:

> Congregation of Franciscan Sisters Servants of the Cross; Polish order established in 1918 for the purpose of caring for the blind. In 1939, a hundred and six sisters worked in eighteen homes. In Zakopane, Sister Klara Jaroszynska saved the life of a little Jewish girl.

We were all speechless. This had to be the right convent, and the little Jewish girl had to be me! The next day, I tried to contact the convent in Warsaw with no success. Eventually, I spoke with Sister Jana Pawla, who was in Laski, fifteen miles outside of Warsaw, where the order continues to look after three hundred blind children to this day. I briefly told her the reason for my call and tentatively asked if it could be possible that someone who had been in Zakopane during the war was still alive. She was very warm and interested and told me the most astounding news: Sister Klara, then ninety-four years old, was alive and in Laski. Twice in two days, I was speechless! I recovered enough to ask about Sister Klara's health. Sister Jana Pawla assured me that, despite Sister Klara's present blindness, her mind was clear, her memory intact and accurate, and her sense of humor as good as ever. I was more than delighted, and we arranged a visit to Laski the very same day—September 8, 2005.

Felisa and I met Sister Jana Pawla in front of the convent's beautiful chapel where we entered the chapel for her to say a brief prayer, and then she led us to the house where Sister Klara was cared for by other nuns. Sister Klara, supported by Sister Rut, her close friend and archivist for the Order, came out of the house and opened her arms to embrace me. I went to her, and we held each other close. Everyone was crying. I led her gently to a bench where we sat together, holding each other. She began to talk, recalling those terrible years.

She remembered me well and with great love, saying I had come to the convent after her meeting with Hanka Rembowska, who had pleaded with her to take her little girls because she had become too ill to look after us. Sister Klara told me that I had been holding Hanka's hand, but I soon dropped it and ran to Sister Klara, putting my arms around her, asking her to pick me up. When she did and I cuddled into her shoulder, she simply could not refuse. Sister Klara corroborated my own sketchy memories of that time and added detail and information previously unknown to me. Hearing her stories was a very emotional experience for me. Those three years in the convent had been a void in my life. I knew no one who could tell me what had happened and what I had been like as a three-year-old child under those difficult conditions.

Eva Kuper with her rescuer, Sister Klara, Warsaw, 2005.

Sister Klara described me as being the size of a two-year-old, bright, intelligent, and very cooperative. She told me that I was gentle with the other children, most of whom were blind except for Zosia and Sister Klara's three nieces. She told me I was the smallest child they had in their care and everyone's favorite.

Sister Klara validated many of my memories and corrected others. She told me that when news reached her that the Nazis were nearby, if time allowed, I had indeed been hidden in a hole, but one that had been excavated beneath the earthen floor of the cellar. A board and a mat covered the hole, and a small table was placed on top. If time did not allow, she would put me into bed together with her little niece who, along with her mother and two other siblings, had taken refuge in the convent to escape the bombardment of Warsaw. Sister Klara's sister had three children, two of whom had blond hair, but one had darker hair, more like mine. The two of us would hide under her covers and pretend to be sleeping until the danger passed.

I asked Sister Klara how she found the courage to risk the lives of the other children, the nuns, and her own sister and her children for the sake of saving one child. She said, "I had to do it. It was right, and besides, God sent you to me, so there really was no choice."

Now I feel I was given life four times: the first when I was born; the second when my mother passed me to be thrown from the cattle car going to Treblinka; the third when I survived the near-death illness of dysentery; and the fourth when Sister Klara agreed to hide me.

I am convinced that the love and kindness I received then helped me to be the person I am today. After the loss of my mother and the separation from my father, the nuns taught me the meaning of love. It is a gift I treasure and benefit from every day of my life.

On October 10, 2007, Sister Klara, along with fifty-three other Poles who had been instrumental in saving Jewish lives, was honored by the Polish government in a special ceremony at the Grand Theater in Warsaw.

Eva Kuper *immigrated to Canada with her family in 1949 and lives in Montreal. She's spent a career as a teacher and an administrator, managing educational centers and schools. After her retirement in 2005, she served on the boards of several organizations, including the Board of Directors of the Montreal Holocaust Museum where she often speaks to large groups of students and adults.*

One Family's Wartime Chronicle

By Jacques Silberman

(Excerpted from My Story, *Volume XXIV, September 2022.)*

While still in his teens, my father saw no future for a Jew in his native Poland, so he boldly left for Belgium. It would take four attempts before he would legalize his stay with the Belgian authorities. Once settled in Brussels, he arranged for his three younger siblings—Pinkas, Samuel, and Rachel—to join him. And he returned to Poland to bring back a wife, Sabina (née Strahl). My father's three siblings married, had children, and except for Uncle Pinkas, who opted for Paris, all became part of the thriving prewar Jewish community in Brussels. Only my father's youngest sister, Secha, remained with her parents in their hometown of Tarnow. My mother was the sole member of her immediate family to leave Poland. Her three siblings found no reason to emigrate.

The only photo we have of the Strahls, taken shortly after WWI, recovered after WWII from a relative in America.

I was born in Brussels in 1932, and my sister Rachelle was born in 1939. We

Pinkas, Alter, and Samuel. Tarnow, 1928.

lived in an industrial area of the city. My aunt Rachel and her family lived down the street, Uncle Samuel and his family were a short walk away, and my father's cousin, Berl, and his family lived around the corner. My father manufactured whatever he could—sometimes clothing but mostly hats—from a workshop a few steps from our home.

My family watched Hitler's rise to power with great anxiety. As the invasion of Belgium became imminent when I was seven and my sister was nine months old, we left our apartment, carrying suitcases crammed with all the possessions we could handle, and we joined the thousands of refugees fleeing to France to seek any port that would allow us to cross the seas. Along the roadways, we made use of an abandoned cart, found shelter in barns, bore the loss of most of our belongings, and endured the strafing. But it was all for naught. By the time we arrived at Dunkirk, we had

Aunt Rachel, undated.

My parents' wedding photo, Tarnow, Poland.

no choice but to return home.

After the invasion, the Nazi military governed Belgium. Although life was restricted, we managed somehow. I attended a nearby *école communale*, which turned out to be the only formal education I received for most of the war. By spring 1942, the situation became dire. Denunciations of Jews and raids occurred on an almost daily basis. Somehow, my parents were placed into contact with the CDJ (*Le Comité de défense des Juifs*), an organization that was linked to the Belgian Resistance and affiliated with the left-wing faction, *Front de l'Indépendance*, founded by Hertz Jospa and his wife Yvonne Jospa. The CDJ had some thirty members in a special section tasked with hiding children. They saved about two thousand of the approximately five thousand Jewish children who went into hiding in Belgium.

In the early summer of 1942, at the age of nine, I became one of those hidden children, and so did my three-year-old sister, and my cousins (Uncle Samuel's children), Charles, almost six, and Liliane, four. It wasn't until 1991, at the First International Gathering of Hidden Children in New York City, that we discovered the CDJ's vital role in our survival. The celebrated leaders of the CDJ's children section, Yvonne Jospa and Andrée Geulen-Herscovici, brought to the conference the precious *carnets* or booklets that held information about every hidden child. To safeguard their data during the war, the CDJ had given each child a number, and all information—real names, false names, hiding addresses of children and parents, etc.—was linked to that number and kept in separate booklets. In case of seizure, no single booklet held all the information. I was number 1206, my sister was number 1207, Charles was number 1209, and Liliane was number 1210.

All four of us were placed at the Protestant orphanage in Uccle under the direction of Marcel and Irène Noël. The Noëls were recognized by Yad Vashem as Righteous Among the Nations in February 1982. According to Yad Vashem's website, there were about eighty orphans at this institution, of which some eighteen were hidden Jewish children.

My cousins were a few years younger than I was, and my sister was barely three years old. I kept watch over the three of them as best I could, and at my sister's insistence, I combed her hair each day.

A highlight of my education at Uccle is that I taught myself to ride a bicycle. I also have a vivid memory of playing Joseph in the Christmas pageant. At the beginning, I felt homesick, and I contemplated fleeing. The orphanage had a large yard that abutted the street. My plan was to walk through the yard onto the street and find my way home to my parents. I would carry some bread stuffed into a matchbox in case I got hungry. The plan remained wishful thinking, of course.

The four of us stayed in Uccle for about nine months until March 1943, when we were suddenly sent back to our homes because a runaway girl had left a note threatening to denounce all the Jewish children if anyone came after her. This was a most perilous time. Our parents knew they could not keep us, and they had to make another agonizing decision.

At this crucial juncture, our downstairs neighbors, Henriette and Théophile Willems, whose last name my sister and I adopted during the war, introduced our parents to Father Bruno Reynders. It was Henriette Willems's young cousin, Irma, whose boyfriend was in the *Résistance*, who made the connection. Père Bruno met my parents in the Willems's apartment, and he assured them that he would take responsibility for our safety, as well as that of our cousins. The next day, he took my sister and cousins to Bruges, where my sister was placed in the Convent of the Franciscan Sisters, and my cousins went to the nearby Convent of the Sisters of Charity.

Père Bruno had created his own elaborate system of resistors, including his nephew, Michel Reynders, and other teenagers. All networked together with the CDJ as a formidable group of people who defied the Nazis and who, at great peril to themselves, delivered children to various hiding places. Members of the Père Bruno network took me to several destinations.

From April to June 1943, I stayed with a family on their small farm. They were decent people who treated me kindly, but I received no schooling. On occasion, I was charged with herding their goats. Then I was taken to the Home de Leffe in Dinant, from June 1943 until March 1944, where I learned to play chess from another Jewish boy about my age.

It did not take long before denunciations of Jewish children in nearby places precipitated another move to the Couvent de la Miséricorde in Louvain. It was the only place where I felt uncomfortable because of its very religious atmosphere. I was relieved to go to my next and final destination, from April through September 1944, at Fexhe-le-Haut-Clocher in Noville, under a new name, Gilles Van Raemsdonck. I lived with the village priest and, at last, went to public school. I took my meals at a nearby farm with many other children. The priest was very understanding. When I went to confession, we discussed aspects of the Old and New Testaments. My parents had made it clear to Père Bruno that we were not to be converted, and their request was respected at every place I stayed. While I was always treated well, I knew that I could be denounced at any time.

Left, Jacques Silberman, with two other Jewish boys, Dinant 1944.

Meanwhile, my parents felt extremely insecure in their own apartment because they faced a double vulnerability. Not only were the Nazis looking for Jews but also for young Belgian males to fill their work camps in

Sister Rachelle at the Convent of the Franciscan Sisters.

Nazi Germany. One such young man on their list was being harbored by our next-door neighbor, Mademoiselle Yvonne. While the young man was there, my parents hid with Aunt Rachel, but this became untenable and risky for everyone. So, they returned to their home, emptied it of all its contents, and placed everything in storage to give the appearance of an empty apartment. They kept just a mattress to sleep on and a deck of cards to while away the time. To maintain the ruse of inoccupancy, they kept the mattress angled against the wall during the day, and they used a real unoccupied kitchen down the street to prepare and eat meals for themselves and for Aunt Rachel and her husband as they pooled their meager resources.

Everyone on our street knew that my parents were there, yet no one betrayed them. In fact, our neighbors helped as much as they could. Whenever rue Ransfort was cordoned off during a raid (*rafle*), cautionary signals came from the people across the street, and Monsieur Willems would lead my parents to his large atelier behind the inner courtyard, where a second-floor rear window, accessible by a ladder only, led to an outside ledge just large enough to hold the two of them. Monsieur Willems would then remove and hide the ladder until the danger had passed. This perch, exposed to all the challenges of the Belgian weather, kept my parents alive throughout the war. However, the terror of those experiences would never be erased from their memories!

My sister and I returned to our home in the fall of 1944, after Brussels was liberated but before Belgium was totally free.

Liliane, Rachelle, Jacques, and Charles. The girls are wearing rabbit fur coats, hats, and hand muffs made by my father. Winter 1945–46.

(The Battle of the Bulge was yet to come.) Our cousins were eventually reunited with their parents in the US in 1946. During the war, Uncle Samuel and Aunt Bronka had made their way to Italy and were among the first one thousand Jewish evacuees to be liberated and brought to the US in the summer of 1944. The story of these evacuees was told by Ruth Gruber in the book *Haven*. They came to the US at the invitation of President Franklin D. Roosevelt and were housed at Fort Ontario, Oswego, in what would be the only refugee center in the United States during World War II.

Remarkably, all my father's siblings who had left Poland survived. Secha, who had remained, was murdered by the Nazis along with my paternal grandparents. Uncle Pinkas and his family survived in France.

Rachelle and Liliane in front, my parents in the rear with Cousin Berl on extreme right, and a visiting cousin from America in between. Brussels, c. 1945–46.

For as long as they lived, our parents bore the pain of losing their families during the Holocaust. My mother's parents, older brother Zygmunt, and her young sister Ida, were killed. Only her younger brother Maurice survived the death marches and the camps, the last of which was Mauthausen. I remember well the whispered postwar conversations about our family's tragedies.

Still, we had to reconstruct as normal a life as we could. We

Jacques Silberman at about age sixteen or seventeen, wearing a suit sent from America by Uncle Samuel.

came to the US in September of 1950, shortly after the Korean War began, and a few weeks before I had to register for the draft. I tried to adjust to my new life, learning English and working in the garment district with my father, who continued to manufacture hats. By the time I was drafted, in 1953, the Korean War was coming to an end, and I escaped going to another war zone! Since I spoke French, I spent two years in France in the Quartermaster Corps. After the army, I went back to school and became a field engineer, working for IBM in various roles for my entire career.

Although I experienced great danger in my childhood, I have had a fortunate life. Marsha and I have two daughters and five grandchildren. I have never felt that my story carried the same weight as that of those who survived under great duress, or those who died either in camps or as the Nazi army swept through their countries. Still, I have come to understand that each survivor's story is important and must be told.

A Childhood on the Run

By Albert Hepner

(Excerpted from The Hidden Child, *Volume XXIII, 2015.)*

Prewar photo of Albert Hepner.

Sometime in the summer of 1942, Motl rushed over to tell my mother he had found a hiding place for me. She screamed with horror, no doubt because the last family member was about to be taken from her. My father had died only a few months earlier, and we didn't know if my brother Max had made it to Switzerland. We had to leave right away "before curfew and the Nazi patrols," Motl said. He grabbed a handful of clothes and, tugging gently at my arm, insisted my mother let go.

We all loved and respected my first cousin, Motl. He'd come to Belgium from Pinsk, Belarus, to complete his medical degree, and during his student days, he had often depended on the hospitality of his aunt, my mother. He'd graduated from medical school in 1938, and by wartime, he'd gotten his own place. Still, he often had dinner with us, and in many ways, he had become a substitute father to Max and me.

By then, Motl was working with the underground, and he knew that the *abbé* at the church on rue de Meersman was hiding Jewish children. As a medical doctor, he had some latitude to roam the streets, but he did not want to press his luck. Before long, he lifted me in his arms so we could move faster.

Motl knocked on the rectory door, and almost immediately, Father Jan Bruylandts, a tall, lean man, greeted us warmly. His smile, though kind, told me I would be left there, alone. Until that moment, I had thought Motl and I would remain together. But Motl hurriedly kissed my cheek, told me to listen to the priest, and was out the door as quickly as we'd gone in.

Father Bruylandts took my hand and guided me through a hidden door, down a few steps, and to another door that opened into a small room where several children were sleeping on cots. We squeezed between six cots to a bed. I felt empty and cold with fear. This must have been obvious to Father Bruylandts because he covered me with care before shutting off the only light bulb and walking out.

Mira Hepner, the author's mother, with her older son, Max, and nephew, Dr. Motl Globerson. Prewar, Brussels.

My first hiding place did not last long. Warned that he had just been denounced to the Nazis, Father Bruylandts immediately called the underground, and Motl barely beat the Gestapo to our door. In the dark of night, Motl dressed me faster than I had ever dressed before, and hoisting me into his arms, we ran out. The reason became clear when I saw cars and trucks, lights flashing, racing toward the church. I was certain we were heading back to our apartment and my mother. But we turned into a doorway on rue de Fiennes. Motl rang the doorbell frantically and repeatedly while leaning hard against the door to be less visible.

An old man opened the door without asking who was calling and smiled at Motl. Barely looking at me, the man took my hand as Motl thanked him profusely. Motl uttered, "Listen to Monsieur," kissed my cheek, and sped out.

Climbing the stairs with this stranger who didn't say anything instilled some calm in me. We walked into a very large room with many pieces of "straw" furniture. In a corner, a woman sat silently, holding on to what I subsequently discovered were strands of wicker. She took one very long look at me, and finally smiled a deep, warm smile that made me feel comfortable. She summoned me with her free index finger, and when I got close to her, she held out a warm hand to shake mine. That might have been the first time I'd greeted someone with a handshake. Monsieur went into the kitchen and came back with a cookie and a small glass of milk.

Despite a stay of several weeks with these kind people, I don't remember any exchanges of words between us. They communicated by signing to each other and eventually to me. Without ever using a word, they quickly taught me how to weave the wicker. The calm I felt from being industrious at this craft overwhelmed me. Whenever anyone came to pick up their wares, Monsieur and Madame would gently lead me into the next room where I'd stand at the window—the place I wanted most to be. Crying quiet tears of envy, I'd watch schoolboys playing on the street below.

The peace and serenity I experienced with this couple never returned. Almost as quickly and as terrifyingly as I had gotten to this haven is how I left. It was the first time anyone had ever explained anything, or perhaps the first time I'd asked why. Motl said that Monsieur had been asked by one of his neighbors about the little boy at the window making funny faces at the schoolboys across the street. My protectors had told their neighbor I was the son of distant cousins in Malines, but they became worried that the neighbor would become more curious and suspicious. So, a few days later, Motl came to get me.

This time we walked to Avenue du Midi, an area I did not recognize. We entered a house with overwhelmingly large rooms and glistening furniture. Motl spoke softly and less hurriedly to a tall man he seemed to know. Then he hugged me, adding that he'd see me soon, and, of course, pressed me to listen to the man, a colleague from the hospital. My new hosts weren't particularly nice, nor were they mean. I had my own room and busied myself with crayons and other simple games. But even a young child knows when he's a burden to someone. Fortunately, my stay here was very short.

Less than a week later, I was taken in by a woman and her mother. The two played games with me, but it was to be another temporary stay. In the end, they simply didn't want me.

Motl brought me to the next encampment, only a few houses away. Here, a very pleasant couple greeted us ever so kindly. Either they knew, or sensed, I had been shuffled from one place to another. By then, I had learned to hide my feelings of despair and isolation. Often, I'd just look idly at my hosts without feeling anything. Somehow, this couple felt different. When Motl left, he didn't tell me to listen to the man. He just said, "Have a good time."

I was put to bed in my own room and was told they'd have a surprise for me in the morning. It was the first time in a long time that I fell asleep feeling really safe. As calm as I had felt with the weavers, I had never really trusted that all would go well. Now I did. The next morning, three smiling children walked in, saying it was time for breakfast. They were the most wonderful gift I'd ever had!

Nevertheless, this haven didn't last long either. A month later, I woke up unable to open my eyes. At first, I rubbed them, but that didn't help. I started to panic but didn't want to call out because I was afraid of what my caretakers would say. I hid under the covers, wishing over and over again for my eyes to open. When Madame came in, I cried through closed eyelids and asked her to forgive me. Monsieur tried a warm washcloth, but that did nothing. For the first time, I cried for my mother. Then I wanted Motl. I was in bed all day before he arrived with eye drops. When that didn't help, Motl seemed angry. He left without hugging or kissing me. I knew he'd come back but thought he'd never love me again. I was petrified.

Two days later, Motl came to get me. My wonderful hosts had been too afraid to call another doctor for fear of being discovered, and they hadn't allowed their children near me because they feared I might be contagious. Once more, I was unwanted. Motl took me to the only place that would have me, his apartment.

As we walked into Motl's home, a woman's voice called out from the bedroom. Motl had told me we were going to his place, so thinking he had lied, I cried. Motl then told me that Marie-Louise was his special friend. She approached me gingerly, and picked me up in her arms, holding me close. It seemed odd how I felt immediately comfortable with this stranger. I could see Motl's face over her shoulder. I think it was the first time I saw him smile since before the Nazis had come to Brussels. She put me down on the couch that was to be my bed. When she rose to hug Motl, I fantasized I was back in a family.

The following morning, Motl was out. Marie-Louise explained that she and I would be spending a lot of time together because Motl was very busy at the hospital and with other work. It was only after the war that I discovered Motl's involvement with the underground. Because he treated Nazis as well as Belgians, he had a special identity card that allowed him to evade any detention, even when stopped during a *rafle* (raid).

By this time, I was seven and would sometimes roam about the busy neighborhood by myself. I'd wander off as I accompanied Marie-Louise on her errands. Nazi soldiers walking along the wide avenues would pat my head and greet me in German. I am blue-eyed and was then very blond. Though extremely frightened, the first time a soldier put his hand on my shoulder and then on my head, telling me what a good little boy I was, I knew enough to smile and say *danke*. Feeling more gregarious and confident, I explained to Motl that he didn't have to worry about me because the Nazis found me so appealing. After that, Motl had me deliver envelopes buried under my clothes to a man who lived several blocks away. I didn't exactly know what I was doing, but I knew enough to feel proud. These feelings of pride didn't last long. The Nazis kept raiding apartments, looking for Jews. So Motl enlisted the help of a family friend, also very active in the underground. Vinnik, a diminutive man with a magnanimous heart and sharp mind, found a farmhouse outside of Brussels where my mother and I could stay.

Mother and I made our way to Odegien. It was my first time in a place with woods and open farmland. The stone farmhouse looked old but solid. A narrow walkway led to the back door where an elderly woman, Madame Lebecq, greeted us with an ambiguous smile, clearly indicating her reluctance. I learned after the war that the underground paid our rent, which no doubt kept her from denouncing us to the Nazis or the Belgian gendarmes. Her husband, Philippe, was an invalid. When we got to our room, my mother said she'd been warned that Philippe hated Jews. The Lebecqs could barely eke out a living on their small farm; they had to hire a young farmhand and rent their upstairs rooms.

My lot seemed hopeless until I stepped out just before dusk and discovered the rabbit hutch. Madame Lebecq and I came to an agreement: I was given the job of feeding the rabbits. That evening, the adults laughed as I mimicked my new charges. Another diversion came through Pierre, the teenage farmhand. One day, as I saw him hitching a large horse to a plow, I ventured a shy hello that brought on such a welcoming, wide smile that I thought I'd made a new friend. Pierre asked my name and what I was doing there. I realized I wasn't supposed to talk to him. I told him we were renting a room but answered his other questions with, "I don't remember." Still, he invited me to walk along the row he was about to hoe, and then to ride the horse. I was already in big trouble for speaking to Pierre; now I would have to explain being out so long. But after my first few rides on the horse, my fearful frown turned into an exhilarated smile.

Soon after our arrival, a family of three—the Finkelsteins and their daughter, Michelle, about my age—moved into the room across the hall from us. Michelle and I became friends immediately and played together while our parents spoke in somber, quiet tones.

Some weeks later, Mr. Vinnik came to tell us he'd been able to enroll Michelle and me at the one-room schoolhouse. Odegien had the sweetest teacher in the world. She treated us so well that we could not wait to run to school every day. Mademoiselle Viviane made learning fun and easy, a far cry from what had been my previous experience with my teacher in Anderlecht, where, with a callous smile, my first-grade teacher had consented to my being marched out of class, along with two other Jewish boys, as requested by a school administrator and a Nazi official.

Michelle and I loved school. Those were the only times we thought things might become normal. Before, the other boys had ridiculed me for not going to school and for not knowing where I came from. Though they still teased me, now that we got to know one another, I risked going to their gathering place, a nearby lake past the rows of corn. While the boys engaged in horseplay, I—a non-swimmer—would sit around the edge. One day, I fell in. In a panic, I thrashed about, but this pulled me away from the edge. I sank twice, each time coming up farther away. I could see some boys laughing. After sinking a third time, I rose close enough to the edge for Pierre to pull me out.

Something must have been said to my mother, for out of the blue, she said, "If anybody asks if you're Jewish, say no." Later that day, Michelle and I talked about being Jewish. She said her father had also told her she was to deny it. Neither one of us understood why. This became even more important when, either by coincidence or because our parents knew something, Pierre asked me flat out, "Are you Jewish?" "*No*," I screamed. My rescuer asked, "Really?" as though he knew more. I'm sure what happened then was an epiphany. I was seven, a stranger in unfamiliar territory, and I had to lie to the one person, besides my mother, who seemed to be a true friend! Until my mother told me to say I wasn't a Jew, I only vaguely knew I was. Six months earlier, I had walked the streets of Brussels with a yellow star covering the entire pocket of my jacket. Now, I felt either naked or ignorant. That episode may explain why for the rest of my life I've often insisted, unnecessarily, on revealing the Jewish part of my identity while hiding the rest of me.

After **Albert Hepner** *and his mother immigrated to the US, Albert joined the US Army. He married and had three* *daughters. Eventually, he built his own tool distribution business. He later went back to school and became an ESL instructor. His book,* Avrumele: Recollections of a Hidden Child, *was published in 2017.*

A Public Thank-you to Chavagnes-en-Paillers

By Odette Meyers

(Excerpted from The Hidden Child, *Volume IX, Number 1, spring 2000.)*

Decades after the war, the townspeople of Chavagnes-en-Paillers, a pretty little French burg in Northern Vendée, discovered that during the war, the village had been a secret refuge for as many as sixty Jewish children. At the time, each of the children thought they were the only ones living clandestine lives, but decades later when some survivors and children of the rescuers started to piece it together, they realized that dozens of Jews owed their lives to someone in the village, described in the press as "The Village of the Righteous Gentiles."

Most of the children, including three friends and me, had arrived after the July 16, 1942, major roundup in Paris. Although we kept our Eastern European Jewish names, we were passed off as children of Catholic prisoners of war and sent to the nuns' school. We learned to say our prayers and not to pay attention to the many Nazi soldiers in the priests' seminary across the street. We were treated well, and we had as normal a Catholic childhood as children separated from their Jewish parents could have.

After the war, we were fetched back to Paris and, essentially, we lost touch with our rescuers. As we got older, some of us went back to Chavagnes to discover that we had not forgotten the town or our foster families, and that they had not forgotten us. Still, it did not occur to us that we had not been the only Jewish children to be saved by local families—at least not until 1998, when the son of my rescuers had a visit from an old friend and neighbor. She admired my memoir, *Doors to Madame Marie*, and the medal from Yad Vashem that Jacques and Jean's parents, Moisette and Gustave Raffin, had been given in early 1999, and she announced that her parents had also saved Jewish children. She said that they had never seen the children again and that she would like help finding them.

A notice in the Hidden Children Bulletin in Paris, a couple of responses, and some long and arduous detective work with the help of a 1943 school register, led to our finding thirty-three of the hidden children. We first met in twos or threes, and later in a larger group, we decided to hold a public thank-you celebration in Chavagnes on October 3, 1993. The townspeople were cooperative. They respected our wish to keep the event low-key, free of politicians—just between the townspeople and us. Fifteen of us had made our way to Chavagnes. Worshippers came out of Sunday mass onto the church plaza where many others had already gathered. After the pealing of joyous bells, there was the sound of solemn music, our signal to start.

The mayor introduced the event. Three children, all descendants, unveiled the plaque on a city hall wall as cameras clicked and everyone held their breath. In white letters on a black background, the inscription read, "To those inhabitants of Chavagnes-en-Paillers and its villages who had the courage to shelter and protect, from 1941 to 1944, children at risk of death because they were born Jewish." It was signed "The former hidden children of Chavagnes." Then, three of us gave speeches to a large and attentive crowd.

Even the children listened. When the ceremony was over, everyone rushed to the wine and refreshments table. Gratitude, reunions, laughter, tears, and shared memories ended the public part of our celebration. We had arranged for a locally catered meal, and except for two older women, the guests were the local children who had shared our Chavagnes childhood. Like us, they had brought families and photos to introduce, explain, and catch up.

The historical society had placed on one wall a display of old photographs from our time, and, on a small table, a copy of the

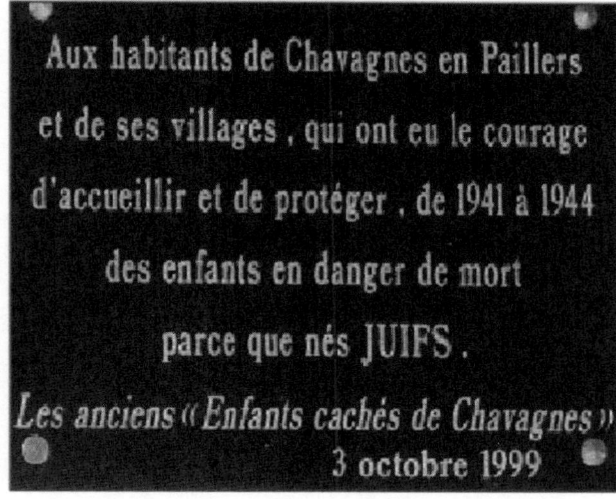

Plaque on the wall of the town's city hall.

1943 register. We milled around, pointing and talking, eating, showing pictures, visiting other tables, mixing more and more, promising to write, phone, send photos, and to see each other again—soon.

That evening, back with my Chavagnes "family," we watched our celebration once more on the local news. What an extraordinary day! Although we had lived separate lives since the end of 1944, we were bound by the simple yet complex human experience of temporarily sharing, as a "family," daily life with strangers. And through the years, we remained attached to the same memories and to the same country landscape. What a relief to have at long last publicly and permanently thanked our rescuers! And what joy to bring Chavagnes-en-Paillers back into our lives!

A month later, Chavagnes had another event. This time, Yad Vashem gave a medal to rescuer Marie-Elise Roger. Again, the event was well attended. Of the many newspaper clippings I received, there were two remarks that particularly moved me. The first from Mme Roger: "I did nothing unusual…I only took in a little guy who had just lost his parents…I loved him and gave him [something] to eat. If I hadn't done this, that would not have been normal."

In 1942, **Odette Meyers** *(1934–2001) immigrated to Los Angeles with her parents in 1949. She earned her bachelor's degree from UCLA, and a master's degree and a doctorate from UC Riverside, and taught French literature at several universities, including UC Berkeley.*

Rabbi Zalman Schneerson Saved the Teitelbaum Sisters

By Bertha Teitelbaum Schwarz

(Excerpted from The Hidden Child, *Volume XIX, 2011.)*

In the summer of 1942, after our father was arrested by the French police and interned at Septfonds, Rabbi René-Samuel Kapel warned my mother that we too risked imminent capture. My father had told Rabbi Kapel, one of the few chaplains authorized to enter France's internment camps, where to find us. The rabbi urged us, and the other four Jewish refugee families hidden in Orgueil, a small village near Toulouse in the Unoccupied Zone, to leave immediately.

With my youngest sister Bella sick, my mother didn't know what to do. She packed a small suitcase for Malka and me, took us to the bus stop, and purchased two one-way tickets to Montauban. She told me that we were to go to the office where, the year before, our family had obtained false names and papers. I was to meet someone who would take us to Marseille. I was nine years old and Malka was six. Although I understood the danger, I was very apprehensive about leaving Mother and Bella. I wondered if I would remember the place and the person we were to meet. And if I didn't find this person, what would I do?

These anxious thoughts and others rumbled through my mind. What if curious passengers asked our names, our addresses, and why we were traveling alone? In the end, no one asked, but I remained terribly frightened. We had been taught never to talk to anybody lest we give away important information that would hurt us later. By then, I certainly knew collaborators lurked everywhere.

We arrived, pale and trembling, in Montauban. I held Malka's hand tightly as we walked toward the train station. I found the office easily and knocked on the door. No one came. I thought it might be lunchtime, so we waited. I knocked again. Still no response. My heart was pounding. What should I do? I had no money to return to Orgueil and no way to let Mother know what was happening to us. I did not know whom to turn to, and I was afraid a *gendarme* would arrest us.

A man stopped and asked, "Little girl, why are you crying?" I said I was supposed to meet someone at this office and nobody was there. He asked for my name, and I told him. "I am looking for you!" he said. Still, I wondered if it was safe to go with him. Was he a collaborator? Will he bring us to Marseille? And how will our mother know that we arrived?

The Teitelbaum sisters at Rabbi Schneerson's Château de Seignebon in Dému: Malka, age seven; Bella, age six; and Bertha, age ten.

After giving us false papers with new names, the man took us to the Montauban train station and traveled with us to Marseille. He was kind; throughout the eight-hour trip, he tried to keep us calm by playing games. Upon our arrival in Marseille, the French police checked our papers. I was very much aware of the danger. They asked me, "Who is this man?" I answered, "He is my father!" They looked at us. "But you do not have the same name." The gendarmes arrested him, and Malka and I were taken to l'Hôtel du Levant in a rundown neighborhood of Marseille near the train station. We never saw that man again or learned his name. The French authorities used l'Hôtel du Levant and a few others to house women and children slated for deportation. We did not know then that we were waiting to be placed on the next transport to Drancy, the antechamber to the death camps. At that time, few knew about exterminations. Yet "deportation" had traumatic implications for everyone.

Conditions at l'Hôtel du Levant were very bad: there was no hot water, and, twice a day, food was piled on a table. The halls and public rooms were overflowing with rows of triple–bunk beds. The older women could not climb high, so we, the children, were assigned the top tiers. I was afraid that Malka would fall. And I kept thinking about ways to tell my mother where we were, but I couldn't. My biggest fear was that we might end up in a terrible place like Septfonds, where I had once visited my father.

There were other children at the hotel, and we ran around the building with them. We could not play outside. One morning, a voice called out, "Someone wants to see you, the Teitelbaum sisters." Two Yeshiva boys appeared, saying, "We've come to take you to Rabbi Schneerson's children's home." I packed our things as quickly as possible, and Malka and I got into a van. They took us to our new home, a safe place, thirty to forty-five minutes away.

Rabbi Zalman Schneerson, long-bearded and distinguished-looking in his long black coat, was happy to see us. To this day I do not know how he found out about Malka and me. I will never know how he obtained permission from the police to take us out of that terrible hotel, but I have no doubt he saved us from deportation.

Although we were treated kindly, it took time for us to adapt. Malka did not understand where she was or why. She kept asking, "When is Mother coming to pick us up?" I had no answer. One month later, Bella joined us. All three sisters were together, just as our mother had hoped.

Almost every day, other children arrived in the same way. Rabbi Schneerson's mission to save Jewish children from deportation coexisted with his vision for the future of the Jewish people, a future steeped in ethical and religious beliefs. His commitment to these principles required that we become observant of the Torah and devoted to Jewish law. Therefore, we all learned our prayers and took our studies seriously. The girls had to wear long-sleeved blouses and skirts, even in the summer heat. The young Yeshiva boys were our teachers. Our schedule included morning studies and afternoon chores: laundry (no washing machines) and kitchen and dining-room duties as well as making our beds and cleaning our rooms and bathrooms. We learned early on that we had to take care of all our needs. This was not home!

All the children spoke different languages, so we had to learn to live together and to communicate in one common tongue: French. There was no choice but to adapt to that and to a new discipline for communal Hasidic life. Rabbi Schneerson was very firm about our listening to grown-ups and not answering back.

I have vivid memories of this period. We had to stand in front of the *château* when the gendarmes came to check on the number of children living there. Rabbi Schneerson had permission to keep no more than sixty children. So, we had to warn the older students to run into the forest behind the château to hide.

Food was in short supply. Rationing created a constant struggle for the rabbi and his wife, who oversaw the food and cooking. They needed coupons and permission to buy produce (when available) and, with the number of people exceeding the stamp allowance, more than once we left the table hungry.

Life at the château became routine; we could not go out and had to play with toys we created and games we invented. Clothes and shoes, mostly clogs, were handed down from one child to the next. We slept with army blankets on straw mattresses that were very itchy.

I remember baking the *matzos* for Passover. Rabbi Schneerson sent packages of matzos to people in the internment and labor camps throughout southern France. For this task, he had a large outdoor oven constructed behind the building. Passover was a special holiday. It reminded us that God had saved the Jews before and gave us hope that He would do so again. For a short while, we felt safe and happy.

Finally, after months of not hearing a word from our mother, we received news that she was hiding and working as a maid for a French Jewish family. Separated from our entire family—with our father in a labor camp and our grandparents away—she was the only one we had left. I kept worrying that it was but a matter of time until she too would be arrested.

Then we received a letter stating that she was now with her aunt Pepi, her mother's youngest sister. A French citizen by marriage, Aunt Pepi was able to travel and to bring Mother to Lectoure, a town in southern France. She was hidden in the attic of their apartment house.

In the meantime, there were rumors that Rabbi Schneerson was trying to obtain authorization for all of us to sail to America. I had to let Mother know that we might leave for America and wrote to her, "How will you ever find us in such a big country?"

After the Nazis took over southern France, leaving for America was no longer possible. Rabbi Schneerson concluded we all had to leave Marseille immediately. Overnight, we packed our belongings and escaped via trucks and train to Dému, about half an hour from Montauban. How could I let our mother know that we were leaving Marseille? Having lost contact with her, I worried that we would never find one another again. Was she arrested or still hiding, and if so, where?

In the meantime, we arrived, tired and hungry, at our new home, a château called Seignebon near the village of Dému. The Red Cross and Quakers gave us blankets and straw mattresses for our beds. The premises were dirty and rundown, with broken windows and no electricity; in short, we had to make our surroundings livable.

As ever, food was Rabbi Schneerson's main concern. But with little cooperation from the local farmers, he had to buy a milking cow and chickens, and we children started a vegetable garden. Soon we all became sick, lice-infested, and had to have our heads shaven. Yet we were busy studying the Torah and trying to live a normal life. Located on the outskirts of the village, the château was very quiet. The children could not leave the premises, but with such a large property, there was enough room to play and run around.

One dark night, we heard loud sounds of a car and voices by the small bridge spanning our brook. It seems that people were attempting to cross the bridge but, failing to do so, they drove away. In the morning, we heard that they had been Nazi soldiers looking for us! This is how close we came to being arrested!

One Shabbat morning, I was told to see the rabbi. When I opened the door, my mother was before me. I jumped into her arms, became very emotional, and asked question after question: "How did you find us? How did you get here? Do you have legal papers?" After many hugs and kisses, Mother asked for Malka and Bella. There were many more hugs and kisses all around. Then Mother looked at our shaven heads and strange clothes, and she began to cry. I told her not to, that our hair would grow back. We were alive and together, and that's all that mattered. Had she come to take us away? She could not then but promised we would be together soon. After a few hours, she left us—not knowing if she would ever see us again.

Mother had been so worried about her children that she had dared to come see us. She had taken a local train with many stops and had gotten off at the station closest to Dému. There, she found herself walking next to a woman who had also gotten off that train. Mother asked the Frenchwoman how far to Dému. When told that it was seven miles, Mother asked her about overnight lodging in the area. She said, "There is nothing around here, so why don't you stay with me at my daughter's house?" That night, they slept in the same bed. The next morning, Mother walked the seven miles to see us.

The Teitelbaum sisters and their mother in Morgin, Switzerland, after their escape from occupied France, c. winter 1944.

After Mother left, we found it very hard to return to a normal routine. Seeing her had been a shock, and we wondered what would come next. When adults can't give assurances or answers, life can be difficult. All we could do was to try our best to be good Jews, to keep faith in our future, and to be helpful to one another—as we were taught every day by the good rabbi and his staff.

A few months later, around May or June 1943, a member of the *Résistance* came to take us by train to Megève, next to the Swiss border, where we would meet our mother and await our crossing into Switzerland. We said goodbye to our friends and to our teachers and the staff, to whom I am very grateful for their kindness and care. I realize that our mother, alone, would not have been able to save us. We owe Rabbi Schneerson our deepest respect and gratitude for the enormous task he took upon himself—the rescue of Jewish children, including the three Teitelbaum sisters.

Postscript: The Teitelbaum family had fled from Antwerp, Belgium, in May 1940, and the grandparents, Yechiel and Leah Ksias, had escaped from Cologne, Germany. Prior to their arrest and incarceration at the Camp of St. Sulpice, the grandparents had been hidden in Lacaune, where their names, and those of other Jewish deportees, are engraved on a memorial plaque in the village square. Usher (in Yiddish), or Asher (in Hebrew), Teitelbaum was only thirty-two when he was killed. The other four Jewish families in Orgueil did not survive the war. The Teitelbaum sisters and their mother crossed the border into Switzerland on September 4, 1943.

Jews Rescuing Jews

By Mordecai Paldiel, PhD

(Excerpted from The Hidden Child, *Volume XIX, 2011.)*

At Yad Vashem, the title of "Righteous Among the Nations" is reserved to non-Jews who, during the Holocaust, risked their lives to save Jews from the Nazis and their accomplices. Major Jewish rescuers are not distinguished by any honors. The reasoning behind this is that while Jews who saved their brethren were fulfilling their obligation, non-Jews had no such responsibility toward their Jewish neighbors; therefore, only non-Jews who braved the risks to themselves by extending help to Jews merit a special distinction. Marion Pritchard, a Dutch Righteous honoree who saved many Jews, has criticized this thinking: not honoring Jewish rescuers of Jews who, "if caught were at much higher risk of the most punitive measures than the gentiles, is a distortion of history. It also contributes to the widespread fallacious impression that the Jews were cowards, who allowed themselves to be led like 'lambs to slaughter.' Nothing is farther from the truth."

Indeed, there were many Jewish rescuers who saved one or several of their colleagues, but I want to focus on Jews who, alone, or in unison with others, created rescue networks and saved dozens and hundreds of Jews. This Jewish Roll of Honor includes persons like Joachim Simon (known as "Shushu") in the Netherlands, who operated a rescue network together with the legendary Joop Westerweel, and was killed by the Nazis; as well as Max ("Nico") Leons, who masqueraded as a seminarian, and in partnership with Arnold Douwes, organized a large-scale rescue of Jews in the off-the-beaten-track village of Nieuwlande. Westerweel and Douwes were bestowed the Righteous title; Simon and Leons were forgotten and received no comparable distinction.

In Amsterdam, the German Jewish refugee Walter Süskind was instrumental in saving hundreds of Jews under the eyes of the Nazis. Equally overlooked are Fela Perlman and Yvonne Jospa, in nearby Belgium, who created the Jewish Defense Committee, a clandestine Jewish organization that helped Jews pass as non-Jews and found hiding places for them—especially children. Ida Sterno, one of the organization's Jewish couriers, traveled widely through the Belgian countryside in search of suitable homes for Jewish children on the run.

In France, the multifaceted panorama of Jewish networks is largely credited for the tremendous Jewish survival rate in that country—over two hundred thousand. To mention the most prominent networks, one would have to include the OSE children's organization and its many operatives, especially Georges Loinger, Jacques Salon, Elisabeth Hirsch, Vivette Samuel, Nicole Weil-Salon, Huguette Wahl (the last two were arrested in Nice and sent to Auschwitz, where they were gassed upon arrival), Andrée Salomon, and Dr. Joseph Weill, all of whom, in combination, were active in the rescue of thousands of Jewish children.

Marianne Cohn and Mila Racine escorted many Jewish youths to and across the Swiss border. Both these brave women paid with their lives—Mila Racine dying in the Mauthausen camp, while Marianne Cohn was brutally murdered by the pro-Nazi French *Milice* on the eve of France's liberation. Others meriting mention are Georges Garel, who created his own rescue network and played a leading role in spiriting out a large group of children from Venissieux camp, near Lyon, and the Hassidic Rabbi Zalman Schneerson, who moved from one place to another through the French countryside with several dozen Jewish children. Also, Emmanuel Racine (the brother of the tragic Mila), Robert Gamzon (known as "Castor"), head of the Jewish Scout Movement, David Rapoport, who fabricated false papers, and had his base in Paris on rue Amelot. Last, but not least in

France, Joseph Bass, Denise Siekierski, and Moussa and Odette Abadi, saved well over a thousand Jewish adults and children in separate rescue operations.

In Poland, Avraham Berman was active in helping Jewish children inside the Warsaw Ghetto; then on the Aryan side, he represented the Jewish underground in Zegota, the sole Polish organization committed to the rescue of Jews. Further north, in Belarus, in the forest vicinity of Novgrodek, Tuvia Bielski organized a family camp, which included a synagogue, school, dispensary, and workshop, as well as a fighting unit. Jews of all ages were admitted into this forest community. Some twelve hundred Jews were saved by the Bielski brothers.

In Slovakia, Gisi Fleischmann and Dov Weissmandel negotiated with SS commander Dieter Wisliceny to save the remainder of the country's Jews under a project known as the Europe Plan. Fleischmann wound up in Auschwitz, where she perished. In Hungary, the Zionist youth underground (led by Rafi Friedl-Benshalom, David Gur, and others) worked tirelessly to smuggle Jews out of the country, or to provide them with false credentials, and to rescue hundreds of children—the latter with the help of Friedrich Born, the Red Cross representative in Budapest. Born earned the Righteous title, while the superhuman efforts of some of the principals of the Zionist youth movement still remain largely unknown to the Jewish public.

Finally, in Switzerland, Georges Mantello and Recha and Isaac Sternbuch worked tirelessly and frantically, through various channels, to save as many Jews as possible, enlisting the aid of any possible source—the pro-Fascist former president of the Swiss confederation, Jean-Marie Musy, in the case of the Sternbuchs; the El Salvador government and its Geneva diplomatic representative, Jose Castellanos (a Righteous), in the case of Mantello. Space does not allow us to expand on all these major Jewish rescuers, so I will only briefly relate the two stories of Walter Süskind and Moussa and Odette (née Rosenstock) Abadi.

In the Netherlands, in the heart of Amsterdam, the Nazis converted a theater known as *Hollandsche Schouwburg* (Dutch Theater) to serve as a makeshift prison for at least fifty thousand Jews, who moved through its doors on their way to concentration camps in distant Poland. Inside the theater, the SS team in charge refused to deal directly with their victims. They issued orders through Nazi-appointed Jewish intermediaries, such as Walter Süskind, who used the special latitude afforded him to smuggle out hundreds of Jews (some say close to a thousand) before their deportation to the camps.

Süskind had fled Germany to nearby Holland upon the Nazi takeover of power. Thanks to his Dutch Theater, SS officer Ferdinand aus der Fünten. Süskind decided, judiciously, to pull the wool over the eyes of the SS, and to save as many imprisoned Jews as possible. In the words of the non-Jewish Righteous honoree Piet Meerburg, "Walter viewed his mission from the beginning as being just one thing: to sabotage the transports. For this, he put on an extraordinary act...." One such deception was the doctoring of the list of internees, which carried Ferdinand aus der Fünten's signature, behind the backs of the unsuspecting SS guards. Süskind and his trustworthy aides changed and deleted the names of those for whom he had arranged an escape and a hiding place. Those fortunate enough to be chosen by Süskind were generally spirited out of the theater's windows or back entrance, at times in connivance with one or several bribed SS guards. As the man responsible for the administrative side of the operation, Süskind made sure that the paperwork was kept in a disorderly—rather "chaotic"—condition, the better to be able to tamper with the names when the time seemed ripe.

Another of Süskind's ruses involved the release of persons already sitting on trains, ready to be taken to Westerbork. This happened after his network had discovered that the keys of the lockers in an Amsterdam bathhouse fitted the locks of some transport railcars, which had been pressed into use for the transport of Jews. Sam de Hond, one of Süskind's secret operatives, remembers many Jews being freed with the help of these keys after Süskind had ensured that their names had been removed from the official register.

Süskind's greatest effort was expended in saving the children who, upon arrival at the theater, had been separated from their parents and taken across the street to the *crèche*. There, they were to be kept and cared for by Jewish nurses until they were to be reunited with their parents for their joint departure to the concentration camps. Whenever parents could supply a safe address for their child, Süskind's accomplices would verify on the outside if the people were indeed ready to conceal a Jewish child. In the words of Lisette Lamon, one of Süskind's associates, "Walter—the heart and soul of Operation Kidnap—would only allow a child to be smuggled out if it had a verified home. Children were smuggled out of the nursery in rucksacks, laundry bags, crates, bread baskets, burlap bags, or held under a coat. One infant passed through a cordon of SS men in a cake box. Occasionally, they were given tranquilizers or sleeping pills to minimize their chance of detection."

The lowest estimate of children saved through Süskind's operation is six hundred. Some place it as high as one thousand. In light of the estimated total of four thousand five hundred Jewish children saved in the Netherlands, Süskind's achievement is quite amazing. Close to a dozen of the many people on the outside, who coalesced with Süskind in this extensive child-rescue operation, earned the Righteous title from Yad Vashem. As for Walter Süskind, when his wife and daughter were arrested, he joined them on their deportation to the camps, where they all perished. While he was neither able to save himself nor his family, in the words of Lamon, "Well over a thousand are living today because of him and those who were his accomplices."

In southern France, two Jewish names come up frequently among survivors, the Syrian Jewish–born Moussa Abadi and his consort Odette Rosenstock (the two married after the war). They headed a private clandestine network in the region of Nice, specifically dedicated to finding hiding places for Jewish children whose parents had been snatched and deported by French and Nazi police units. In one such story, the two Engel brothers were aided by the Abadis upon being stranded after the arrest of their parents in a Nazi raid. The two brothers were moved to a children's home, headed by Alban and Germaine Fort, both of whom were awarded the Righteous title. Abadi's name came up again in the cases of Monsignor Paul Rémond, the Catholic bishop of Nice, and several clergies of the Don Bosco Order in Nice, who were also awarded the Righteous title for sheltering Jewish children turned over to them by the Abadi network.

Born in Damascus, Syria, in 1910, Moussa Abadi studied at the local French-speaking Jewish Alliance school, where he earned a scholarship for further studies in France. At the Sorbonne, he took a liking to the theater and appeared in several university-sponsored plays. However, the war disrupted his acting career. Fleeing to Nice, in the Vichy non-occupied zone, he met Odette Rosenstock, a pediatrician and medical school inspector, who was forced to give up her job because of the newly promulgated anti-Jewish discriminatory laws by the Vichy regime.

In Nice, Abadi was hired by the Catholic Church to give grammar and diction lessons to seminarians who needed to brush up on their French language. In 1943, fearing that Nice would fall under direct Nazi rule, Abadi asked for an audience with Monsignor Rémond, the bishop of Nice, and told him, "I am Jewish, and I come from one of the oldest ghettos in the world. Try to live up according to your Gospels as I try according to my Bible. You may take me to the door and throw me out. But without your help, I cannot save children." Rémond responded that he needed time to think. "As he accompanied me to the door, he stopped and said, 'You have convinced me. You have converted me.'" Abadi was assigned a room at the Diocese for use in planning the rescue of as many children as possible should the occasion suddenly arise. It was still the idyllic period of the Italian occupation.

The situation altered drastically upon the Italian capitulation, in September 1943, when the Nazis swept into Nice and Cannes. Headed by the notorious SS commander Alois Brunner, they began a hunt of Jews in homes, hotels, and on the streets. At this point, Moussa Abadi and Odette Rosenstock moved into action, picking up abandoned Jewish children after their parents had been suddenly arrested, or were themselves in hiding, and finding for them secure hiding places. False credentials, such as new identity cards, baptismal certificates, and ration cards were manufactured in the room that Bishop Rémond had placed at the disposal of Abadi. Rémond also handed Abadi a personal letter of introduction, which opened many doors of Catholic institutions.

To cover their tracks, Moussa and Odette assumed new identities, now appearing respectively as Monsieur Marcel and Sylvie Delatre—ostensibly educational aides and medical assistants for the Catholic diocese of Nice. It was a two-person operation, with Odette making house calls at the homes of prospective host families, paying for the upkeep of the children, and taking note of the children's health and good treatment. Financial aid came through the USA-based Joint, the OSE, and the Quakers. During the one-year rescue period, from September 1943 to August 1944 (when France was liberated), the Abadi network, known under the code-word *Marcel*, secured safe places for over five hundred hundred Jewish children in various private and children's homes in the Cannes/Nice region.

To keep track of all the children under their care, the Abadis established three separate card indexes: one for the Red Cross, to be stored in Geneva for safekeeping; another, for day-to-day work; and a third, to serve as a reserve index, in case the two others were misplaced. Children were first collected and brought to a secret place, where they were given new names and false credentials before being escorted to their hiding destinations. French-sounding names were substituted for too conspicuously sounding Jewish ones, such as Arthieu instead of Artsztein; Bernier for Bernstein; and Barot for Borenstein.

In April 1944, Odette Rosenstock was arrested and moved to Drancy after undergoing a brutal interrogation, during which she held her own. She did not divulge any information on the scope of the rescue operation. A month later, she was deported to Auschwitz, then to Bergen-Belsen, which she survived. With the police frantically looking for him, Moussa spent nights in a school's classroom and vacated the room early each morning. He'd pass the next three hours attending continuous masses in the city's Catholic churches and chapels. "No practicing Catholic attended so many masses in such a short time as I did," Abadi facetiously recalls.

With danger his constant companion, Abadi continued his rescue operation almost single-handed until Nice's liberation in August 1944. Immediately after the war, he turned over the children's list to Jewish organizations, including information on the current whereabouts of the 527 children, so they could be fetched and reunited with their families and loved ones. After marrying Odette, upon her miraculous survival, he returned to his old interest, the theater, this time as a dramatic art critic on French radio, where he hosted a special program for twenty-two years. While still alive, Moussa and Odette Abadi were overlooked by the Jewish community, and no honors were bestowed on them.

Understandably, the title of "Righteous Among the Nations" is reserved for non-Jews who risked their lives to save Jews. At the same time, cannot the Jewish people, through the Yad Vashem or other Holocaust memorials, devise a similar honorific to Jewish rescuers, such as Walter Süskind and the Abadis? And what of the dozens of other outstanding rescuers who added risk upon risk to themselves in their efforts to save their brethren? Such a program would go a long way to instill a measure of self-esteem to Jews everywhere—especially the young generation. It would demonstrate that not all Jews went to the slaughter like sheep: some tried their very best to save as many as they could. It does not take courage to devise such a program, but it does require the will to do it. It is high time for this to happen.

Dr. **Mordecai Paldiel** *was born in Antwerp, Belgium, in 1937. Upon the onset of WWII, he and his family fled to Switzerland. He was the director of the Righteous Among the Nations Department at Yad Vashem from 1982 until 2007. During that twenty-four-year period, some eighteen thousand non-Jewish persons were awarded the "Righteous Among the Nations" honor for saving Jews from the Nazis. Dr. Paldiel has authored fourteen books, numerous articles, and he lectures before various organizations and institutions on the rescue of Jews during the Holocaust.*

PART IX

Refugees on the Run

Editor's Note: The World's Response to the Crisis of War in Europe

By Rachelle L. Goldstein

Within a few years of Hitler's rise to power in 1933, the lives of European Jews were increasingly in peril. The world's response? Nearly all countries shut their doors. On December 2, 1938, a few days after *Kristallnacht*, Great Britain admitted the first *Kindertransport*, 196 children from a Berlin Jewish orphanage that had been destroyed. By May 14, 1940, the day Holland fell, England had welcomed to its shores close to 10,000 Jewish children from Germany, Austria, Czechoslovakia, and Poland. British immigration policy loosened partly because of intense pro-refugee lobbying and partly because of political embarrassment over the campaign against Jewish immigration into Palestine. The Netherlands and Belgium also took in Jewish children, with The Netherlands admitting 1,700 Jewish children and Belgium several hundred more.

In the United States, the Child Refugee Bill, known as the Wagner-Rogers Bill and proposed in early 1939, aimed to allow twenty thousand children—Jewish or otherwise—to enter the US between 1939 and 1941, apart from and above the regular German immigration quota.

The bill had strong support from influential people, including Eleanor Roosevelt, and from all religious denominations. The Quakers worked out the complex logistics, and within a day of the plan's announcement, four thousand families had offered to adopt the children.

But the bill faced fierce opposition by numerous groups, including the Allied Patriotic Societies, American Women Against Communism, Veterans of Foreign Wars, and the Sons and Daughters of the American Revolution. The American Legion, for one, announced its support for a more popular and restrictive bill, which would abolish all immigration to the US for the next ten years. Typical of the hostile witnesses at the House Committee on Immigration hearing was a representative of the widows of World War I veterans, who declared that the country could not guarantee its children their Constitutional rights "if this country is to become the dumping ground for the persecuted minorities of Europe."

President Franklin D. Roosevelt, reluctant to antagonize the isolationist Congress, chose not to support the bill actively in order to obtain the expansion of the Air Corps and construction of naval bases. The bill was withdrawn. The Jewish children had lost. The isolationists had won.

The opposition to letting German refugee children into the US stood in sharp contrast to the public and Congressional willingness to allow besieged British children to bypass the immigration regulations. Within weeks of the Battle of Britain, the US Department of State had the procedures that would enable these children to enter the United States. A special organization, the United States Committee for the Care of European Children (USCOM), was formed to facilitate their entry. By the time this evacuation was canceled, in the fall of 1940, 835 British children were removed from peril. The USCOM then focused its attention on the Jewish refugee children in Vichy France.

Between 1940 and the summer of 1942, the Quakers (the American Friends Service Committee) worked closely with the *Oeuvre de Secours Aux Enfants* (OSE) in selecting children from Jewish orphanages and from internment camps in southern France for transport to America.

With dreadful reports of arrests and deportations in the summer of 1942, the State Department relented to the pleas of American relief workers in Vichy France, and, by the end of September, authorized five thousand visas for Jewish children. The problem became one of extracting exit visas from the Vichy regime.

Vichy, resistant to American officials' appeals, resorted to contorted arguments: allowing some children who had been "illegally" hidden to emigrate would justify and maybe even encourage such unlawfulness; and sending children to another continent might impede future reunions. This great "concern" for maintaining family unity was also cited for deporting children along with their parents to "destinations unknown."

Very reluctantly, Vichy agreed to release an initial five hundred children, insisting, however, that these be "bona fide orphans." Since no information on the fate of deported Jews was available, such proofs were unattainable. Yet the Quakers worked nonstop to satisfy such intractable obstacles.

Meanwhile, the Allies landed in North Africa in early November, and consequently, on November 11, the Nazis took over the unoccupied zone. Diplomatic relations between the US and Vichy were severed, thus dashing all hope of rescuing any children.

During the entire period of 1934 to 1945, only about one thousand unaccompanied Jewish children, mostly from Nazi Germany, managed to reach the safety of the United States. Of these, 590 came prior to 1941. From the summer of 1941 to the end of the war, 350 Jewish refugee children entered the US, most of them arriving after spending some time in France. To escape the Nazi assault, there were but a few places of "last resort," such as Shanghai and the Philippines, where no visas were required.

Between 1933 and 1941, more than twenty thousand desperate people fled to Shanghai, one of the few places they were guaranteed to be accepted. Also in the late 1930s, Philippines President Manuel Quezon welcomed over twelve hundred Jews from Nazi Germany and Austria with his Open Doors policy.

Though their stories are among the least known, the largest group of survivors to outlast the Nazi slaughter are those who "Fled to the East." Between 1939 and 1941, nearly three hundred thousand Polish Jews, about 10 percent of the Polish Jewish population, escaped Nazi-occupied parts of Poland and crossed into the Soviet zone. The Russians transported tens of thousands of Jews to Siberia, central Asia, and although conditions there were very difficult, most survived. After Nazi Germany attacked the Soviet Union in June 1941, more than a million Soviet Jews also fled eastward into the Asian parts of the USSR, where most survived.

Bibliography:

Israel Gutman, *Encyclopedia of the Holocaust*, Macmillan, 1990.

Arthur D. Morse, *While Six Million Died: A Chronicle of American Apathy*, Random House, 1968.

David S. Wyman, *The Abandonment of the Jews: America and the Holocaust 1941–1945*, Pantheon Books, 1984.

M.R. Marrus and R.O. Paxton, *Vichy France and the Jews*, Calmann-Levy, 1981.

I Remember

By Johanna Franklin Saper

(Excerpted from The Hidden Child, *Volume XIII, 2005.)*

On March 13, 1938, I was home on spring vacation. My older brothers were listening to the radio all day. There was agitation and apprehension as we heard of the Nazis' arrival in Vienna. As a ten-year-old, I had no idea what all this would mean for me.

I felt happy and secure. My brother Josef, in his twenties, worked during the day and attended lectures and political activities every night. My brother Harry was in his last year at the *gymnasium*; he had many friends and was active in sports. My father worked until late in the evening. My mother usually awaited my return from school with many questions and a pastry with whipped cream. As the youngest, my brothers, aunts, uncles, and cousins indulged me. Everyone called me "Hannerl."

Our apartment faced a busy street, and on this day, we all stared out the front windows. There was none of the usual flurry. As we watched, we could see movement in an abandoned building across the street. Suddenly, as the radio trumpeted the triumphant entry of Adolf Hitler into Austria, hundreds of people streamed out of the building bearing large flags with swastikas and singing victory songs. The building had been transformed into Nazi headquarters. Although we were all very apprehensive and could hardly believe what we were seeing, my mother was optimistic. She said, "We will survive this."

Overnight, our lives changed. My father's Christian business partner told him not to return. Though their enterprise was lucrative, my father received nothing for his share of the business.

My brother Harry was imprisoned for "associating with communists." He was released after a few weeks. I could no longer attend classes and was sent to a Jewish school where about eighty children were crammed into one classroom. There was confusion and disorder all around. On my way to school, children threw stones at me and yelled, "Jew, Jew, get out!" I wasn't learning anything, and with the risk of getting hurt, my mother said I didn't have to attend the Jewish school any longer.

One spring afternoon, two SS troopers intruded into our apartment. As I held my mother's hand, I watched them open every drawer and closet, stuffing silverware, jewelry, and embroidered linens into one of our pillowcases. When one found a small gold watch, my mother pleaded, "This is a birthday present for my little girl here. She'll be eleven next month." The trooper pushed her aside and stuffed the watch in with the other loot. As they were leaving, my brother Harry walked in. "We want him to come with us," they said in unison. My father pleaded that they take him instead, but they refused. Harry was put to work, scrubbing floors and cleaning toilets of the newly renovated Nazi headquarters across the street. At one point, I spotted him on a tall ladder, washing windows while neighborhood boys taunted him, "Red Harry, Jew boy!"

With more restrictions and atrocities, we began to prepare for a new life. I took English lessons. In June 1938, my parents placed an ad in a Jewish paper in England, asking for a family willing to take in an eleven-year-old girl, preferably a family with a child of similar age. We narrowed the few answers to one family living in a suburb of Manchester. Sol and Clara Glickman had a daughter, Rosetta, almost eleven years old. Many years later, I learned that on the day our ad appeared in the newspaper, Mr. Glickman had been in a car accident. The two other passengers had been killed. As an observant Jew, he felt that since God had spared his life, he should save another, and they answered my parents' ad.

Meanwhile, my cousin Inge came to live with us because her family had been expelled from their home. Inge and I had a great time, never realizing our imminent disaster. My brother Harry had a pen pal in the United States. After months of exchanging letters and forms, the American Gentile family kindly sponsored him. Harry left Vienna for North Carolina in November 1938, the day before *Kristallnacht*.

Suddenly, old men were beaten, windows were smashed, synagogues were pillaged, and the activities across the street intensified. We were frightened. My father became very quiet and appeared older. If all went well, I would be leaving for Manchester by the end of 1938. Inge and her mother had also secured places in England: Inge with one family, her mother working as a maid for another. The three of us would leave together, and I was looking forward to it. While Christmas trees and sparkling lights could be seen in the parks and streets, my mother was carefully packing my suitcase. When we arrived at the Central Railroad Station, about fifteen people had come to say goodbye to us—parents, aunts, uncles, cousins, friends. I never saw any of them again.

I was looking forward to an adventure—a new country, a new language. I was sure that in a few months, I would see my parents and brothers again. I could not imagine that there was no return, and that the life I knew was over.

As we approached the German border, the train stopped, and people were ordered off the train. Inge's mother told us to lie down on the benches and pretend to be sleeping. Two Nazi soldiers entered our compartment. They looked at our passports and just as they were about to evict us, Inge's mother said in her best Viennese accent, "Please officer, the children are sleeping, I'd hate to wake them up." She smiled and flattered the young soldiers, and we were allowed to stay on the train. Those who had been taken off did not return.

I started calling the Glickmans Mum and Dad and to consider Rosetta a sister. I acclimated to a new school, language, and culture, and corresponded with my parents weekly. After seven months in England, the war began, and all communication stopped. The Glickmans and their neighbors built an air raid shelter in the back of their houses. We spent many nights in the shelter, wondering if our lives would be spared.

My brother, Josef, who had also gone to England, was interned as an enemy alien as soon as the war broke out. Josef married Berty, a cousin ten years his senior. He met her need for a better quota to get into the United States, and he was able to leave the camp. They adopted me as their "child," and two years after living in Manchester, I left England with them.

In early January 1941, we arrived at my cousin Friedl's house on Long Island. It had been a long trip from Manchester to Scotland, where we boarded a South African ship to Canada; we continued by train from Montreal to Grand Central Station in New York. The three of us were exhausted. My cousin Friedl, her husband, and four-year-old daughter were waiting for us. Meeting them seemed less traumatic than when I'd met the Glickmans in 1939. Now, I spoke English, and at the age of thirteen, I had been reshuffled, re-cultured, and felt I could handle anything.

At an ensuing family gathering, I was told that my father had died a week earlier. I was stunned. My first thoughts were, "Where is my mother?" but, overwhelmed, I was unable to speak those words.

After several decades of pursuing one reliable lead after another about what happened to my mother, on August 17, 2001, I received the following letter from the American Red Cross:

> *...Charlotte Hirschbein, born June 22, 1890 (maiden name Frankovits) was deported to Maly Trostinec near Minsk on May 6, 1942...she was probably shot immediately after her arrival. Please note that almost all of the deportees to Maly Trostinec during that time met this fate.*

I will never forget...on the eve of my departure from Vienna, my mother sat me down and said, "You are going to live with a family of good Orthodox Jews in England. If, during the religious rituals, they ask whether we observed in the same way, say that we did. I am sorry that we have not been more observant." Then she took out a bible, placed my hand on it, put her hand on my head, and blessed me, "You are my baby, my only daughter, and I love you. Remember everything I taught you and be an observant Jew, my golden child, Hannerl."

Throughout my teens in the US, I attended a different school every year and lived with relatives, friends, and with my brother, Josef. The recurrent theme in my life was, "Forget the past, be a good student, improve yourself, acclimate!"

Johanna Saper *received a bachelor of science degree in occupational therapy from NYU and a master of education in special education from the University of Maine.*

An Ill-fated Voyage and Return to Danger

By Judith Koeppel Steel

(Excerpted from My Story, *Volume VII, April 2021.)*

Editor's note: On June 6, 1939, after neither Cuba nor any port in the Western Hemisphere allowed its passengers to disembark, the MS St. Louis *sailed back to Europe. Jewish organizations negotiated with four European governments to secure entry visas for the passengers. According to the Holocaust Encyclopedia: Great Britain took 288 passengers, the Netherlands admitted 181, Belgium took in 214, and France gave 224 passengers temporary refuge.*

Of the 288 passengers admitted by Great Britain, all survived WWII except one who was killed during an air raid in 1940. Of the 620 passengers who returned to the continent, 87 (14 percent) managed to emigrate before the Nazi invasion of western Europe in May 1940. At that time, 532 former passengers were trapped there. Just over half, 278 survived the Holocaust. In total, 254 former passengers of the MS St. Louis *died: 84 who had been in Belgium, 84 who had found refuge in Holland, and 86 who had been admitted to France.*

In Germany, on *Kristallnacht*—the night of November 9 to 10, 1938—some thirty thousand Jewish men were arrested and sent to Nazi concentration camps. My father, Josef Koeppel, was one

Irmgard and Josef Koeppel, with Jacob Koeppel holding Judith.

of them. During his incarceration, my father learned he would be released on the condition he leave Germany within eight weeks or he and his family would be arrested. I was fourteen months old when my parents and my grandfather managed to book passage on the luxury ship MS *St. Louis*, bound for Havana, Cuba.

Despite the difficulties, my mother, Irmgard, and my father, along with my grandfather, Jacob Koeppel, felt safe and secure aboard the ship. They wined, dined, and danced, not knowing that the MS *St. Louis* would become a large prison whose 937 passengers would not disembark into Cuba or any other country in the Western Hemisphere. My parents' world was quickly changing. The fear on my mother's face was clear. Our ship stayed ten days in Havana Harbor, and only a few souls disembarked. According to government officials, our visas were invalid, and we were turned away.

We tried to enter Miami but again were told to move on because according to the US State Department, we were in violation of US territorial laws. After pleading with other countries, including Canada, and getting rejected numerous times, we had to go back to Europe and an uncertain fate. The ship returned to the Port of Antwerp, Belgium, where we had to choose a country that would give us refuge from the Nazis. My parents and my grandfather (Opa) chose France, where we rented an apartment in a town called Nay, in the Pyrenees. We stayed there together until September 9, 1942.

I remember the landlady, Eletta Carapezzi Enard, whom we called "Maman," as a tall French woman with movie-star looks.

The Koeppels with another passenger on the MS *St. Louis.*

My parents and my grandfather rented a small apartment above a furniture factory that belonged to Maman.

Early one morning, there was a knock on our door. It was the Vichy police coming to arrest us—because we were Jews! I remember my grandfather in his bed, crying uncontrollably. At that time, I didn't understand why. I just tried to console him as only a four-year-old could. I said goodbye to him and went with my parents. I recall seeing my mom whisper something to Maman before we were taken by the police. I've often wondered what my mother said to her.

We were first taken to Gurs, a detention camp in the south of France, and later to Rivesaltes, another camp. From Gurs, I only remember soldiers standing with machine guns. Although I was only four and a half years old, I have some vivid memories of Rivesaltes. I recall a beautiful family, a mother and her three children, that were across from me in the barracks.

One day, as my mother was playing with me, she said with a sadness in her eyes I cannot forget, "Judy, Mommy and Daddy have to go away, and we don't know when we will be back." Of course, I could not comprehend this, and we continued to play. But the sadness remained. Later that day, my father said, "Judy, let's take a walk."

"Okay!" I replied. My mother gave me a quick kiss on the cheek and cheerfully told us to have a good time. Her kiss meant, "Goodbye."

My dad and I walked into the darkness until we came to a lit room where someone greeted us. I was given something warm

Judith Koeppel, left, poses with Suzy, the daughter of her rescuer, and another child. Nay, France; June 1946.

and sweet to drink. I held my dad's hand with my left one. He pointed to my right side to distract me and said, "Look over there, Judy!" I looked, and then I heard him say, "Just a minute." Then, he let go of my hand.

My hand was picked up by someone else. My father was gone, and I never saw him or my mother again. In that one instant, my life changed forever.

I remember screaming inside a room along with many other children who were also crying for their parents. That night, I fell asleep from sheer exhaustion, or maybe because of the hot drink I was given earlier.

The next morning, I woke up to find the Rivesaltes barracks empty. Papa Enard came for me and brought me back to Opa at his apartment. All the prisoners were put onto trains to Drancy and then to Auschwitz. My parents had been warned by the mother of the "beautiful family" not to take me on the train with them since Auschwitz wasn't a work camp. My mother was so right to listen to her.

Now, I can't help but to imagine how my dad returned to my mom after handing me over to the OSE (*Oeuvre de Secours aux Enfants*). How they must have clung to one another, supporting each other, and praying together. I hope my parents knew that, somehow, I would survive.

I was covered with sores. Maman had to douse the sores with iodine, and I remember screaming from the sting of the medicine. Later, Maman sent for a doctor who said I suffered from malnutrition, and he wasn't sure if I would survive. I believe Maman's loving, healing hands helped me to recover. I loved hearing Maman sing to me in French, Spanish, and Italian.

Maman risked her life and the lives of her family in order to keep me alive. Without her, I would never have survived. As she tended to my sores, she was also healing my broken heart.

Shortly, after arriving at Maman's, my grandfather suffered a major stroke and was hospitalized. I visited him in the hospital once before he passed away. I believe he died from a broken heart.

I soon became a little French girl who went to school and church. Out of respect for my Jewish background, they never tried to convert me to Christianity. From time to time, I would

Judith, second from right in the front row (wearing hat) with other children at the OSE home in France. August 1946, before boarding a ship to the US.

ask Maman, "When are my mother and father coming back?" But unfortunately, there was no answer.

Today, I look at my early childhood with much gratitude. I am thankful for the love I received from Maman, and of course, from my natural parents. It is only through their love that I survived the Holocaust.

The war in Europe ended when the Americans liberated France. It was a joyous time. But it also meant that I would have to leave the home, where I felt loved for four and a half years. The Enards had protected me and kept me alive, and I wanted to stay with Maman, the only mother I knew outside of my real mom.

I stayed with Maman for another year and a half. Then the time came when Maman had to take me to Paris to the OSE headquarters. Maman and I checked into a hotel, and she put me to bed, chanting a beautiful lullaby with her sweet voice.

I had come to Maman with a doctor doubting my survival. It was Maman who loved me and took care of me as if I were her own child. Thinking of my life without her was unimaginable. She did try to prepare me, but I was now an eight-year-old who couldn't understand the concept of leaving her.

The next day, when we got to the office of the OSE, Maman told me she had to leave me there. The news made all my fears of abandonment and rage resurface. It was the same feeling of my

Judy with Maman Enard in 1992.

father giving me away four years earlier. I held onto her hand, begging her not to leave me. It took two or three people to pry me away from her. I screamed at the top of my lungs, "Please Maman! Don't go! Don't abandon me!" The pain of it all was happening again.

The next day, I was taken to an OSE orphanage called Villa des Glycines, where I stayed with other war orphans until the OSE was able to book me on a ship to America. I was told that I would live with my aunt, uncle, and two cousins, who were "very rich." But it didn't matter to me. I wanted to stay in the only home that I knew, where I was very much loved. Through all of this, I kept the hope that Maman would come to get me. When I saw her years later, she told me how she could not stop crying, how she felt her heart breaking that day, and how life was never the same for her.

Cantor **Judith Steel** *is an Interfaith minister and an active speaker for organizations, schools, and places of worship. She recently published a memoir,* Love Brought Me Through the Holocaust: A Daughter's Memories.

Survival in Shanghai, China, During World War II

By Evelyn Pike Rubin

(From The Hidden Child, *Volume XIII, 2005.)*

I was born in Breslau, now Wroczław, Poland, at the onset of the Nazi era, to an Orthodox, Zionist family that had been in Germany for many generations. My father, a patriotic German, had fought for Germany during World War I and had been awarded the Iron Cross Second Class by Kaiser Wilhelm II.

In 1935, after the promulgation of the Nuremberg Laws, my parents began looking for countries to which we could immigrate. They tried Brazil, Palestine (under British Mandate), Cuba, England, and America—all to no avail.

Evelyn on her first day of school in Breslau, Germany, 1935.

In the spring of 1938, after the annexation of Austria, we heard that, as victors of the Sino-Japanese war of 1937, the Japanese had established Shanghai as an "open city." There was a good possibility one could go there without a visa just for the price of a steamship ticket.

November 9 and 10, 1938, *Kristallnacht*, was the beginning of the end. My father was among those arrested and sent to the camp of Buchenwald. During his incarceration, my mother purchased tickets for us to leave for Shanghai the following February. This was most fortuitous, for the Nazis decided to release almost all those arrested during the Kristallnacht pogrom, with the proviso that they leave Germany within two months. My father was released in December. On February 9, 1939, we took the train over the Brenner Pass for the month-long voyage into the unknown.

We arrived in Shanghai on March 14, 1939. Although the Japanese controlled the city, the French administered the French Concession, the westernized residential area; the British administered the International Settlement, the business sector; and the Japanese administered Hongkew, a mostly slum area that had taken the brunt of the 1937 war. The city had a population of approximately eight million, consisting of a large number of foreigners besides the local people. There were Russians—Jewish and non-Jewish—who had fled the 1917 Revolution, Baghdadi Jews, and businesspeople from many European countries and from the United States, who were in charge of branch offices of their respective firms. Also present were staff members of the American Joint Distribution Committee, who provided funds to help the refugees settle in what was thought to be a temporary refuge.

What greeted us was shocking—horrific, unhygienic conditions, which produced widespread epidemics. We had to be inoculated against cholera, typhoid, and paratyphoid three times a year, and smallpox once a year. All drinking water, fruits, and vegetables had to be boiled or cooked for at least five minutes.

My mother sold our personal possessions to purchase an apartment in the French Concession and to establish a typewriter business. My father did the repairs with the help of a hired Chinese mechanic, and my mother handled the bookkeeping, appointments, and paperwork.

We then arranged for my paternal grandmother—the only grandparent left—to come to Shanghai. She arrived on a hot, sultry day in June 1941, wearing her *sheitl*, a long black dress, and high boots. My mother persuaded her to discard the sheitl because of the oppressive heat. I had never seen her without it, and it seemed strange to see her gray, wispy hair. She looked

第 926 號
無國籍避難民
通行許可證
住所 四九八弄 八 號
職業 上海猶太學校生徒
氏名 Popielarz Evelyn
年齡 12 年
右無國籍避難民指定地域外ノ通行ヲ許可ス
上海無國籍避難民處理事務所
0 MAY 1944
0 OCT 1944

Special pass issued by Japanese occupation authorities to leave ghetto area, 1943–45.

very different. What she would not discard, however, was the featherbed she had brought with her.

I continued my interrupted schooling at the Shanghai Jewish School, a British school founded, administered, and subsidized by two philanthropic Baghdadi families—the Kadooris and the Sassoons. I learned English rather quickly, as well as French and Hebrew.

The attrition rate of the refugee community, which was to number approximately eighteen thousand by 1941, was tremendous. Many could not endure the subtropical climate, the cold, wet winters, the monsoon rains that overflowed the sewer system, leaving streets constantly flooded, and the unbearably hot summers.

My grandmother was happy to take care of the household. It gave her a purpose. We had a Chinese servant called "Number One Boy" who shopped for groceries while my grandmother took care of the cooking. He did not speak German and she did not speak English or Chinese. They would yell at each other constantly—and yet over time, a mutual respect developed.

Then, my father who had always been very healthy, became ill. The doctors were baffled. First, they pulled out all his teeth; then they put him on all kinds of medications. He did get better. But suddenly, he was sick again. It started with a sprained ankle; one week later, he was dead. The only diagnosis that the doctors could offer was that he must have gotten a parasite while in Buchenwald, where his old war wound had acted up and been left untreated. (As a German soldier during World War I, my father had been wounded at Verdun and imprisoned by the French.) In a different climate, with better surroundings, he might have survived. Of course, we'll never know. It was March 1941, and he was only forty-three years old. This left my grieving mother, my seventy-two-year-old grandmother, and me.

My mother continued operating the typewriter business, together with the Chinese mechanic, doing quite well by putting in long hours. Of course, we still observed the Sabbath, so she worked on Sundays, *shlepping* typewriters in a rickshaw to customers all over the city. These were mostly American and English with some French and German.

We awoke to a tremendous explosion in Shanghai's harbor, followed by a parade of the Imperial Japanese Army and Navy. Shortly thereafter, enemy aliens of Japan and Nazi Germany were interned in camps, where they were to stay for the duration of the war. So far, we refugees were left alone. A tremendous food shortage developed, only slightly alleviated by sugar, flour, and rice rations. The American staff members of the Joint were repatriated to the United States and the stranded refugee community no longer received financial assistance. My mother now ran the typewriter business by herself, but there was not much business. Her American and other foreign customers were either interned or had liquidated their businesses. Shanghai was now isolated from the rest of the world.

I continued attending the Shanghai Jewish School, which remained open even though the Japanese had interned most of our instructors. We were left with a few of our Russian and Iraqi teachers.

On February 18, 1943, the Japanese issued a proclamation: the refugee community had three months to "relocate to a designated area." In effect, we were relegated into a ghetto area within Hongkew.

My grandmother died just before our move. My mother sold our apartment to a Japanese family, and with three other families, we moved into a three-room hovel with one bathroom, cold running water, and no heat. We cooked over a little rooftop stove, forming egg-shaped coals from coal dust mixed with cold water. Hot water or boiling water could be purchased from the hot water stand. The food shortage became even more acute, and refugees were not just dying of disease but also of starvation and despondency.

Many students at the Shanghai Jewish School transferred to the Kadoorie School in the ghetto area. This school, established by the wealthy Kadoorie family on a piece of land they had purchased, was staffed with refugee teachers. Even though it could take us up to two hours or more to continue to attend the Shanghai Jewish School, my friends and I opted for this. In order to leave the ghetto area, a *Tung*, or special pass, had to be obtained from the Japanese authorities. Mr. Ghoya, who proclaimed himself "King of the Jews," administered the passes. Most applicants who could demonstrate a need to make a living outside the ghetto received one. My friends and I received our passes from Mr. Ghoya without a problem. Adult applicants did not have it quite as easy.

My mother also applied, declaring that as a typewriter mechanic she still had customers in the French Concession. Actually, she had none! She used her pass to seek out Chinese peddlers in parts of the city that were not often frequented by westerners. There, she purchased sundries, such as scarves, sunglasses, and belts, which she brought back to sell to refugee street peddlers. This did not bring in much money, but it kept us one step above starvation.

My mother and I were the only ones in our ghetto house to continue to observe the Sabbath and Kashrut. While others rendered pork lard on their little stoves, we rendered beef fat, pretending it was chicken. It smelled up the whole house. Ailments such as malaria, jaundice, intestinal worms, and the usual colds were rampant. Medicine was available from the refugee doctors who received their supplies from the Health Department run by the Japanese authorities. And vermin such as huge, flying cockroaches, red spiders, centipedes, mosquitoes, mice, and rats abounded.

My mother improvised our meals. From young Chinese boys, she bought noodles that they had obtained by chasing grocery trucks and slitting sacks. The scattered noodles would be swept up from the gutter and sold very cheaply. My mother and I would sit by the light of the kerosene lamp to separate the street debris from the noodles. To make a spread, she would mix about one ounce of peanut butter with five or six ounces of syrup. The one egg that we could sometimes afford became a delicious dessert lasting two or three days. Salami, bought by the slice from the refugee grocer, was cut into four pieces. Each day, one piece filled a sandwich. For Shabbat, Yom Tov, and Chanukah, my mother fashioned "candles" out of small, rounded pieces of metal, oil, and a piece of cotton to serve as a wick. The *Juedische Gemeinde* (Jewish community) baked *matzoth* for Pesach by having all of us contribute our flour coupons.

Sometime in 1944, the Joint in New York managed to get funds for refugees, and soup kitchens were again established. While there were already a number of refugees who had died of starvation, many more were saved by this.

We were constantly being strafed by American planes, and, as we watched the American and Japanese fighter planes above, the children's favorite pastime was to bet with marbles as to who would shoot down whom. The Japanese had an excellent air raid alert system that warned us about attacks.

In May 1945, when we heard that the war had ended in Europe, we were euphoric—until we heard the horrific news. Only then did we learn how lucky we were. After all, we were still alive, even though, being in the Pacific Theater, we were still at war. When would it also end for us? Not so quickly. We were very worried when we heard about the atomic bombs being dropped on Hiroshima and subsequently on Nagasaki. Would the Americans also drop this bomb on us in Shanghai?

They did drop bombs, though not atomic ones. On July 17, 1945, American fighter planes appeared suddenly over the Shanghai sky and bombed the ghetto, hitting the radio station. The bombs, unfortunately, also killed thirty refugees and wounded hundreds, as well as a great number of the Chinese inhabitants.

A month later, Maj. Gen. Claire Chenault came with the American Liberation Forces from Chungking. We were free at last!

It would take another two to three years for the refugees to find new homes in many corners of the world—Australia, Israel, America. Almost no one went back to Europe.

Thus ended another chapter of Holocaust survival. When the world closed their doors to the Jews, Emperor Hirohito of Japan left one door open, through which approximately eighteen thousand entered. And when the Nazi Fifth Column, active even in Shanghai, tried to impose their "final solution" on this refugee colony by asking the Japanese authorities to either shoot us or put us out to sea on boats without any food or water, they refused to comply. Their compromise was to put us into a ghetto area.

Evelyn Pike Rubin *is the author of* Ghetto Shanghai *(Shengold Publishers, 1993), an amazing story of sanctuary and survival.*

The Saga of the Tehran Children

By Dorit B. Whiteman, PhD

(Excerpted from The Hidden Child, *Volume XIII, 2005.)*

Almost one thousand Polish Jewish children who fled from Poland into Russian-occupied territory during WWII came to be known as the Tehran Children. The Nazis had hunted them for being Jewish, and once in Russian territory, they were persecuted for being Polish. The ultimate rescue of some of these children was due to innumerable, unexpected political twists as well as to the combined humanitarian efforts by England, the United States, the Jewish Agency in Palestine, and the resolute and resourceful leadership of the Hadassah. Ultimately, the Tehran Children endured endless hardships, but in the end, they prevailed.

When Hitler invaded Poland, many Poles—Jews and Christians—fled to the eastern part of the country. This territory had become Russian as a result of a prewar, non-aggression pact between Hitler and Stalin. In return for allowing the Nazis to take over Poland, Hitler gave Stalin the eastern section of Poland and promised not to invade Russia. The fleeing Poles hoped that the Russians would be more benign than the Nazis. They were wrong. The Russians immediately arrested all former Polish soldiers, sending them to Siberia. Thousands of Polish officers were murdered. It is not generally known that during the Russian occupation of Poland, the Russians killed more Poles than the Nazis did.

Many of the Jews who fled from the Nazis made their way to Lvov (now Lviv). Under Russian occupation, the once beautiful city had become wasted and overcrowded. Whatever was

The "Tehran Children" arrive in Israel, February 1943.

movable was requisitioned and sent back to Russia, leaving the local inhabitants without food and clothing. People were arrested for the slightest transgressions and frequently disappeared forever. The Jewish population tried to survive. But in 1940, the Russians began a roundup of thousands of Poles, both Jewish and Christian, hurtling them in cattle cars and shipping them to Siberia. Many people perished during the agonizing journey north. Their bodies were tossed out of the train and left near the tracks. In the chaos, many children became separated from their parents. Many adults succumbed to the dreadful conditions, and their children became orphans.

Once the deportees reached the gulags, they lived under the most primitive conditions. Food rations were based on unreachable work quotas. If prisoners failed to reach these, their meager food rations were decreased. The resulting evil cycle all too often led to death.

Soon, there were many pathetic orphans resorting to any means to stay alive. One girl carried soup from the kitchen to adults, who, after a fourteen-hour workday, were too tired to fetch their portion. In return for each portion delivered, she received one spoonful of soup. Another child went from shack to shack, singing in the hope of receiving a morsel of food. Working in a flour mill was an enviable job. When unobserved, the children ate the raw flour. Many people lost hope of ever being able to leave.

The fate of the prisoners changed suddenly, however. In 1941, Hitler broke the non-aggression pact and invaded Russia. Stalin was shocked by Hitler's action. Not only was he totally unprepared, but, in his paranoia, he had executed so many Russian officers that the army lacked leadership. In desperation, he turned to England for help. The British agreed, but they demanded that the Russians release the Polish soldiers and allow them to join the allied forces. Trapped and desperate, Stalin agreed to release seventy thousand Polish soldiers and thirty thousand Polish civilians. They were to be allowed to leave Russia under the command of Polish General Wladyslaw Anders, who was being held prisoner in Lubianka, one of Russia's worst prisons.

Upon their release, the prisoners had to make their own way from Siberia to General Anders's assembly point, Tashkent, located in the south of Russia. The orphaned children left the gulags as well. The Polish government-in-exile in London sent Polish social workers from England to Russia. They were assigned the very difficult job of searching for these children and placing them in orphanages. The NKVD, the Russian secret police, pursued the social workers and tried to incarcerate them.

The orphanages were wretched places. There was little food. The children infected one another with illnesses that their weakened state could not resist. The death toll continued to be high. The Jewish children had an additional problem. Many of the orphanages were antisemitic and refused to accept them. Even when they did, the Jewish children were taunted by the others and frequently were not given their share of food. All the orphanages were supposed to follow Anders' Army. But frequently, counselors would not allow Jewish children to join the exodus.

Since only thirty thousand civilians could follow General Anders, they believed that the more Jewish children were excluded, the more Christian children would find places. Desperate to be accepted, some Jewish children pretended to be Christian. Fortunately, there were also Christian directors of orphanages and local priests who insisted on including Jewish children. However, the percentage of Jews accepted was relatively small.

From the collection point in Tashkent, the children were brought on trucks to the eastern side of the Caspian Sea. Among them were nearly one thousand Jewish children. Not all were orphans. Some, often at their parents' urging, pretended not to have parents since the *Kindertransport* was basically meant for orphans. The children sailed across the Caspian Sea. Once they reached the western shore and they were no longer in Russia, their joy was enormous. The NKVD and the SS could no longer reach them, but their suffering was not over.

From the Caspian Sea, they traveled in rickety trucks to Tehran. There was very little food or drinking water. Their clothes were in tatters and illnesses were rampant. By the time the children reached Tehran, they were half-dead. Asked to examine them, a physician exclaimed, "I thought you were bringing me children, not corpses."

After fleeing the Nazis and losing family, after horrific experiences in the gulags, the children's emotional state was fragile. Added to all this, antisemitism was still rampant. The Jewish head counselor, David Laor, saw that the children needed stability and security. He received permission to organize a separate camp for the Jewish children. He established a routine and organized classes and sports activities. Still, conditions remained primitive, food was sparse, and medical supplies were limited.

The Jewish children were to be sent to Palestine. In order to do so, it was necessary for them to cross Iraq. But the Iraqi government was uncooperative. Weeks went by, then months, while the children languished in Tehran. The British and American governments, as well as the Jewish Agency in Palestine, made every effort to persuade the Iraqis to allow the Jewish children to pass. The resolute women of the Hadassah in the US used every connection they had to help the children. All to no avail. They stayed on and on in Tehran and became known as the Tehran Children.

When the British and American governments became convinced that the Iraqis would never allow the children to cross Iraq, they realized they had to find another way. Since planes could not be freed from their wartime use, the British government decided to take the children through a long and dangerous route by sea. The children were to sail through the Persian Gulf to Karachi and from there, across the Red Sea to Egypt on an ancient vessel. From Port Said, it was only a short train ride away to Palestine.

The journey was extremely dangerous. The seas were filled with mines. There was the danger of submarines, torpedoes, and air attacks. The children stopped in Karachi. Hearing that nearly one thousand exhausted Jewish children were arriving, the Bombay Jewish community sent badly needed clothes. After a two-week stay in Karachi, the children continued their journey on a different, equally ancient ship. There were not enough life preservers, food, or fresh water, and danger was continual. When the children finally arrived in Palestine, hundreds of Jewish men, women, and children came to welcome them, ecstatic that nearly one thousand Jewish children had survived in the middle of the war.

It is impossible in one article to convey the daily tragedies and triumphs, the children's emotional reactions, and the dedication of the people caring for them. In *Escape via Siberia*, I relate the story as told to me by one of the Tehran Children. Reading about him brings the story of the Tehran Children to life. The sheer luck, courage, resourcefulness, and physical strength necessary for survival can best be conveyed through the odyssey of one individual. By the age of thirteen, Lonek had fled from the Nazis, endured months in a gulag, and traveled on his own on the *Kindertransport* leaving Russia. He triumphed over hunger, loneliness, and temporary blindness to survive and fight in Israel's War of Independence. He is a worthy representative of the Tehran Children's ordeal, survival, and victory.

Dr. **Dorit B. Whiteman** *is the author of* The Uprooted: A Hitler Legacy, *and of* Escape via Siberia: A Jewish Child's Odyssey of Survival.

Escape to Russia and Beyond

By Ruth L. Weiss Hohberg

(Excerpted from My Story, *Volume XVI, January 2022.)*

In the summer of 1939, when I was four years old, my mother and I were vacationing in Zakopane. In an effort to keep us safe from Hitler's advance, my father instructed us not to return home but to continue east to Krakow to join his twin sister. From there, we took a train to Lvov (now Lviv) to stay with another relative. During that time, my father remained in the three-story home my Grandpa built in Bielitz to help Grandpa. They left eventually, crossing Poland on foot to join Mother and me.

One early morning, there was insistent pounding on the door and a group of angry, shouting Russian soldiers broke in. They ransacked all the rooms but couldn't find whatever they were looking for. They ordered us to pack a few essentials and leave within thirty minutes. We were rushed into lorries and taken to the railway station, where trains of cattle wagons stood waiting. Four weeks of travel later, we arrived somewhere empty and were unloaded.

On a low, bare hill in a cleared part of the forest, partially built log cabins with gaping holes for windows and doors awaited. They stood silent, empty, waiting for windowpanes and people. Inside, there were no accommodations of civilized life—no plumbing, no lighting—such as we had previously taken for granted.

The weather had turned bitter cold. We still had no clear idea where in the world we were. Later, we learned we were in a Soviet Republic in Siberia called Yakutsk, three hundred miles from the nearest railway station. My parents and I, my grandparents, aunts Sala and Peppi, and a couple named Kaminski, were assigned to our cabin.

In the first section nearest the entrance was a stove, to provide heat and a cooking surface, and a rough wooden table and benches. The space was to serve as the communal room, kitchen, and laundry. Each family group had a room. This was home from now on.

It was October 1939. Doors and windows had to be provided and installed quickly, lest we freeze to death. Somehow, with the help of the new arrivals and the military in charge, the essentials were accomplished. Gray, quilted, Chinese-style jackets (*fufaikas*), pants, caps with furry ear flaps, and felt boots (*valenki*) were distributed, and everyone of working age was assigned a job. Roll call was every evening at six.

Felling forests, clearing boulders to build roads, fighting fires, and occasional farm-related work were the most common tasks assigned. Per regulations, the workweek was six days, from dawn to dusk. Often a seventh day was required as a "voluntary" gesture for the war effort. When a forest fire was out of control, people were temporarily pulled from their other jobs to help. My mother, always slender and delicate, was put to work fertilizing potato fields with buckets of liquefied manure, which had to be lifted out of a huge vat. There were many unhappy incidents of spills, leaving bad smells and memories for all concerned.

My father's job was clearing forests. Being rational by nature, making the best of a bad situation and not wanting to get killed by a falling tree, he managed to make this dangerous occupation interesting for himself by using his knowledge of physics to calculate the direction and timing of a tree's fall. He found joy in the awesome landscape and pointed out its unspoiled wild beauty to his fellow prisoners as they trudged through the forest in the dark, before dawn, on their way to their workstations. The temperatures reached minus sixty degrees centigrade. The air was so clean, the snow never looked dirty. It was very deep, its crystals glistening when the sun shone, and it remained packed hard until it began to melt in mid-May.

For his midday meal, Father carried a piece of black bread saved from the previous day's ration and black coffee in a tin can that had frozen into a block of ice during the night. I stayed with my grandmother and my great aunts because I was too young to go to work. My grandma made sure I observed the Sabbath by keeping me from doing anything playful or useful that day. I wasn't very enthusiastic. She told me that God sees and knows all things, even my secret thoughts, and that he wants me to observe the day.

Occasionally, a few *kulaks*, the remaining Russian farmers dispossessed from their lands and exiled to these frozen wastes earlier in the century by Stalin's orders, appeared in this sparsely populated Taiga region. Sometimes, an old Chinese man selling bok choy came around our settlement. It appeared that we were probably not very far from the Chinese border. What follows are some recollections of life in the "northern winter wonderland."

While playing with children from a nearby cabin, a boy tossed a rock that hit me in the forehead, making it spring a torrent of blood. Grandma comforted me and said I shouldn't be angry but had to be compassionate and pray for him. Remarkable lady.

It was a crisis when I lost one of my mittens in a snowbank while playing. That loss took on potentially tragic dimensions when my mother found out. She scolded and cried, while my father went to search the snowbank with me and tried to soothe and assure us both that somehow, we would keep my hand from freezing for the remainder of the winter. Mother knew that we had no materials available to knit a replacement. She also knew that frostbite often resulted in the loss of a digit or the entire limb; this posed a serious problem. I don't remember what the resolution was, but I have all my fingers, although they bear the effects of frostbite.

Our food rations were quite stringent at this time. Bread was one half a kilogram (about a pound) per adult per day with something like a quarter pound of butter per month, if it was available. Sugar, flour, eggs, coffee, and tea were sporadically brought in by truck and doled out until supplies ran out. Those who were not so lucky as to be in the front of the queue returned to their cabins empty-handed, despite having stood in line for many hours no matter the weather.

Sometimes, even frills like hair-ribbons were delivered. For my fifth birthday, I was given two sets: one red, the other maroon. The maroon ones were for "every day," the red ones were plaited into my pigtails on special occasions, like Saturdays and holidays, for the next five years.

The men found they could plant potatoes secretly, thus, often frozen, they were more readily available than other foods. One of my mother's earliest culinary efforts that winter was a potato soup, which was much too salty for my taste. I refused to eat it. My mother, already on edge, became hysterical; in the heat of the moment, she tried to pull me from the table by the arms and to force me out of the house into the cold. She was convinced I would starve unless I ate that watery, salty concoction. Aunt Peppi came to my rescue, and while the two women engaged in an argument over me, she convinced my mother that I wouldn't starve in spite of not eating that particular soup. It was my mother's lowest point of despair, sanity, and civility.

One afternoon, my mother arrived back from work earlier than usual. Working hours were not over. She was distraught and in tears. She was rubbing her nose. It had become white with frostbite eleven times that day. She could not take any more of the bitter cold. I don't know how she managed not to be jailed for this break in discipline; perhaps the authorities and the doctor worked it out.

Luckily, there was a medical doctor in the group on our transport. There was no hospital or medical facility where a sick person could turn for help. He was supplied with minimal basic medications, syringes for injections, and whatever else became available at intervals of varying length, until the road became impassable.

In this northern winter wonderland, considered to be the end of the earth in those days, the long icicles melted into potable water. In the short summer, edible plants such as mushrooms, blueberries, raspberries, pine nuts, and onions grew wild. I was too young

Ruth in 1946.

to appreciate its awesome natural beauty. City folks like us had to learn to use these to stave off starvation and as many symptoms of malnutrition as possible. Those who failed to learn, quickly died.

We were cut off from communication with the outside world, but occasionally mail did come through, and my parents were called upon to translate English, French, or German correspondence. Any news was an occasion, and it made the rounds. Whenever my parents translated a letter, I got the stamps. There was one with the likeness of a dark-haired handsome man with an intense, direct look. I liked him a lot. When I grew older, I discovered that he was the Shah of Iran.

To leave the settlement for any reason, one had to obtain a signed permit from the commandant. One day, my grandfather received permission to go to the only established town in the area. The village commandant gave him the pass and asked him, as a favor, to deliver an envelope to the government building.

Grandpa did not return to us that evening, and all inquiries to our commandant were met with a shrug. The following days

Ruth with her father in 1946.

and nights were awful. We had no idea what may have befallen him. Did he get sick? Eaten by wolves? By bears? Or did he lose his way in the unending taiga where there were no landmarks? There was nothing we could do to find him. The official who gave him the envelope had no answers, only that shrug. We were very upset and totally helpless.

Ten days later, Grandpa appeared gaunt, hollow-eyed, and permanently saddened. Much later we found out that the envelope contained an order for his arrest. The reason? "Exploitation of labor." During the summer, Grandpa had arranged to pay two young men for their help to chop wood for the winter. The Soviet system was so hypersensitive to having anyone perform a task that looked even remotely as if it might be servitude that common sense was entirely absent. Justice was not even in the vocabulary. We had no recourse but to bless the day he returned to us, considerably aged by his experience in a Siberian jail.

After the signing of a pact between General Sikorsky and Stalin in 1941, we were permitted to leave the Siberian settlement and to travel within the Soviet Union, provided we stayed away from metropolitan areas.

Ruth L. Weiss Hohberg *is an artist and a writer. She graduated from the High School of Music and Art, Cooper Union School of Art, City College (BA), the College of New Rochelle (MA), and finally Yeshiva University (MSW). She enjoys painting and photography and has exhibited her work and won a few prizes. Her published pieces are,* Getting Here: An Odyssey through World War II, A Girl from Bielsko, Vignettes from Life, Here and There, Going Places, Witness and Survivor, *and* The View from Jerusalem. *The last two books are translations from German of parts of her great-uncle's journal of the war and subsequent life in Jerusalem.*

PART X

The Aftermath

Yaakov's Story: A Jewish Child in Christian Disguise

By Jack Kuper (born Yaakov Kuperblum)

(Excerpted from The Hidden Child, *Volume XXIII, 2015.)*

Since my arrival at the Kozaks, I had attended church on Sundays. After the liberation, I continued doing so even though I understood little of what went on. When others knelt, I knelt; when others stood, I stood. I wanted to stop this charade and found myself going to church instinctively. My daily prayers were no longer aimed at fooling people; I said them with conviction and sincerity. Such discoveries upset me, for now I realized how far removed I had become from Jankele Kuperblum. There seemed to be two of me: one Jankele Kuperblum, the other Franek Zielinski. I could visualize the latter, but Jankele Kuperblum was almost a blur. I feared forgetting my real name and repeated it often to myself in the dark of night.

Terrible guilt beset me, and my inner voice rebuked me. Shame Jankele! Shame! You're free and yet you make no attempt to return to the fold. I had survived, I thought, but for what? Where are the others?

In the village, stories circulated of returning Jews reclaiming their properties and being found floating in the river. "Mr. Kozak!" I addressed my employer. He puffed on his pipe and kept turning the wheel of the chaff-cutting machine. "Mr. Kozak," I blurted out with a trembling voice, "I'm a Jew! I think it would be better if I left." His eyes bulged with anger. "Never!" he shouted. "I saved your life, boy! All of us could have been killed and everything we own could have been burned to the ground! You'll

Jack Kuper, age eight, with little brother Josele in the Warsaw Ghetto.

stay right here and work for me the rest of your life!" Nevertheless, I made plans to leave. Another week went by. Although it was a warm day, I put on my two pairs of underwear, two shirts, and both of my trousers.

I returned to the shtetl where I had last seen my mother. No one was waiting for me. At a time when Jewish boys have their bar mitzvahs, I entered a church and asked to be baptized. The priest suggested I come back when I turned twenty-one and advised I go to Lublin where I would find other survivors.

On the train, I met a boy returning home to Lublin and asked him if it's true that the Nazis had left and the *Yids* are back. "They're crawling like bed bugs out of a mattress," he replied. I spent the night on the station floor and, early the next morning, faced the city covered in mist. I started to walk, seeing only a few meters in front of me. I saw no one but heard footsteps and motor vehicles coming from all directions. I was hesitant, uncertain, and fearful. Soon, a glowing sun made its appearance, and a full street came into view. I felt like a forest animal lured out into the open. If I could, I would have gladly returned to the safety of the Kozak farm.

In a store window, I caught the image of a young boy with cropped hair, torn trousers, and bare feet caked in dirt. Is it really me? Would my family recognize me? Where shall I go? I approached a stranger but quickly turned from him. If I asked him about Jews, he might suspect, and....

In the end, I chose an individual walking in my direction and casually asked, as if the question carried no importance, "I hear the Jews are back?" He grabbed me by the sleeve. "You're a Jew!" I protested and loosened his grip. "Wait!" he called after me. We turned a corner. "Look," he pointed to a droshky with a mustached driver with two well-dressed passengers reclining in comfort. "Yours!"

My heart pounded. "Come! Come!" called my guide, and I followed.

"There!" he said, pointing to a short, stocky man leaning against a courtyard gate. "One of yours," he pushed me and disappeared into the crowd.

The stocky man took a puff on a cigarette, eyeing me with suspicion. "Are you a Jew?" I asked with a mixture of repulsion and kinship. He turned from me and proceeded toward the courtyard. "I'm a Jew, from Pulawy." I ran after him. "Be on your way, boy!" he barked angrily over his shoulder and opened a door, about to enter, but I held onto his jacket.

"Please believe me!" I pleaded. "This *shagitz* says he's a Jew," he addressed a passing neighbor. Both rocked with laughter. Before I knew it, the two vanished into a building and bolted the door. I pounded on it. "If you don't go away, I'll call the police," I heard the threatening voice. "Please," I begged, "I'll pull down my pants to prove it." The door slowly opened. "Come," he said and led me down a dark hallway and into a dimly lit room.

A bear of a man with curly red hair laid on an iron bed as a brood of children jumped on him. Finally focusing on me, he asked in a hoarse voice, "What have we here?"

"He claims he's from Pulawy."

The bear motioned to come closer. "Who's your father?" he snapped. "Zelik Kuperblum," I answered somewhat afraid. "Zelik's son? You're Zelik's son? The baker Chaya-Yeta's grandson then!" I nodded. "A relative of yours lives down the street," he said. A chill raced through my veins, wondering who it might be. "Follow me," said the man who had brought me there and, after a short walk, led me into a courtyard and there, in a shop, introduced me to a barber busily shaving a customer. After hearing me out, the barber bolted from the shop shouting toward a window above! "Sarah!" A young woman stuck her head out. "Come down quickly!" Panting, she flew down the rickety stairs. "Who do you think this is? Take a guess," urged her husband. "What's to guess? A peasant."

They both shot questions at me. How had I survived? What happened to my parents? They, in turn, explained how we were related.

The connection was nebulous, but I was pleased to be attached to someone...anyone. The apartment consisted of two tiny rooms. The freshly scrubbed floors were covered with newspaper. Cousin Sarah began to chop fish, and the staccato sound conjured up so many images, as did the aromas emanating from the stove, which brought back memories of my childhood in Pulawy. At dinner, Sarah covered her head with a white shawl and, closing her eyes, she blessed the candles with circling hand motions. I looked at her face and was reminded of my mother.

First, we ate gefilte fish with horseradish and challah, followed by chicken soup with noodles and lima beans. The taste was so familiar and yet so very foreign. Mesmerized by the flickering candles, I stopped eating. When I glanced up, I caught my hosts studying me. "What's the matter, Jankele, don't you like it?" asked Cousin Sarah. My tears dropped into the soup. I lowered my head, spooning the soup with the tears. For the first time since leaving home, I rested my head on a real pillow and covered my body with soft feather bedding. Sleep came easily....

The Orphanage

"How come you can't speak Yiddish?" asked some of the orphans after I had been there a while. "I forgot." "Maybe you never knew it, eh? You call yourself Jankele, but you don't look or act like a Jankele. And what's this?" asked one, displaying the Saint Francis medallion I had hidden under the mattress upon my arrival. I felt like a shadow, a ghost, or even less than that. One night, I was awakened by a whisper, "He's a Jew!" I opened my eyes and was blinded by a flashlight. My bedcover was on the floor and faces were staring at my nakedness. Jumping out of bed, I began swinging my arms. The gang quickly scattered. I followed and stumbled. The lights switched on. Eyes peeked out from under blankets. Others feigned sleep. I pulled at their covers and smashed whatever was in my path.

"You jerks! You cowardly bastards! Bloody Christ killers!" I screamed. They stared in silent disbelief. Then I felt a blow in my stomach, another on my head, and I fell to the floor. I was picked up and slugged, kicked, and punched. The next morning when I awoke, my pillow was drenched in blood. My face was bruised, my right eye was half closed, and I was swollen everywhere.

A recent arrival to the orphanage who had witnessed the scuffle befriended me. His survival resembled mine, and like me, he still prayed to Jesus. He even managed to secretly attend church on Sundays. One day, he divulged he had arranged for his priest to baptize us and send us to a place no one could find.

On the appointed day when we reached the church, he scaled the stairs to the open, heavy door and entered the darkness while I watched from below. "What if my mother survived and came looking for me? And my father is probably in the Russian army, and he'll be searching for his Jankele." And with that, I ran to the Registry office where Jews left depositions of their survival on a message wall. Picking up a pencil hanging from a string and locating a blank spot, I scribbled: *Jankele Kuperblum is alive!*

At the age of fifteen, Jankele Kuperblum, now ***Jack Kuper****, went to Canada as one of a thousand war orphans sponsored by the Canadian Jewish community. He was placed in a foster home in Toronto and sent to the local public school. After a six-month English crash course, he enrolled at Central Tech to study commercial art. Upon graduation, in 1952, Jack was offered a job at the Canadian Broadcasting Corporation. He designed graphics, animated show openings, acted, wrote, and directed. By the time he left, thirteen years later, he was head of three departments: Graphics, Animation, and Still Photography.*

His memoir, Child of the Holocaust, *was published in 1967 and has been translated into eight languages. The sequel,* After the Smoke Cleared *(1994), won the Jewish Book Award for Holocaust Literature.*

Reuniting with Family

By Dr. Rose Kfar Rose, PhD

(From The Hidden Child, *Volume X, Number 1, 2001.)*

In August 1942, when over 60,000 Jews had been deported over a three-week period from Lvov (now Lviv), a city with a Jewish population of 135,000, my parents felt that we had to take drastic measures to save our lives. My father purchased false papers of a Christian girl, Janina Gornicka, and persuaded me to assume a Catholic identity. I was fifteen, did not want to leave my parents, and vigorously opposed this plan. But after they assured me that they would also make arrangements to hide from the Nazis, I agreed to escape the ghetto.

My parents instructed me that, should they not survive, I was to turn for help to my American relatives. I knew that my father had four brothers, one sister, and two uncles in the United States. I vaguely remembered my aunt, Entze Kfare, who visited us when I was four years old; and I had fond memories of my uncle, Charles Kfare, who came to Poland when I was eleven.

The arrangement was for me to live with a Polish schoolteacher, Krystyna Moskalik, in the small village of Sieciechowice, about nineteen miles from Krakow. I was to help her with chores around the house. Krystyna told her friends and neighbors that I was the daughter of a cousin, and accordingly I called her *Ciocia* (Aunt). Every day, I feared that I might do or say something that would give me away. In fact, in the summer of 1944, one of Krystyna's friends learned that I was Jewish and tried to blackmail her. But Krystyna refused to be intimidated, reminding the blackmailer that her own husband, a Polish Army officer, was also hiding

Family photo taken in 1938 when Charles Kfare visited Lvov, Poland. Seated, left to right: Charles Kfare, Chaya Sara Kfar (grandmother), Benzion Kfar (father). Standing, left to right: Pola Kfar, Roza Kfar (age eleven), Oscar Wasserman, Esther Kfar (mother), and Friedka Herzer.

from the Nazis. The rebuttal worked, but I lived through many frightening days.

The Russians liberated Sieciechowice in January 1945. During the war, I had continued my education under the guidance of clandestine Polish teachers. After the liberation, Krystyna encouraged me to move to Krakow where I could attend a real Lyceum. I still did not know what had happened to my parents. Krystyna had told me that my father had joined the partisans, and my mother had been hiding in a village near Lvov. On February 12, 1945, when I was seventeen and a half years old, I went to Krakow to live with Krystyna's friends.

Fearing widespread antisemitism, I continued to live under my assumed name, but I did register as Roza Kfar with the newly formed Jewish Committee. I kept checking with the Committee to see if any relatives had survived.

By accident, in March or April 1945, I met a close friend of the family, Mr. Shulim Kanner, who told me that my mother had escaped from the deportation train bound for Belzec but had died of typhus in February 1943. My father had escaped from the infamous Janowska camp in Lvov but had also died of typhus in March of 1943. By the time the ghetto in Lvov had been liquidated, around June 1943, only three of my relatives were alive: my aunt, Pola Kfar Wasserman, her husband, Oskar Wasserman, and my aunt, Friedka Herzer. They had planned to get false papers and pass as Christians.

I was devastated by the news. I asked Krystyna why she hadn't told me about my parents' deaths. She explained that she feared I might become despondent and lose the will to live, and she was determined to have me survive! I felt all alone in the world. I could not forget all my dead relatives. I had nightmares of the atrocities I had witnessed in the ghetto: people shot on the street; young girls jumping to their death to avoid arrest; starving children and adults begging for food; unidentified bodies on the street every morning.... My mind and heart held the fresh scars of all that had happened. I had to learn to cope with my memories, anguish, and loneliness.

Nothing could erase my sad memories or replace my dead family. In my despair, I recalled my parents' fervent wish for me to survive, to be courageous, and to adjust to life's cruel circumstances. I realized then that my most important goals were to complete my education and to build a new life, hopefully in the United States.

I continued to hope that my three relatives who had survived the ghetto had also survived the war. I did not yet know that Oskar Wasserman had been liberated from Buchenwald on April 11, 1945. He managed to place a notice in a Yiddish newspaper in New York looking for his wife's relatives. (Oskar did not yet know that his wife Pola had not survived.) My uncle, David Kfare, spotted the notice, and the family contacted Oskar. He told them to look for me in Krakow. On May 3, 1945, my relatives sent a letter to the Jewish Committee in Krakow. It said, in part:

> *We are very anxious to locate our niece.... Her Yiddish name is Rosie or Rozalia Kwar.... She was born in 1927 and lived with her father Bentchik*

> *and her mother Tinka. Her mother's maiden name was Hercer. They lived in Lemberg at Pod-Debem 6A.... Please try to locate this girl....*

Mail was very slow in the early postwar days and the letter did not reach me until August 27, 1945. I was overjoyed to receive it, and a friend took a picture of me reading this letter. In the meantime, in June 1945, my aunt Friedka Herzer came to Krakow to look for me. She had been arrested in Lvov in June 1943 and had survived Auschwitz and subsequent slave labor in a munitions factory near Leipzig, followed by a grueling death march ordered by the Nazis trying to escape the advancing Allied armies. Russian soldiers liberated her near the Czech border on May 9, 1945. Walking and hitching rides along the way, Friedka slowly made her way to Krakow. I was surprised to run into her on the street, coincidentally at the same spot where I had found Mr. Kanner!

As soon as telegraphic service was reestablished, at the end of July, I sent a telegram to Charles Kfare at 286 Grand Street, New York. It stated:

> *Roza Kfar, Benchik's daughter, and her mother's sister, Friedka Herzer, survived. Please write care of Kanner, Koltek 4, Krakow.*

Correspondence with my American relatives started in a variety of languages: Polish, Russian, Yiddish, and English. Letters took a long time; the main topic was always how to get Friedka and me out of Poland quickly.

At first, Uncle Charles sent an Affidavit of Support to try to get us to immigrate to the United States. However, the US immigration authorities did not give special consideration to Holocaust survivors in Poland, and the waiting time under the restricted Polish quota was very long. The Polish government was willing to issue passports to Jews and to grant them permission to leave, only if they proved that another country would accept them. In the meantime, my uncles determined that it would be faster to get us out of Poland through a visitor's visa to Cuba. On March 23, 1946, I received the following telegram:

Telegram

NLT = ROSE KFARE CARE KANNER KOLOTEK 4 KRAKOW =

463 NEWYORK CNE 59/22 56 21 105 =

VIA IMPERIAL = UC 3219 =

COUSIN RAPHAEL ZILBER OF HAVANA SUCCEEDED IN GETTING VIS
TO CUBA FOR YOU AND AUNT VISA NUMBER TWELVE FORTY SIX
AITING IN OFFICE OF CUBAN CONSUL IN PARIS PHOTOSTATS O
DOCUMENTS AIR MAILED UPON RECEIPT OF COPIES GO TO FRENC
ONSUL FOR TRANSIT VISA ACT FAST = CHARLIE KFARE

Cousin Raphael Zilber of Havana succeeded in getting visa to Cuba for you and Aunt. Visa #1246 waiting in office of Cuban Consul in Paris. Photostats of documents airmailed. Upon receipt of copies, go to French Consul for transit visa. Act fast. Charlie Kfare.

With this and a Polish passport, I could try to obtain the necessary transit visas. The passport was issued on May 28, 1946, clearly stating, in Polish and French, that it was valid for a *single* crossing of the border. Apparently, the Communist Polish authorities were allowing Jews to leave, but they did not want us to return to Poland.

By June 1946, we were able to leave for Paris. In Paris, we obtained the Cuban visa, but we still had to wait around for the transit visa through the US. We left Paris on July 29 via Air France and arrived in New York on June 30.

When we stepped onto the tarmac, I was unexpectedly greeted by Uncle Louis. He had sneaked by, pretending to be an airline "executive." He identified himself but warned not to kiss him. We proceeded to the immigration holding room where we waited two and a half hours for processing. One by one, the other seven relatives sneaked in to welcome me. When they saw all the crying at our reunions, the immigration officials looked aside. I recognized most of my relatives from the pictures we had received before the war. Uncle Dave looked strikingly like my father, and when I told him so, it made him cry.

Once past the official formalities, Uncle Charlie rushed us to Manhattan to see my great-uncle, Sanya Greenstein, who was gravely ill. Uncle Sanya reminded me that he had been in Lvov on a visit in 1927 when I was born. It appears he had been waiting for me, his only relative to survive the Holocaust, to come. He died that night. My first full day in America was spent at a funeral, meeting relatives, friends, and *landsleit*, most of whom told me that they remembered my father, Benzion, nicknamed Bentchik. The funeral was a heartbreaking experience. It was not only Uncle Sanya's burial that I attended. It felt as if I were witnessing the burial of all my dear relatives and friends who had perished in Europe. I cried bitter tears but found relief in being able to cry at last.

Dr. **Rose K. Rose**, *PhD, lived in Havana, Cuba from September 1946 to January 1948 before she was able to immigrate to the United States, where she lived in New York City as a science writer and translator.*

Brussels, 1945–1947

By Albert Hepner

(Excerpted from The Hidden Child, *Volume XXIII, 2015.)*

We moved to a two-room apartment on rue Brognier, a few blocks from where we had lived before the war. My mother constantly worried about what had happened to my brother, Max, who had not been heard from in three years. I didn't have to ask her why she whimpered each day. She only knew that he had hoped to run away to Switzerland with two friends who'd been picked up by the Gestapo before he arrived late at the Gare du Midi station. And she cried for her nephew, Motl, who had been sent to a concentration camp. The more news she heard about others who had been killed, the less she felt the chances of their return.

We were relieved when Max suddenly appeared. Family friends had been able to return to their prewar home, and Max had found them. So few Jews were left in Brussels after the war that each knew where the others lived. After years of hiding, we were relieved to be able to say where they were. Everyone spoke about who survived and who was where, so when Max got to our family friends, they were delighted to tell him.

Max had spent the war as a lumberjack in a Swiss labor camp and came back much taller and stronger. I was immediately proud of him, not only for how he looked but also for how adventurous he'd been. He told us that when he'd discovered his two companions had been picked up by the Gestapo, he'd debated whether to turn back, but then decided to proceed toward Switzerland on his own. He smuggled himself into France with the help of a taxi driver who would take a dirt road through the woods to avoid all barricades and he'd drop off his passengers at the next station on the French side. Max left the train when he felt he was close to the Swiss border and made his way on foot, eventually reaching a work camp for lumberjacks where he worked for the duration of the war. Shortly after Max's return, he met and married the woman who would be his life's companion.

At first, my mother and I felt abandoned rather than happy at the start of the young couple's life together. It felt like another loss. Nevertheless, within a short time, we found a larger apartment, I returned to school, and my mother went back to work. Before the war, she had worked in the assembly of leather goods and now found a job sewing military hats. She became the fastest seamstress in a factory of several hundred women, and the managers, pushing the other women to produce more, used her as the exemplar. One day, the other employees attacked her because her work made them seem inept. She came home bloodied and unsure she'd be able to go back to work at that plant. The next day, she received a letter from the Belgian government, and she was overjoyed. She'd been instructed to go to a downtown warehouse to retrieve furniture that the Nazis had confiscated if she could prove it was ours.

As I was returning home from school, my buddy André from down the street yelled out his window that he'd seen in the newspaper, *Le Soir*, that my mother had tried to commit suicide by throwing herself under a streetcar in front of La Bourse (the stock exchange). He said she had not succeeded. I ran home crying, hoping it wasn't true. When I found our apartment empty, I headed toward my brother's apartment but found him running toward me. He explained that she had not found any furniture. The one hope that something of our past would help us go on had come crashing down on her. My father's death, five years of insecurity, and precariousness fed by the war, two years of hiding in a cabin in the woods, getting beaten up in a hat factory, and having to take care of an eleven-year-old by herself without even a semblance of comfort from our old apartment, had been too much.

At that time, Belgian law required that anyone who attempted suicide be committed to an "insane" asylum. My brother, who didn't feel equipped to take care of me, found an orphanage in Antwerp. Its mission was to teach the orphans not only Hebrew, so they could form a religious kibbutz in Israel, but also to have them learn all that was expected of religious boys. My convent experience had served me well: I was able to fulfill all expectations without believing in any of the rites. I had been assured by my brother that my mother would likely be out of the asylum way before we'd move to Israel. Hence, it felt even more temporary. The uncertainty and tenuousness I'd experienced at the convent resurfaced. The entire experience seemed false. By the time I was eleven, I had learned to question the purpose of religion.

When my mother returned from the asylum, my brother brought me back to our little apartment. I'm not sure that life returned exactly to where it had been. After some initial educational difficulties in fifth grade, my mother got me a tutor, a British woman, who was paying for the rent of our attic by teaching me. I resisted reading anything about history, but she was so enthusiastic about making learning fun that she helped me enter sixth grade with a great deal of confidence.

Mr. Roggemans, the teacher who had not concealed his pleasure when the Nazis had pulled me out of first grade, was now my fifth and sixth grade teacher. Despite hating Mr. Roggemans, in 1947, I graduated second in my class. Two other Jewish boys (numbers one and three) and I walked with great pride up to the dais outside of the Anderlecht Municipal Hall on Place Communale, only two blocks from where I had been hidden by Father Bruylandts in his church. In full view of the entire community and stern-faced Roggemans, the three Jewish hidden children received their grade's top awards from the *burgermeister* of Anderlecht.

After **Albert Hepner** *and his mother immigrated to the US, Albert worked for his uncles. He joined the US Army, married, and had three daughters. Eventually, he built his own tool distribution business. After many years of commerce, he sold his business, went back to school, and became an instructor of English to second language learners. His book,* Avrumele: Recollections of a Hidden Child, *was published in 2017.*

The Postwar Years, 1945-1953

By Joseph Gosler

(Excerpted from The Hidden Child, *Volume XXVIII, 2020, and from the author's book,* Searching for Home: The Impact of WWII on a Hidden Child, *published worldwide by Amsterdam Publishers.)*

The Netherlands

In the beginning of spring 1945, in the south near Maastricht, the fighting had ceased, and the people were free to walk the streets. It would take until May 11 before the rest of Holland was freed. It was a period of euphoria. Yet, it was also a time of hysteria, hate, and vengeance. These were fluid days, and many victims felt all these emotions simultaneously. Adding to this and the physical turmoil, the economy was in shambles.

It took weeks before my mother, Yetta, knew whether my father, Maurice, was alive. They reunited after he made his way back to Gelderland on a bicycle with wooden wheels. The two months at Westerbork had taken a toll on my father. His feet were bleeding, his lower back was debilitated, and he had lost 35 percent of his body weight. The stress and hopelessness he felt and the oppressive labor had left him gaunt and listless. But at least they were together again, and my mother became pregnant with my sister, Marja. It took them another four weeks to search the underground records to find me and to finish the legal paperwork before they could embrace the child they had given away.

Nearly three years had passed. Their infant son had not only changed physically but had wrapped himself, emotionally and psychologically, in the arms of the Dijkstra family. My parents were strangers. I did not recognize them and wanted to return to the only parents I'd known. At age three, I was confused and upset by the loss of my underground family. My biological family was back together again, but each of us was irrevocably damaged by the experience of war. We returned to Groningen. My parents were devastated by the loss of their family—parents, brothers, sisters, aunts, uncles, and cousins. Also, they lost their homes, jobs, careers, friends, and—most importantly—their spirit. Every day was consumed by painful memories. My parents were in an endless state of mourning.

At three years old, I was still wrapped in innocence, but cracks were beginning to form in my fragile psyche. I felt abandoned by the only family I had known. I cried for Moeder. I trusted no one. The war ravaged us all in so many ways. In early summer, my mother suffered a nervous breakdown. The feelings she held in so valiantly during the war, tied up in neat, little, locked boxes, now burst out, and she was overwhelmed by sadness and rage. She barely functioned.

My father, emotionally void, could not tend to her either, because he was desperately seeking work. My parents were so needy and self-absorbed that the normal bonding between child and parent did not occur for me until much later in life. It is also possible that my longing for Moeder and Vader and my inability to forgive my own parents delayed the bonding even more.

Still struggling with severe depression and fatigue, my mother experienced the life forming inside her, and the healing grace of time helped her regain some emotional footing. My father found a job as an electrical appliance salesman. There was now a semblance of order in the home.

I did not know it at the time, but the cracks in my soul were ever more apparent. What could a three-year-old know about the lasting effects of being a hidden child? For that matter, what could anyone know? I was disoriented and could not understand or accept why I was separated from Moeder and Vader.

Within weeks after being reunited, I found a box of matches and promptly set the bathroom window curtains on fire. My parents were alarmed, but this was not a time when adults were psychologically attuned. They did not understand it as a cry for help, an outward expression of my inner anguish, my way of displaying rage, and my longing for Moeder and Vader. I wanted to go home. I yearned for my other life. The pain was pervasive, cumulative, and remained raw.

In time, the family gained some normalcy: Poppy had a job and Mommy tended to us. Marja was nearly two, and I made friends with Dimo, a boy who lived nearby. Yet, my restlessness persisted. I felt stuck, controlled, and possibly still exposed to danger.

At our home, Marja and I would play together; I liked playing with finger and hand puppets, using different voices to personify different emotions and characters. Marja was a great audience. But she was more than that, she filled part of the emptiness I felt. Guiding her, and being the "big" brother, gave me stature and meaning, which helped counterbalance the distance I felt toward my parents—a separation I could not understand, a distance they could never seem to reduce.

Mommy and Poppy were planning to move. The postwar economy in the Netherlands had not rebounded. My father was dissatisfied with his job, and the nightmares of the war were ever present. They needed to distance themselves from the memories that continued to haunt them.

They attempted to get visas for America but applied very late. It would be years before visas to America could be secured and our parents were desperate to leave. Israel was in its first year of existence and was eager to embrace new arrivals. After months of planning, packing, and a series of goodbyes to a small group of family and friends who also survived the war, our family waved our final goodbye and boarded the train for Marseille, France. Once again, I was displaced, separated from all that was "home" and secure.

Israel, 1949–1953

We were not prepared for kibbutz life, and we each experienced it very differently. The separation of children from their parents, a heavenly reality for me, was a form of purgatory for my parents and sister. At age six, I craved the distance from my parents, the independence to roam, and the camaraderie of children my age. The distance from my parents allowed me the space to sort things out and to begin to understand who I was. I felt totally smothered, bewildered, and resistant to my parents' attention, and unknowingly still mourned my own losses. The kibbutz was a perfect haven.

My parents and sister, on the other hand, found it difficult to adapt. The traditional family unit so ingrained in their consciousness was disrupted and everything they used or wore was communally shared. While I needed distance from my parents, Marja's needs were just the opposite. Even in Holland, Marja intuited that our mother was emotionally fragile and self-absorbed, and she felt neglected. At least a few evenings per week, for quite a while, she made her way to our parents' cottage and would wake up sleeping in their bed.

As she grew older, she became more independent, so much so that at age five, she was hitchhiking and wandering by herself along the main road outside Beit HaShita. This sense of independence that I also shared was very much the result of living on the kibbutz. No longer was the traditional home and family the only place of safety, the kibbutz and the surrounding community were as well.

My father, now "Moshe," worked as a shepherd and spent most days outdoors, taking his flock to the valley and low hillsides where there were many streams and lush grasses. The warm breezes, the occasional sounds of a turtle dove, and the incessant baas of sheep created a soothing rhythm to his day. He found refuge outdoors and was deeply consoled by nature's hum. My father flourished in the kibbutz, but the same could not be said for my mother. She was prone to headaches, and depending on the heat and humidity, she sometimes struggled to breathe. Her daily work shifted between the cafeteria, the laundry, and the library. She washed the dishes and pots, and washed and ironed the clothing. My mother didn't mind working indoors, but she felt that this work was beneath her.

She was lonely. In Holland, she had her own home, her own clothing, and her children nearby. Now, everything was shared: clothing, property, and children. Her children no longer identified only with their parents, they identified with an extended family, a whole community. This was difficult to accept, especially for a Holocaust survivor.

The daily routines for a six-year-old were quite uniform. I didn't mind it being so specific; in fact, it gave me structure and security. I knew what to expect and what was expected of me. I awoke at 6:30, washed, brushed my teeth, and dressed. All the young children dressed alike: short khaki pants with shoulder straps that buttoned in front and back and a short-sleeved, light-colored shirt. Then we went outside, and led by an adult, we ran barefoot cross-country style, through various terrain in and around the kibbutz.

I enjoyed those vigorous daily runs and looked forward to breakfast. After three hours of class time, we took our lunch to the fields. I never grew tired of the black bread, slathered with mayonnaise and filled with scallion greens, that was toasted by the noonday sun. We spent two hours working in the fields, harvesting grapes, eating some, and taking little snoozes in the shade of the vines. Sometimes, we set large tarps around olive trees and milked the branches of green olives, scooped them off the canvas and packed them into wooden crates.

Free time after dinner was devoted to playing on the big lawn near the dining hall. The lights would go out in the dorms about eight. For me, the daily experience was rich, sweet, predictable, and secure, and created a rhythm that was as soothing as it was exhausting. The sky was clear, and I slept well. But this bounty of joy was not to last. While my father, sister, and I thrived in kibbutz life, my mom couldn't adjust. Four years had passed, and she still had the headaches and occasional shortness of breath. She still longed to be closer to her extended family and was less and less happy with the climate and the communal nature of the kibbutz.

In early 1953, we left the kibbutz, with the intent of immigrating to the US. The move itself seemed quite simple because all we carried were our meager belongings: some clothing, photos, jewelry, and other small mementos. Marja and I felt a tremendous loss. Uprooted once again, I felt a loss of community, security, and friendships that I had finally attained. Those feelings could never mend, and trust was ever fleeting.

For nearly forty years, **Joseph Gosler** *worked as a business manager in the field of day care centers. He and his wife founded a pre-school called Beginnings Nursery in New York City.*

An American Summer Camp

By William Donat

(Excerpted from The Hidden Child, *Volume XVII, 2009.)*

We came to New York in 1946, right after the war. I was placed in the second grade at P.S. 41 in Greenwich Village, where all my classmates accepted me and tried somehow to communicate though I spoke no English. To my surprise, no one called me "*zhidek*" (little Yid), and most of the kids genuinely wanted to befriend me.

My parents were fortunate enough to have found a nearby two-room, walk-up apartment on the fourth floor. They slept on a sofa that opened into a bed at night, though they never complained. We had survived an ordeal that had killed 90 percent of Polish Jews. We were all in the Warsaw ghetto at the start of the war, and in 1943, I was smuggled out. My parents were taken to Hitler's concentration camps, where they spent two years, not knowing if the other was alive.

In Poland, my parents, both graduates of the University of Warsaw, had experienced many frustrating restrictions to their aspirations because they were Jews. Now, they quickly saw that their son would be able to achieve greater things in this wonderful new country. My father was working in a printing plant, and my mother was taking evening courses in English. Both told me my educational possibilities in America were endless; all I had to do was work hard.

As an eight-year-old, my reactions were far less sophisticated. For me, to be able to walk the four blocks to school, alone, without fearing that someone in a uniform would grab me and send me away was a great relief. And I knew that I could wander the streets with my friends after school without worrying that my parents wouldn't be there when I came home. Knowing that the Nazis could not take them away and that I would never again be hungry is what America meant to me then, and by the time I could understand the words to *America the Beautiful*, I had wrapped my arms around this country and made it mine forever.

I spent two weeks of my first summer in America at a Labor-Zionist camp where I broke my ankle doing acrobatic stunts. My parents didn't want me to go back there because of the poor medical attention I had received. So, in the summer of 1948, I was sent to Camp Greenkill, which was said to be well managed and, above all, affordable. Camp Greenkill, located in West Huguenot, New York, drew its boys from the New York City area. As a YMCA camp, its counselors were mostly young men studying to become teachers, high school coaches, or clergymen. The members of the administrative staff, full-time employees of the YMCA, were very professional and well-suited to run a nonprofit summer camp. Many were former GIs who had fought in the war. As the summer of 1949 approached, I looked forward to returning to Camp Greenkill. By then, at age eleven, I had lost my accent almost entirely. More and more, I refused to speak Polish with my parents.

From the moment we pulled into the camp, I was enchanted again by the lush greenery and the lake. The boys came from a wide variety of neighborhoods, distinctly divided along ethnic lines, yet the camp was surprisingly integrated, a true melting pot, much as I had learned in school about the entire United States. The kids were of all backgrounds: Irish, and what we then politely called "colored," Italian, Protestant, and surprisingly, there were quite a few Jewish boys. Although we were all required to attend chapel on Sunday morning and sing "Onward Christian Soldiers," this was the extent of our exposure to religion. Having spent much of the war hidden in a Catholic orphanage in Poland, and having then been a devoted Catholic, singing Christian hymns was nothing new for me.

I had made some good friends the previous summer and many had returned. None of my bunkmates knew of my early childhood in the Warsaw ghetto. I had opted not to divulge my past because I wanted to be like the others, an average American boy. I loved being at Camp Greenkill. I looked forward to all the activities, especially swimming, canoeing and, my favorite, rifle shooting.

Our first evening in the mess hall, we were introduced to the various instructors, one of whom was head riflery instructor, Franz Gruber. We were told that Franz had served in the German army in the last war and that he was very familiar with target shooting and with the NRA marksmanship program in which the camp participated.

I liked riflery and went to the range the very next day. We would wait our turn to shoot postcards and stamps when the co-op opened after dinner. Franz had a distinctive German accent and wore an *Afrika Korps* peaked cap. He would line up the five boys who were the next to shoot, repeat the safety procedures, hand us our rifles, and have us assume the prone position on the mattresses that were laid out. He was very watchful as to how we handled the rifles, always pointing the barrel down-range, even if we hadn't loaded it yet. I usually did well, earning my NRA pro-marksman badge quickly. He didn't seem to notice that I didn't pronounce his name like "France," the country, as the other boys did, but in a more accurate, European way, as in my native Polish.

Each morning, we'd choose an activity from many, including crafts, junior lifesaving, canoeing, or riflery. In the afternoon, our bunk would participate in team sports. In the evening, there would be a talent show, boxing, or movies. Sometimes there would be interesting lectures.

Often, we would still be very revved up from the evening's program when taps sounded, and we would continue our boisterous conversations well past lights out. There were always two counselors on duty for each section of the camp in case of an emergency and to keep order. In most cases, the counselors on duty would let the murmured exchanges gradually die down as we finally fell asleep after a fatiguing day.

One evening, the program had been exceptionally interesting for eleven-year-olds—an anthropologist enthralled us about the

William Donat with parents and aunt, c. 1950.

lives of the local Mohawk and Iroquois tribes that had inhabited the region. Our discussion was enthusiastic, animated, and admittedly loud.

The screen door of our bunk was abruptly thrown open and Franz stepped in. He started to growl and shout at us in his high-pitched, German-accented voice. "What do you think you are doing? You will not talk, not a word. We have rules, you know. You will sleep now or there will be trouble." After his harangue, he stepped back outside, slamming the screen door behind him.

Suddenly everything changed for me. The barrier I had been building in my child's mind to the memories of my earlier childhood crumbled. The subconscious effort I had made to lose any trace of an accent, easy for a ten- or eleven-year-old, became meaningless. Franz's guttural screaming brought me back to the Warsaw ghetto where I had been a five-year-old. I was once again in the back room of the last remaining pharmacy in the ghetto, on Zamenhof Street, where my mother was working. A drunken Nazi officer had come into the store looking for alcohol, but when told they didn't have anything drinkable, only the kind used for disinfecting wounds, he became infuriated. I was again hearing the same guttural snarl—the same illogical screaming as had come from that Nazi officer in 1943.

But this time it was directed at me, not at my mother. Once again, it was the same angry Nazi who had ordered his soldiers to take my mother, me, and the other seven women working in the pharmacy to *Umschlagplatz*, the railhead in the ghetto, to be put on the cattle cars bound for the death camp, Treblinka. But this time it was happening *here*, in my wonderful America, in my beloved American Camp Greenkill. Here, where I had been assured by my American relatives that such bad things didn't happen. That everything would always be all right, that I didn't have to be scared, that no Nazi could hurt me, or my parents, again. I was shocked to my eleven-year-old core.

With Franz's screaming, a levee was breached. My desperate three-year attempt to sublimate my foreign beginnings, my attempt to become a real American boy, to lose my Polish accent, was all forgotten. All that we had lived through during the war came rushing back to me.

"That son of a bitch," I said in a loud voice, not caring who heard. He was no longer a Nazi soldier, and I was no longer a fearful Jewish child in the Warsaw ghetto. He couldn't take away my rocking horse, as another Nazi soldier with a rifle had done; he couldn't take my mother's silverware; he could no longer take my father's printing presses from his newspaper. This was Camp Greenkill; this was, after all, my wonderful America!

"He has some nerve," I told my bunkmates. "You know, I'm Jewish and I'm originally from Warsaw, Poland. From 1940, all the Jews of Warsaw were crammed into the ghetto where Nazi bastards like him would come into our homes and take whatever they liked. My parents both spent two years in concentration camps separated and not knowing if the other was alive. My mother got her arm tattooed with a number at a camp called Auschwitz. They were guarded by guys like him, wearing the same kind of caps. Except, we're in America now, but he doesn't seem to know that."

Some of the boys were stunned by my revelation. "I thought you said you were from Manhattan," said Ray.

"I am now. But I was born in Warsaw, and I was there during the war," I responded. "And people like that bullied and killed us because we were Jewish." I felt all right saying that because two other boys in our bunk, Ray and Marvin, were also Jewish. They were from the Bronx, where many other Jewish people lived.

"I'm surprised that they let a son of a bitch—" I had recently learned this expression from my cousins and had practiced it until I could say it without the slightest hint of an accent—"I'm surprised they let him even hold a gun, let alone teach kids to shoot."

"Hey," said Yancy. "I was in your bunk last year too, and you never told us about any of this. But I remember that you did talk a little funny." Yancy, a Black boy from upper Manhattan, whose father worked for the post office, was a great ball player and everyone always wanted to be on his team, especially in games against other bunks.

"Well, to tell you the truth, I don't like to think about it much," I said.

I told them what had happened. How I was smuggled out of the ghetto and my parents were sent to the camps. I told them how lucky my parents were to come back. A lot of uncles and aunts and cousins of my parents were killed.

"At first," I told them, "I lived with the Christian people who were supposed to be my uncle and aunt, but then the Polish police came, and I had to go to an orphanage outside of Warsaw, in a little town called Otwock," I told them. "We were always hungry, and I had sores all over my body, but when the Russian Army came, things got better. Then, after two years, my mother came back for me, just as she had promised to do."

"Is that why you always eat up all the food on your plate?" Marvin asked.

"I guess so; I didn't want to be hungry again," I said. By now, it was a good hour past lights out and everyone was starting to fall asleep. I stayed awake until I was no longer angry and, eventually, also fell asleep.

The next morning, at breakfast in the large dining hall, Franz came over and whispered something to my counselor Bert and went away. Bert then said, "Billy, Franz would like to speak with you after breakfast, do you mind?"

I thought I had gotten in trouble for talking and cursing so loud the night before. I replied, "I really don't want to talk to him, especially if he's going to yell at me again."

Bert said, "I have a feeling it won't be like that, but you don't have to go if you don't want to."

As I was walking out of the mess hall, Franz was waiting. "May I have a moment to speak with you?" he said. I reluctantly nodded and we walked over to a nearby tree that had a bench built around it. He motioned for me to sit down. "I heard the story you told your friends last night. I am so sorry," he said. "When we were young in Germany, we thought we were fighting for our country. Not all of us were involved with what happened to the Jewish people." His face grimaced with remorse. "Please believe that some Germans did not wish it to happen, I'm sorry, I'm so sorry. Do you believe me?"

I gave a slight nod, shrugged my shoulders, and walked away. I never went back to the rifle range again that summer; and Franz never wore his Afrika Korps hat again. The most productive element to come out of this encounter was that I no longer tried to hide my background; I didn't mind if my parents continued to call me by my Polish name, Wlodek, instead of my adopted American one, William—or Billy.

Here, in America, the Germans apologized, and I didn't have to hide my Jewish identity as I had done in the Catholic orphanage. I could go on with my life, enjoying school and camp and living as a real American, even though I had come from Poland as a Jewish refugee after the war.

William H. Donat *retired from his financial printing business in 2002 and later became involved in Holocaust education. He spoke to high school and college classes about his childhood experiences and taught courses on the history of the Holocaust.*

Return to My Mother, Yiddish Culture, and Jewish Identity

By René Lichtman

(Excerpted from My Story, *November 2022.)*

My Mother's Return to Claim Me

My mother survived the war in Paris with the help of her neighbors. After the Liberation, a woman I had never seen came to our farm and was announced to me as "*ta mère*" (your mother), who had come to take me back with her to Paris. The woman was young and did not look like anyone I had ever seen: she dressed differently, wore perfume, and she spoke French with a strong accent.

Thus, I returned to my Jewish mother. This strikes me as a strange combination of words to explain the complex emotional parts of that period: this was the most traumatic aspect of my childhood. When my mother wasn't heard from for the last two years of the war, my hiding parents assumed she was dead. They had me baptized and they prepared me for my new Christian identity. They had plans to send me to an art school, since I drew a lot. (Until the end of her life, Maman Nana had saved many of my drawings.) I had some Christian books with photos of saints and a special ring engraved with an image of the Virgin Mary.

I do not recall the ensuing period as "happy" for either of us. My mother worked at home as a seamstress. She had more than one machine and, during her "busy season," she hired other people to help. They all spoke Yiddish, or a mixture of Yiddish and

French. I was sent to the local school near our Paris apartment. Although I was close to eight years old and had never been to school before, I survived somehow. How did I adapt? I still do not know or understand. My mother and I had fights. One time she threw a shoe at me, which went through the window. I made her very angry.

One reason was that she tried to make me wear a patch on my good eye, because I had a very poor, crossed eye. A doctor had recommended the patch, but I could not see anything with my weak eye, so I rebelled. Eventually, she gave up on me, stopped forcing me, and my poor eye grew weaker until I lost sight.

I must have been quite a sight at my school, with or without a patch—cross-eyed, obviously Jewish, not "real" French. But after the war, all the kids had some kind of history. The only negative experience I recall was being called a "*sale Juif*" (dirty Jew) after a Christian holiday. I ran home crying, telling my mother I did not want to be Jewish. "Kids make fun of me…you lost your whole family because they were Jewish…."

While staying with my hiding parents, the Lepages, during the 1950 summer break, I received a letter from my mother telling me she had remarried and we were to move to the US. I was disheartened, but Maman Nana assured me that the US would be great. When I met my new stepfather, a religious Jew, that too was a negative experience. Here I was, a thirteen-year-old kid who spoke no English, with a stepfather so old, he could not speak with me at all. There was nothing wrong or unusual about him except that he had grown kids and grandkids, and I kept wondering what my mother was doing with this guy.… He'd often complain to her that I drank too much milk. Then my mother and he would argue over this. It was just a very strange relationship.

Oscar Hunter, My Surrogate "Father"

Oscar and Bernice Hunter owned a little silkscreen workshop on Christopher Street in New York. Oscar played a particularly important role in my life. In many ways, he was the only father figure I ever had. He was both an intellectual and artistic influence

René with his two mothers on a postwar visit.

on me over the four years I worked for him. Bernice was a very talented artist who designed the patterns, while Oscar processed her creations onto the silkscreens. I met them when I came out of the military in 1961. I had received two scholarships, one to Cooper Union Art School and the other to the Brooklyn Museum Art School, and I was attending the Brooklyn Museum Art School in the morning and Cooper Union in the evening. But I needed a job. Oscar hired me part-time for the afternoon. My task was to hang the freshly screened wallpaper to dry. So, I stood next to Oscar as he worked, and we talked and listened to WBAI radio—very far left—but I did not know that. I loved it!

Oscar was a light-complexioned African American man who had gone to Hampton College and been an athlete. Then, he went to Spain as part of the Abraham Lincoln Brigade. He came back to the States in the 1950s, amid the crackdown on communists, and at some point, he was blacklisted. That was when Oscar and Bernice, who was Jewish, opened their silk-screening business together.

We discussed a lot of things, including communism and fascism and the Jewish experience. Talking with Oscar, I began to understand why, in America, young idealistic people—mostly young working-class Italians and Jews—went off to fight fascism. My reason for joining the Army had been to get away from a home where my mother and stepfather argued a lot.

Ever since we'd arrived in the US, I'd had stomach pains. Oscar sent me to his own doctor, Dr. Louis Finger, a Jew from Germany, who examined me and said I had a duodenal ulcer that needed to heal. Dr. Finger told me to tell my mother that he did not want me to see her every Friday night. And if she wants to, "she can call me." So, I told my mother that, and she screamed back: "What kinda *meshigenne* doctor you got there!" Still, I visited her less frequently, and with a strict diet, my ulcer healed.

René Lichtman, *PhD, graduated from the Cooper Union Art School and was the recipient of a Fulbright Scholarship in painting. He holds degrees in fine arts, mass communication, and a PhD in instructional technology from Wayne State University in Detroit, Michigan. As an artist, he continues to paint and has had solo exhibits in Michigan. As a filmmaker, he has done documentaries on autoworkers and on Jewish children in Poland during the Second World War.*

Photo Credits

Pages 8, 27, 85, 272, 273, 274, and 275 - Courtesy of the United States Holocaust Memorial Museum

Page xv - Courtesy of the Anti-Defamation League

Page xviii - Courtesy of Abraham Foxman

Pages 11 and 12 - Courtesy of Lillian Boraks-Nemetz

Page 15 - Courtesy of Charles Stevens

Page 16 - Courtesy of Lili Silberman

Page 19 - Courtesy of Moshe Bar-Semech

Pages 20, 21, 22, 24, 25, and 26 - Jack Goldstein

Pages 30 and 32 - Courtesy of Cordula Hahn

Page 35 - Courtesy of Yetty Derschowitz

Pages 40, 42, 44, and 45 - Courtesy of Ellen Bachner Greenberg

Page 47 - Courtesy of Renée Roth-Hano

Page 51 - Courtesy of William H. Donat

Page 55 - Courtesy of Rena Hass

Page 65 - Courtesy of Robert Krell

Pages 67 and 68 - Courtesy of Maya Freed Brown

Pages 71 and 73 - Courtesy of Esther Franco

Pages 75 and 77 - Courtesy of Andrew Griffel

Pages 99, 100, 106, 107, and 110 - Courtesy of Joanne Ashe

Page 115 - Courtesy of Manfred Segal

Page 118 - With permission of The Lodz Archives; Archivum Panstwowe, Lodz

Page 127 - Courtesy of Susan Thumin Silk

Pages 132, 133, 134, 135, 141, 142, and 143 - Courtesy of Erna Stopper Bindelglas

Pages 141, 142, and 143 - Courtesy of Sharon Goldman

Page 147 - Courtesy of Semmy Riekerk

Pages 148, 149, and 150 - Courtesy of Eva Paula Nathanson

Page 163 - Courtesy of Yolanda Avram Willis

Page 176 - Courtesy of the Joint Distribution Committee

Pages 181 and 182 - Courtesy of Ruth Lavie-Jourgrau

Page 186 - Courtesy of Pinchas Zajonc

Pages 190 and 286 - Courtesy of Yad Vashem

Pages 197 and 198 - Courtesy of Richard Ned Lebow

Page 207 - Courtesy of Mordecai Paldiel

Pages 211 and 327 - Courtesy of René Lichtman

Pages 213, 214, 215, 218, 220, and 222 - Courtesy of Eva Kuper

Page 219 - Courtesy of the Montreal Holocaust Museum

Pages 225, 226, 227, 229, 230, 231, and 232 - Courtesy of Jacques Silberman

Pages 233 and 234 - Courtesy of Albert Hepner

Page 243 - Courtesy of Odette Meyers

Pages 246 and 250 - Courtesy of Bertha Teitelbaum Schwarz

Page 276 - Courtesy of Judith Koeppel Steel

Pages 278 and 280 - Courtesy of Evelyn Pike Rubin

Pages 294 and 295 - Courtesy of Ruth L. Weiss Hohberg

Page 299 - Courtesy of Jack Kuper

Pages 304 and 307 - Courtesy of Rose Kfar Rose

Page 321 - Courtesy of William H. Donat

About the Contributors

Rachelle L. Goldstein was born to Jewish parents in Brussels, Belgium, just before the onset of World War II. She was hidden from the Nazis as a young child in order to save her life. Rachelle is the Co-Director of the Hidden Child Foundation/Anti-Defamation League, based in New York.

The **Anti-Defamation League (ADL)** was founded in 1913. Its timeless mission is "to stop the defamation of the Jewish people and to secure justice and fair treatment to all." Today, the ADL continues to fight all forms of antisemitism and bias, using innovation and partnerships to drive impact.